THE PSYCHOLOGY OF LEARNING AND MOTIVATION

Advances in Research and Theory

VOLUME 10

CONTRIBUTORS TO THIS VOLUME

Raymond C. Battalio
Roger W. Black
John D. Bransford
W. K. Estes
Jeffery J. Franks
Leonard Green
Douglas L. Hintzman
John H. Kagel
Howard Rachlin
K. Edward Renner
Jeanne B. Tinsley

THE PSYCHOLOGY
OF LEARNING AND MOTIVATION

Advances in Research and Theory

EDITED BY GORDON H. BOWER

STANFORD UNIVERSITY, STANFORD, CALIFORNIA

Volume 10

1976

ACADEMIC PRESS New York • San Francisco • London
A SUBSIDIARY OF HARCOURT BRACE JOVANOVICH, PUBLISHERS

Copyright © 1976, by Academic Press, Inc.
ALL RIGHTS RESERVED.
NO PART OF THIS PUBLICATION MAY BE REPRODUCED OR
TRANSMITTED IN ANY FORM OR BY ANY MEANS, ELECTRONIC
OR MECHANICAL, INCLUDING PHOTOCOPY, RECORDING, OR ANY
INFORMATION STORAGE AND RETRIEVAL SYSTEM, WITHOUT
PERMISSION IN WRITING FROM THE PUBLISHER.

ACADEMIC PRESS, INC.
111 Fifth Avenue, New York, New York 10003

United Kingdom Edition published by
ACADEMIC PRESS, INC. (LONDON) LTD.
24/28 Oval Road, London NW1

LIBRARY OF CONGRESS CATALOG CARD NUMBER: 66-30104

ISBN 0-12-543310-7

PRINTED IN THE UNITED STATES OF AMERICA

CONTENTS

List of Contributors ix
Contents of Previous Volumes xi

SOME FUNCTIONS OF MEMORY IN PROBABILITY LEARNING AND CHOICE BEHAVIOR
W. K. Estes

I. Introduction 2
II. An Observation-Transfer Paradigm for the Study of Predictive Behavior 3
III. The Informational Basis of Predictive Behavior 6
IV. Theoretical Interpretation of Probability Learning Series ... 20
V. Differential Reward Learning Relative to Values of Reward Sets ... 30
VI. Theoretical Interpretation of the Differential Reward Series ... 38
VII. General Discussion 42
References 44

REPETITION AND MEMORY
Douglas L. Hintzman

I. Introduction 47
II. The Representation of Frequency 48
III. The Spacing Effect 65
IV. Repetitive and Retrieval 80
References 87

TOWARD A FRAMEWORK FOR UNDERSTANDING LEARNING

John D. Bransford and Jeffery J. Franks

I. The Place of Novelty	94
II. Toward a Stage Setting Metaphor of the Effects of Past Experiences	102
III. Stage Setting and the Problem of Learning	112
IV. Overall Summary and Conclusions	121
References	125

ECONOMIC DEMAND THEORY AND PSYCHOLOGICAL STUDIES OF CHOICE

Howard Rachlin, Leonard Green, John H. Kagel, and Raymond C. Battalio

I. Introduction	129
II. The Purpose of the Experiments	135
III. Experiments on Substitutability: Procedure and Results	136
IV. Experiments on Substitutability: Discussion	141
V. Summary	152
References	152

SELF-PUNITIVE BEHAVIOR

K. Edward Renner and Jeanne B. Tinsley

I. Introduction	156
II. Self-Punitive Behavior	157
III. Experimental Evaluation of the Discrimination-Expectancy Account	161
IV. Effect of the Punishment	176
V. Empirical Constraints	183
VI. Conclusions	188
VII. Implications for Punishment Theory and Research	190
VIII. Generalizations	194
References	196

REWARD VARIABLES IN INSTRUMENTAL CONDITIONING: A THEORY

Roger W. Black

I. Introduction	199
II. Basic Theoretical Formulation	207
III. Implications of the Theory	220
IV. General Discussion	236
References	241
Subject Index	245

LIST OF CONTRIBUTORS

Numbers in parentheses indicate the pages on which the authors' contributions begin.

Raymond C. Battalio, Department of Economics, Texas A & M University, College Station, Texas (129)

Roger W. Black, Department of Psychology, University of South Carolina, Columbia, South Carolina (199)

John D. Bransford, Department of Psychology, Vanderbilt University, Nashville, Tennessee (93)

W. K. Estes, Rockefeller University, New York, New York (1)

Jeffery J. Franks, Department of Psychology, Vanderbilt University, Nashville, Tennessee (93)

Leonard Green, Department of Psychology, Washington University, St. Louis, Missouri (129)

Douglas L. Hintzman, Department of Psychology, University of Oregon, Eugene, Oregon (47)

John H. Kagel, Department of Economics, Texas A & M University, College Station, Texas (129)

Howard Rachlin, Department of Psychology, State University of New York at Stony Brook, Stony Brook, New York (129)

K. Edward Renner,[1] Department of Psychology, University of Illinois, Champaign, Illinois (155)

Jeanne B. Tinsley, Department of Psychology, University of Illinois, Champaign, Illinois (155)

---

[1] Present address: Department of Psychology, Dalhousie University, Halifax, Nova Scotia, Canada.

CONTENTS OF PREVIOUS VOLUMES

Volume 1

Partial Reinforcement Effects on Vigor and Persistence
  Abram Amsel

A Sequential Hypothesis of Instrumental Learning
  E. J. Capaldi

Satiation and Curiosity
  Harry Fowler

A Multicomponent Theory of the Memory Trace
  Gordon Bower

Organization and Memory
  George Mandler

Author Index—Subject Index

Volume 2

Incentive Theory and Changes in Reward
  Frank A. Logan

Shift in Activity and the Concept of Persisting Tendency
  David Birch

Human Memory: A Proposed System and Its Control Processes
  R. C. Atkinson and R. M. Shiffrin

Mediation and Conceptual Behavior
  Howard K. Kendler and Tracy S. Kendler

Author Index—Subject Index

Volume 3

Stimulus Selection and a "Modified Continuity Theory"
  Allan R. Wagner

Abstraction and the Process of Recognition
  Michael I. Posner

Neo-Noncontinuity Theory
  Marvin Levine

Computer Simulation of Short-Term Memory: A Component-Decay Model
  Kenneth R. Laughery

Replication Processes in Human Memory and Learning
  Harley A. Bernbach

Experimental Analysis of Learning to Learn
  Leo Postman

Short-Term Memory in Binary Prediction by Children: Some Stochastic Information Processing Models
  Richard S. Bogartz

Author Index—Subject Index

Volume 4

Learned Associations over Long Delays
  Sam Revusky and John Garcia

On the Theory of Interresponse-Time Reinforcement
  G. S. Reynolds and Alastair McLeod

Sequential Choice Behavior
  Jerome L. Meyers

The Role of Chunking and Organization in the Process of Recall
Neal F. Johnson

Organization of Serial Pattern Learning
Frank Restle and Eric Brown

Author Index—Subject Index

Volume 5

Conditioning and a Decision Theory of Response Evocation
G. Robert Grice

Short-Term Memory
Bennet B. Murdock, Jr.

Storage Mechanisms in Recall
Murray Glanzer

By-Products of Discrimination Learning
H. S. Terrace

Serial Learning and Dimensional Organization
Sheldon M. Ebenholtz

FRAN: A Simulation Model of Free Recall
John Robert Anderson

Author Index—Subject Index

Volume 6

Informational Variables in Pavlovian Conditioning
Robert A. Rescorla

The Operant Conditioning of Central Nervous System Electrical Activity
A. H. Black

The Avoidance Learning Problem
Robert C. Bolles

Mechanisms of Directed Forgetting
William Epstein

Toward a Theory of Redintegrative Memory: Adjective-Noun Phrases
Leonard M. Horowitz and Leon Manelis

Elaborative Strategies in Verbal Learning and Memory
William E. Montague

Author Index—Subject Index

Volume 7

Grammatical Word Classes: A Learning Process and Its Simulation
George R. Kiss

Reaction Time Measurements in the Study of Memory Processes: Theory and Data
John Theios

Individual Differences in Cognition: A New Approach to Intelligence
Earl Hunt, Nancy Frost, and Clifford Lunneborg

Stimulus Encoding Processes in Human Learning and Memory
Henry C. Ellis

Subproblem Analysis of Discrimination Learning
Thomas Tighe

Delayed Matching and Short-Term Memory in Monkeys
M. R. D'Amato

Percentile Reinforcement: Paradigms for Experimental Analysis of Response Shaping
John R. Platt

Prolonged Rewarding Brain Stimulation
J. A. Deutsch

Patterned Reinforcement
Stewart H. Hulse

Author Index—Subject Index

Volume 8

Semantic Memory and Psychological Semantics
Edward E. Smith, Lance J. Rips, and Edward J. Shoben

Working Memory
  Alan D. Baddeley and Graham Hitch

The Role of Adaptation-Level in Stimulus Generalization
  David R. Thomas

Recent Developments in Choice
  Edmund Fantino and Douglas Navarick

Reinforcing Properties of Escape from Frustration Aroused in Various Learning Situations
  Helen B. Daly

Conceptual and Neurobiological Issues in Studies of Treatments Affecting Memory Storage
  James L. McGaugh and Paul E. Gold

The Logic of Memory Representations
  Endel Tulving and Gordon H. Bower

Subject Index

Volume 9

Prose Processing
  Lawrence T. Frase

Analysis and Synthesis of Tutorial Dialogues
  Allan Collins, Eleanor H. Warnock, and Joseph J. Passafiume

On Asking People Questions About What They Are Reading
  Richard C. Anderson and W. Barry Biddle

The Analysis of Sentence Production
  M. F. Garrett

Coding Distinctions and Repetition Effects in Memory
  Allan Paivio

Pavlovian Conditioning and Directed Movements
  Eliot Hearst

A Theory of Context in Discrimination Learning
  Douglas L. Medin

Subject Index

SOME FUNCTIONS OF MEMORY IN PROBABILITY LEARNING AND CHOICE BEHAVIOR[1]

W. K. Estes

ROCKEFELLER UNIVERSITY, NEW YORK, NEW YORK

I.	Introduction	2
II.	An Observation-Transfer Paradigm for the Study of Predictive Behavior	3
III.	The Informational Basis of Predictive Behavior	6
	A. Experiment 1. Probability Learning with Homogeneous Blocks of Observation Trials	7
	B. Experiment 2. Randomized Training Trials and Delayed Tests	10
	C. Experiment 3. Observation Trials with a Common Losing Alternative	12
	D. Experiment 4. Joint Variation of Stimulus Frequency and Outcome Probability	15
	E. Experiment 5. Joint Variation of Stimulus Frequency and Outcome Probability with Overlapping Observation Pairs	17
IV.	Theoretical Interpretation of Probability Learning Series	20
	A. The Associative Coding Model	21
	B. Parameter Estimates and Predictions of Choice Probability	24
	C. Scale Properties of the Model	29
V.	Differential Reward Learning Relative to Values of Reward Sets	30
	A. Experiment 6. Variation in Range of Reward Values and Mean Differences within Acquisition Pairs under a Full Information Condition	31
	B. Experiment 7. Variation in Mean Reward Differences within Acquisition Pairs under a Partial Information Condition	35
	C. Experiment 8. Mean Reward Differences within Disjoint Training Pairs	37
VI.	Theoretical Interpretation of the Differential Reward Series	38
VII.	General Discussion	42
	References	44

[1] The research reported here was supported primarily by USPHS grant MH16100 from the National Institute of Mental Health; the theoretical analyses and the preparation of this chapter were supported also by grant MH23878. I wish to acknowledge the contribution of Edith Skaar to the data collection and processing.

I. Introduction

One of the main paths to generality and elegance in the development of physical theory has been associated with a search for measurable properties of objects and events with respect to which physical laws take on especially simple forms. With the advent of experimental psychology it seemed natural to try the same strategy. We need not pause to dwell on the accomplishments pursuant to this effort in the area of sensory processes where three-quarters of a century of effort has eventuated in a major body of quantitative theory concerning psychological measurement and scaling of sensory attributes. Extended beyond the sensory laboratory into the domain of human decision making and choice, the same methods have led to the concepts of subjective probability and utility. And in this area, the work of a number of theorists, perhaps most notably that of Thurstone (1927, 1959) and Luce (1959), has demonstrated that in many choice situations human beings do indeed behave as though they had recoded objective quantities into psychological magnitudes having simple scale properties.

In this latter line of theorizing, however, form has tended to outrun content. Consequently, we find ourselves in possession of a body of mathematical theory impressive with respect to both elegance and depth (for example, Krantz, Luce, Suppes, & Tversky, 1971) but with almost no demonstrable relevance to research going on in the various areas in which psychologists study decision and choice.

A principal reason for this annoying gap is to be found, I would suggest, in the fact that investigators interested in demonstrating scale properties of human choice behavior have been little concerned with the psychological processes that give rise to the scale properties. We can readily answer questions as to whether particular scales exhibit transitivity or satisfy interval or ratio properties, but if asked where scales come from, we fall silent. Surely scales involved in most choice and decision behavior of adult human beings must be generated by some as yet unidentified learning processes.

The studies to be reported in this chapter represent a first step toward illuminating the problem. I shall focus attention on two types of data, one having to do with subjective probability of events, and the other with utility or reward value. In each case the first step will be to demonstrate that orderly patterns of behavior reflecting scale properties can be generated in controlled learning situations. The next step will be to analyze each situation from the standpoint of current theories of memory and to attempt to bring out experimentally some specific aspects of storage and retrieval that are responsible for the development and maintenance of the orderly patterns of choice behavior associated with psychological scales.

The first group of studies to be reported arose from an interest in problems of probability learning, probability estimates, and subjective probability. In the psychological literature, the term *subjective probability* has arisen primarily in connection with research on bets, gambles, and risk, and represents an inference from observed choice behavior with little attention to the type of memory structure that might underlie it (Cohen, 1964; Luce & Suppes, 1965). In probability learning experiments, on the other hand, it has been possible to show that orderly predictive behavior, and in some cases orderly probability estimates, arise as a function of an individual's experience with a set of alternative events over a series of trials in which the event probabilities remain constant.

In this latter line of research, we know quite a bit about the course of learning but almost nothing about the scale properties of the resulting choice behavior. If, following experience over a series of trials with two events whose probabilities are .75 and .25, an individual comes to predict these events with relative frequencies that match the true probabilities, we can conclude that he has learned something about the probabilities of the events. But we have no basis for concluding that he has developed a memory structure having any properties of a scale of probability. To take the latter step, we should need at least to demonstrate that, following experience with a few pairs of events drawn from a larger set, the individual is able in effect to place the various events on a psychological scale in such a way that he can then exhibit successful predictions or can generate accurate probability estimates concerning any new pairs of events from the set that might confront him on test trials.

II. An Observation-Transfer Paradigm for the Study of Predictive Behavior

In order to examine the acquisition of information regarding event probabilities, we need to simplify the subject's decision problem to the point that his choices can be taken as direct indicators of his state of information. Then at a later stage we may be able to produce specifiable states of information and study the development of decision strategies on a known baseline. Further, it seems essential to restructure the traditional probability learning situation so that subjects can be expected to understand that their task is to learn about probabilities. In the past, the standard practice has been either to give subjects no meaningful orientation or to mislead them concerning the nature of the task (Estes, 1964; Myers, 1976). The reason in part is that orderly acquisition data and asymptotic probability matching seemed to be best attainable when subjects were led to believe that their task was to solve a problem or to make psychological judgments which had nothing to do with probabilities. Thus, in most studies of human probability learning, we were in effect dealing with incidental learning. On the few occasions when subjects were instructed as to the probabilistic nature of the task, learning proved more rapid (Peterson & Ulehla, 1965; Rubinstein, 1959). But then a new problem intruded. Learning curves for a substantial proportion of subjects rose quickly to an asymptote of 100% prediction of the more frequently occurring trial outcome, an inconvenient result if one's purpose is to determine how limits of learning are related to differences in outcome probability.

In the present research we have attempted to circumvent these problems by combining a task situation in which subjects clearly understand that they are dealing with probabilities and an experimental design that permits us to monitor the subject's state of information regarding probabilities without disturbing the learning process.

One widely familiar and well-publicized activity with regard to which nearly everyone in our culture understands the role of probability is the public opinion poll. It seemed that we could capitalize on this familiarity by setting up an experimental situation which would simulate the operation of an opinion poll. Our subjects, who would take on the role of observers of the poll results, could be expected to come to us well instructed by extra-laboratory experience prior to the experiment and to bring to the task whatever habits and skills they might have developed outside of the laboratory for dealing with uncertain events.

In the studies to be reported, our subjects were told that they were to imagine that the computer which operated the experimental apparatus had been programmed to conduct an imaginary opinion poll according to exactly the same principles as those governing the Gallup poll and others with which they were familiar. Prior to each trial of the experiment, a hypothetical individual in the hypothetical population being sampled would be interrogated by the computer as to his preference with regard to a pair of alternatives (these might be candidates for office or treatments, such as headache remedies—for brevity we shall refer to them simply as stimuli) and the results of the inquiry would be transmitted by way of a simulated television screen to the subject who acted as an observer. The subject understood that his task was solely to observe the results of a series of trials, attempting to form a mental impression of the relative likelihoods that different stimuli would be preferred by the individuals being sampled, and that he then would be tested on his ability to predict the results of further polls in which the stimuli were tested in new combinations.

The point of departure for our new experimental paradigm was the observation of Reber and Millward (1968) that they could speed up probability learning considerably by starting their subjects off with a block of trials in which they simply observed the occurrences of the events which were later to be predicted but without making any responses on these trials. This result might well have been anticipated on the basis of analyses of Thorndikian learning situations which demonstrated the excessive information processing load entailed by the usual procedure of requiring a subject both to make responses and to observe outcomes on each learning trial (Buchwald, 1969; Estes, 1969).

Proceeding from these observations, it seemed that we might hope to obtain a more sensitive index of the learning which goes on in probability learning experiments by means of a transfer design which separates the occasions on which the subjects obtain information by observation from the occasions on which they are tested. The design is illustrated in Table I for an experiment in which three pairs of stimulus alternatives, listed at the top, appear on observation trials and then enter into transfer tests in all possible pairwise combinations. The probability that stimulus A_i is the winner (i.e., is reported to have been preferred over the other member of the pair) on any observation trial is customarily denoted by π_i. The π values shown are those used in the first two experiments to be reported.

TABLE I

DESIGN OF EXPERIMENTS 1 AND 2

	Observation pairs					
	A_1 vs. A_2		A_3 vs. A_4		A_5 vs. A_6	
Probability of win (π value)	.62	.38	.58	.42	.54	.46

During the training phase of the experiment, the subject has opportunity to observe the results of a number of simulated preference tests on A_1 versus A_2, a number on A_3 versus A_4, and a number on A_5 versus A_6. Now, in the case shown in Table I, π_1 would be .62 and π_3 would be .58. Over a series of trials the subject would have an opportunity to learn that A_1 was preferred over A_2 62% of the time, and A_3 over A_4 58% of the time. With enough experience he might well come to encode stimuli A_1 and A_3 as "winners" and if asked to predict the results of future polls, always predict that A_1 would be chosen over A_2 and always to predict that A_3 would be chosen over A_4. How then could we determine whether the subject had acquired any information with regard to the differential win probabilities of A_1 versus A_3? Our procedure is to ask the subject to predict the outcome of a new test in which A_1 and A_3 are pitted against each other. He can do so with greater than chance success only if he has stored in memory information about the corresponding π values beyond simply the fact that both A_1 and A_3 have been winners on the average.

This tactic is employed systematically in all of the experiments to be reported. Each experiment is divided into training and test phases. During the training phase the subject is given the results of repeated simulated preference tests on the observation pairs, then during the block of test trials he is asked to predict the results of surveys in which these stimuli are paired in all possible ways.

III. The Informational Basis of Predictive Behavior

In the initial exploratory studies conducted with the observation-test design I wished, first, to appraise the speed and precision of probability learning under these conditions and, second, to narrow down the range of tenable hypotheses concerning the basis of predictive behavior in memory. With respect to the latter objective, I began with the assumption that an individual's predictive behavior is based on his state of information regarding event probabilities. The information need not be numerical, nor even verbal, in character. Rather, the representation in memory of an event probability may be conceived as a cumulation of the residual effects ("memory traces") of previous trial outcomes. Further, the development of such a representation in memory need not depend on counting or other heuristics, but may be the result of a learning process which proceeds automatically as a function of observation trials and is reflected directly in predictive behavior unless masked by hypothesis-testing activities on the part of the learner.

A. EXPERIMENT 1. PROBABILITY LEARNING WITH HOMOGENEOUS BLOCKS OF OBSERVATION TRIALS

1. *Method*

The design of this experiment required the subject to acquire information concerning the preferences that a hypothetical population of voters would exhibit concerning three pairs of candidates and to make predictions concerning results of elections.

The subjects were given full information concerning the probabilistic nature of the situation and the fact that their sole task was to gain sufficient information concerning probabilities of winning and losing on the part of various candidates during the observation blocks to improve their predictions for the various possible pairs on test blocks.

The candidates were represented by initials—single letters displayed on an oscilloscope screen interfaced to a PDP-8/I computer. In this experiment the basic plan for each session involved three pairs of letters; for each pair there were preassigned probabilities (π values) that each of the two members would be the winner or loser on each observation trial. The probability combinations were .62–.38, .58–.42, and .54–.46.

In Part 1 of the experiment, nine subjects were each studied for a single session in which they received eight replications of a basic cycle, each cycle comprising 72 observation trials, 24 on each of the three pairs of alternatives, followed by 30 test trials. An observation trial began with the display on the oscilloscope screen of the two letters corresponding to one of the pairs of hypothetical candidates for 500 msec, for example,

$$A$$
$$B,$$

after which a row of tallies appeared following each of the two letters, for example,

$$A\ III$$
$$B\ I,$$

and remained in view for 750 msec; then the screen went blank for a 1-sec intertrial interval. The numbers of tallies that might appear ranged from 1 through 8 and the subject understood that on each trial the candidate who received the larger number of tallies was to be regarded as the majority choice, that is the "winner" of an opinion poll conducted with the sample of potential voters. When the tallies appeared on each observation trial, the subject pronounced the initial of the winner.

The computer program governing the experimental routine prescribed in advance which of the two alternatives would be the winner on each observation trial; the winner always received 5, 6, 7, or 8 tallies and the loser 1, 2, 3, or 4 tallies, the only constraint being that each particular value appear equally often within the winner and loser categories.

Within any observation series, each of the three pairs of alternatives was assigned to a block of 24 consecutive trials, the blocks occurring in random orders from one cycle to the next. Within a block, the same pair of alternatives appeared on each trial, the winner of each trial being determined by a random number generator with the constraint that in a .62–.38 block A_1 and A_2 were designated as winners exactly 15 and 9 times, respectively; in a .58–.42 block, A_3 and A_4 were winners 14 and 10 times; and in a .54–.46 block, A_5 and A_6 were winners 13 and 11 times, respectively.

During the block of test trials which followed each 72-trial observation series, all possible pairs of the six candidates were tested, each pair appearing once in each of the two possible left–right orders on the screen, resulting in a block of 30 test trials. The test trials were subject paced. At the beginning of the trial, two alternatives were presented (for example, A_1 versus A_4) and remained on the screen until the subject indicated his choice by pressing the response key under one of the two stimuli. The choice and the response time were recorded by the computer but no immediate feedback was given the subject regarding the actual winner of the hypothetical election in which the two candidates were paired. However, in order to maintain motivation, at the end of each 30-trial test block, the subject was shown the number of times on which his predictions of winners agreed with those generated by the computer, which had a full knowledge of the true probabilities of winning and losing for the population being sampled in the simulated opinion polls and elections.

Subjects in all of the experiments to be reported were young adults, not necessarily students, who in most cases were recruited via newspaper advertisements and who were paid for their services.

2. Results

For a group of nine subjects run under the procedure just described, the first overall result was a surprisingly rapid rate of learning, especially considering that the differences in π value between the members of observation pairs are rather small compared to those involved in most classical probability learning experiments. For convenience in assessing learning, we define as a correct response on any test trial a choice of the alternative with the higher π value. In these terms, the learning curves in terms of proportion of correct responses per test block rise from the initial value near .5 to a level slightly above .7 by the beginning of the fifth test block, then remain constant over the remainder of the session, never rising above .72. This terminal level is far above probability matching, which would be .56 over all test combinations of π values.

The test results on particular pairs of alternatives are summarized in Table II in the form of a paired-comparison table. The rows from top to bottom and columns from left to right correspond to the stimulus alternatives (candidates) in order of π values. The value in each cell represents the percentage of test trials on which the row alternative was chosen over the column alternative and the marginal values in the right-hand column represent the average proportions of cases in which each alternative was chosen over all others with which it was paired on test trials. These values represent data pooled over the entire session. The values in the upper right quadrant of the table, representing proportions of choices of the three highest valued stimuli (the winners on the observation trials) over the three lowest

TABLE II

RESPONSES[a] ON PAIRED-COMPARISON TESTS OF EXPERIMENT 1
(BLOCKED OBSERVATION TRIALS)

π Value	π Value						Average
	.62	.58	.54	.46	.42	.38	
.62	—	59	72	79	83	89	76
.58	41	—	55	77	83	85	68
.54	28	45	—	80	80	84	64
.46	21	23	20	—	60	63	37
.42	17	17	20	40	—	51	29
.38	11	15	16	37	49	—	26

[a] Percentage choice of row over column alternative.

valued (the losers) are uniformly high. Further, the marginal values in the right-hand column of the table line up nicely in the order of the π values of the alternatives even though π values of adjacent stimuli within the winner and loser sets differ from each other by only .04.

Clearly the subjects could not have achieved these results entirely by encoding the stimuli as "winners" and "losers," for their percentages of correct predictions were somewhat above chance even when winners were paired with winners and losers with losers on transfer tests.

B. EXPERIMENT 2. RANDOMIZED TRAINING TRIALS AND DELAYED TESTS

It seemed possible that the exceedingly efficient learning in Experiment 1 might have been attributable, in part, to the procedure of utilizing homogeneous blocks of observation trials on specific pairs of alternatives. This procedure might have enabled the subjects to do a certain amount of counting or encoding of event runs as units in order to facilitate their estimates of probabilities. Also, although the subjects' principal source of information concerning event probabilities was the observation trials, we had no way to determine whether the feedback given at the end of each test block might have had any influence on performance. The present experiment was designed to obtain evidence on both of these questions.

1. Method

The general procedures, the stimulus sets, and the π values were all the same as in the preceding experiment. There were just two changes in design. First, on the observation trials the three pairs of alternatives were presented in a completely random order rather than being segregated into homogeneous blocks. With this change in procedure it appeared quite impossible for the subjects to utilize counting or to keep track of properties of the preceding sequences on the various individual pairs during a 72-trial observation block. Second, for half of the subjects in this experiment, no test trials were given until after the fourth 72-trial observation block. There were seven subjects in each group.

2. Results

The terminal overall level of correct responding on test trials was approximately .67 as compared to approximately .71 in the first experiment. The rate of approach to this terminal level also was similar, with little increase in correct response level over the last half of the session. For subjects receiving test blocks after every 72-trial block the proportion of correct responses after the fourth observation cycle was .66, whereas, for the group that did not receive tests following the first three observation blocks, the corresponding value was .65. Thus it appears that the information given at the end of the test blocks had little effect on learning.

Three additional groups of 10 subjects were run under the same procedures, but with a different set of letters for each group, and with test trials after each observation block. In the pooled data for all 37 subjects run under this condition, the overall percentage of correct responses increased from an average of 62 over test blocks 1 and 2 to 64 over blocks 3 and 4 and then 66 over blocks 5 to 8, where again 56% would constitute probability matching.

But principal interest attaches to the paired-comparison matrix for the transfer tests, presented in Table III for the data pooled over all test blocks. These choice percentages increase quite uniformly across the rows and up the columns of the table in just the manner one would expect if the choices were based on a representation in memory of the positions of the stimuli on a scale of subjective probability. And, considering the considerable increase in difficulty of the task over that of Experiment 1, the subjects exhibit rather striking proficiency at acquiring information concerning event probabilities, even under circumstances contrived to rule out the use of the heuristic devices or strategies that may supplement sheer learning by observation under less strictly constrained experimental conditions.

The results of this first series of studies offer some support for our

TABLE III

RESPONSES ON PAIRED-COMPARISON TESTS OF EXPERIMENT 2
(RANDOMIZED OBSERVATION TRIALS)

π Value	π Value						
	.62	.58	.54	.46	.42	.38	Average
.62	—	57	64	69	78	75	69
.58	43	—	59	69	71	76	64
.54	36	41	—	58	65	66	53
.46	31	31	42	—	59	56	44
.42	22	29	35	41	—	48	35
.38	25	24	34	44	52	—	36

preliminary analysis. The slow and variable course of probability learning characteristic of studies using traditional procedures is evidently attributable to extraneous activities on the part of the subjects that mask the course of acquisition. When normal adults understand fully the probabilistic nature of the task and are motivated to base their choices directly on their states of information, we obtain a picture of rapid and precise probability learning, with only tens rather than hundreds of observation trials being required to establish significant discriminations of very small differences in probabilities of events.

Further, the data clearly exhibit properties signifying the development of a memory structure that functions as a scale of a psychological magnitude. Following observational experience with only three of the pairs that can be formed from a set of six alternatives, our subjects generate orderly predictive responses to all possible test pairs, and, when training has been given with randomized observation trials, predict as well on new test pairs as on those included in the observation series. This transfer pattern is just what one would expect if the subjects had been given information regarding the relative placement of the candidates on a probability scale.

C. EXPERIMENT 3. OBSERVATION TRIALS WITH A COMMON LOSING ALTERNATIVE

The results of the first two experiments, and especially the second, appear quite compatible with the idea that the learner is rather directly translating objective into subjective probabilities and performing transfer tests on the basis of the placement of the various alternatives on the subjective probability scale. Now we wish to begin to look at experimental manipulations that might be more sharply diagnostic with respect to alternative interpretations. The main alternative to be considered, on the basis of theoretical considerations of memory, is that the individual is actually storing frequency counts in memory and then converting these to probability estimates at the time of transfer tests. In this experiment we examined a situation that should be the equivalent of the one studied in Experiment 2 from the standpoint of a subjective probability model but that might raise some new problems for an information processing system based on the acquisition of frequency information.

For this purpose we introduced the design exhibited in Table IV. The general procedures are the same as those of Experiment 2 except that on observation trials each of four candidates A_i (i=1–4) is paired

TABLE IV

DESIGN OF EXPERIMENT 3 (COMMON LOSER)

	Observation pairs							
	A_1 vs. CL		A_2 vs. CL		A_3 vs. CL		A_4 vs. CL	
Probability of win (π value)	.75	.25	.67	.33	.62	.38	.58	.42

with a common alternative candidate who, on the average, is a loser with respect to all of the others.

All subjects were given six cycles each comprising 96 observation trials followed by 30 test trials. The tests included pairings of each of the five candidates that had appeared on observation trials with each other and also pairings of these with a novel alternative (N), introduced to the subject as a new candidate about whom they had to make predictions even though he had not participated in the simulated preelection opinion poll.

On observation trials the two candidates for whom simulated opinion poll data were to be presented were displayed in a vertical arrangement on the CRT screen with the common loser (CL) always in the lower position, whereas on test trials, the members of the various pairs appeared in a horizontal arrangement with left–right orders counterbalanced. The detailed procedure on observation trials differed for two experimental conditions. Sixteen subjects were assigned to Condition W, in which they were required on each observation trial to pronounce the initial of the candidate who received more votes on the trial; 32 subjects were assigned to Condition A, in which they were required on each observation trial to pronounce the name of the candidate appearing in the upper position and then to state whether he won or lost on the given trial. These manipulations were introduced in an attempt to influence the combinations of events to which the subjects would attend and therefore those which, on a frequency hypothesis, they might be expected to encode and store in memory.

The data are assembled in Table V, again in the form of paired-comparison matrices, the upper and lower panels representing Groups W and A, respectively. The overall rate and course of learning were similar to those of Experiment 2 and, if we look only at the transfer tests involving various pairings of the form A_iA_j, the results also are similar. At first glance the differentiation among these candidates (shown in the upper left-hand portion of each of the

TABLE V

RESPONSES ON PAIRED-COMPARISON TESTS OF EXPERIMENT 3
(COMMON LOSER)

Alternative		A_1	A_2	A_3	A_4	CL	N	
Condition W	π Value	.75	.67	.62	.58	.34	—	Average
A_1	.75	—	55	60	61	61	88	65
A_2	.67	45	—	51	47	50	89	56
A_3	.62	40	49	—	47	54	87	55
A_4	.58	39	53	53	—	53	86	57
CL	.34	39	50	46	47	—	91	55
N	—	12	11	13	14	9	—	12
Condition A								
A_1	.75	—	52	54	58	73	87	65
A_2	.67	48	—	53	50	70	89	62
A_3	.62	46	47	—	52	68	90	61
A_4	.58	42	50	48	—	68	87	59
CL	.34	27	30	32	32	—	79	40
N	—	13	11	10	13	21	—	14

paired comparison matrices), seems rather small; however, in view of the π values used, larger differences could not be expected on the basis of such theories as the stimulus sampling model. One can readily confirm, for example, that none of these observed transfer proportions for any pair A_iA_j are far from the value $\pi i/(\pi_i + \pi_j)$, which would represent the analog of probability matching in a simple noncontingent situation.

The transfer results for the A_i alternatives pitted against the CL prove to depend strongly on the conditions of vocalization of observation trial outcomes, yielding choice proportions much below probability matching for Condition W (name the "winner" on the trial) but above, on the average, for Condition A (report whether the A alternative won or lost). The critical differentiating factor appears to be the extent to which the instructions led subjects to attend to, and therefore encode in memory, the trial outcomes for the CL during the observation series.

The results on tests pitting the various alternatives that had been presented on observation trials against the novel candidate also present some surprises. Since the subjects had no information concerning the novel candidate, one might have expected them to assign him an average position, that is one close to the adaptation level value on a probability scale. The high proportion of choices of the A_i alternatives over the novel candidate are compatible with this idea, but the fact that the CL was chosen over the novel candidate with similarly high probabilities (even higher than for A_i candidates in Condition W and only slightly lower in Condition A) is hard to fit in with the idea that the subjects were performing in accord with a scale of subjective probabilities. Evidently the subjects were in a sense misled by the fact that candidate CL, though always a loser on the average with respect to each of the candidates paired with him on observation trials, had accumulated a larger total number of winning outcomes during the observation series than any one of the A_i candidates. Thus in these data, as well as those for A_i vs. CL, we have a hint that the subjects' test performance is based at least in part on frequency information as distinguished from a rationally constructed scale of subjective probabilities.

D. EXPERIMENT 4. JOINT VARIATION OF STIMULUS FREQUENCY AND OUTCOME PROBABILITY

The hint emerging from Experiment 3 that subjects' performance reflects memory for total frequencies of winning outcomes on given alternatives as well as estimates of outcome probabilities is not unprecedented. In a related study (Estes, 1976) even more direct evidence of a similar tendency appeared. That study involved an observation-transfer design similar to that of the experiments reported above but a slightly different task orientation. Further, there was a major departure from the design of Experiment 2 of the present investigation in that some of the observation pairs occurred more often than others so that, for example, a stimulus with a π value of .42 occurred twice as often during the observation series as a stimulus with a π value of .54; thus the former stimulus accrued a larger total number of winning outcomes even though it had the lower probability of winning on any observation trial. The data for a transfer test on this pair of alternatives yielded a choice probability of .64 on the part of the subjects for the stimulus that had occurred more often but with actually the lower π value. If the subjects' test performance was governed by a scale of subjective probabilities, then the scale was not related in a monotone fashion to objective probabilities but rather was grossly perturbed by the variations in stimulus frequency.

Owing to its central importance to the objectives of the present study, that experiment was replicated with the present task orientation and the design illustrated in Table VI. The rows of the table labeled Conditions 1 and 2 indicate the relative frequencies with which the observation pairs above occurred during the observation series; for example, in Condition 1 the pair A_3 versus A_4 occurred twice as often as the pair A_5 versus A_6. Sixteen subjects were assigned to each condition and all were given six cycles of 72 observations followed by 30 test trials under conditions otherwise identical to those of Experiment 2 of the present paper. The way in which stimulus frequency and outcome probability interact in this situation is brought out most strikingly in the comparison shown in Table VII. These data represent proportions of choices of alternatives A_1 and A_2 over each of the other four alternatives. In both the upper and lower parts of the table the columns represent the alternatives $A_3 - A_6$ in decreasing order of π value. However, one can see at a glance that, quite contrary to the results of the first three experiments, the relative probabilities of winning outcomes associated with the alternatives are exceedingly poor predictors of subjects' choices. Rather, the pattern of test performance reflects closely to the assignment of the stimulus alternatives to the high (H) or low (L) frequency condition.

One can readily infer from this last result that if we were to summarize the full test data for this experiment in paired-comparison tables like those presented for Experiment 2, and with the rows and columns again ordered in terms of π values, we would not obtain a similarly orderly pattern of data in the table. However, the paired-comparison table does provide us some leverage on the problem of determining just how stimulus frequency and outcome probability interact. We need only seek a function of these two variables such that, when the alternatives are properly ordered in terms of the function, the orderly pattern is restored to the paired-comparison table.

TABLE VI

DESIGN OF EXPERIMENT 4: VARIATION IN STIMULUS FREQUENCIES AND OUTCOME PROBABILITIES

	Observation pairs					
	A_1 vs. A_2		A_3 vs. A_4		A_5 vs. A_6	
Probability of win	.62	.38	.58	.42	.54	.46
Relative frequency of pair						
Cond. 1	3		4		2	
Cond. 2	3		2		4	

TABLE VII

INDEPENDENT EFFECTS OF HIGH (H) OR LOW (L) STIMULUS FREQUENCY AND WIN PROBABILITY ON TEST PERFORMANCE IN EXPERIMENT 4

π Value	.58	.54	.46	.42
Condition 1	H	L	L	H
.62	36	67	78	58
.38	21	49	60	31
Condition 2	L	H	H	L
.62	66	48	55	78
.38	36	18	26	56

A solution turns out to be engagingly simple. We need only multiply the π value for each stimulus times the total number of times that it appeared during the observation series, thus in effect computing the total number of winning outcomes observed for the given alternative. The paired-comparison tables for the two conditions, ordered in terms of this index, are presented in Table VIII; and one may see at once that we have indeed restored the orderly pattern, with choice percentages increasing across the rows and up the columns as uniformly as one could expect for data which have some inherent variability. Further, the trends are not only qualitatively similar but quantitatively in very close agreement with the data obtained from the corresponding experiment in the study utilizing simulated preference surveys (Estes, 1976). Thus it appears that this result is highly reliable and replicable across variations in task orientation. The combined results appear to support strongly the suggestion emerging from Experiment 3 to the effect that our subjects' predictive behavior is based primarily on memory for event frequencies rather than upon accurate estimates of outcome probabilities.

E. EXPERIMENT 5. JOINT VARIATION OF STIMULUS FREQUENCY AND OUTCOME PROBABILITY WITH OVERLAPPING OBSERVATION PAIRS

Those who are attached to the idea of man as a rational decision maker might raise a question about the previous experiment on the grounds that the experimental design may not provide a fully adequate opportunity for learners to gain the information they need to establish a subjective probability scale. The possible weak point is that none of the observation pairs overlapped, so that, for example,

TABLE VIII

RESPONSES ON PAIRED-COMPARISON TESTS OF EXPERIMENT 4[a]

Condition 1	112	90	80	54	52	44	Average
112	–	64	69	79	79	80	74
90	36	–	58	68	67	78	63
80	31	42	–	69	54	64	52
54	21	22	31	–	49	60	37
52	21	33	46	51	–	61	42
44	20	22	36	40	39	–	31
Condition 2	104	90	88	56	54	40	Average
104	–	52	70	74	82	82	72
90	48	–	55	66	78	78	63
88	30	45	–	61	74	76	57
56	26	34	39	–	64	76	48
54	18	32	26	36	–	56	34
40	18	22	24	24	44	–	26

[a] Entries ordered by total win frequency over observation trials.

the learner had an opportunity to observe the relative probabilities of winning and losing on the part of alternatives A_1 and A_2 relative to each other but had no observation trials in which either of these was paired with any other member of the set of alternatives. Perhaps the necessary condition for the establishment of a rational scale of subjective probabilities is that the learner's observations include pairings of each alternative with every other, either directly, or at least by way of intermediary links (for example, A_1 versus A_2 and A_2 versus A_3). This possibility is investigated in the present experiment with procedures similar to those of Experiment 4 except for a change in design.

The present experiment included four stimulus alternatives and two π values, combined into observation pairs according to the following scheme:

A_1 vs. A_2 A_3 vs. A_4 A_1 vs. A_4
.58   .42   .58   .42   .58   .42

Now all of the alternatives are connected in the sense mentioned above. Considering A_2 versus A_3, for example, the observation series provides information on A_2 versus A_1, A_1 versus A_4, and A_4 versus A_3, thus providing the basis for placing all of the alternatives in their appropriate positions on a probability scale. Twenty-eight subjects were all given the same procedure, which involved eight cycles of 72 observation trials on the three observation pairs (in random sequence) and 12 test trials, including all possible pairings of the four alternatives in each of the two left—right orders.

During the observation series, the three observation pairs occurred equally often, but owing to the overlap the individual alternatives did not occur with equal frequency. Within a 72-trial observation block, of the $\pi = .58$ alternatives, A_1 occurred together with a winning outcome 28 times and A_3 14 times, whereas for the $\pi = .42$ alternatives, A_4 occurred 20 times and A_2 only 10. Thus we again will be in a position to determine any effects of the independent variation of stimulus frequency and outcome probability.

The full paired-comparison data pooled over all eight test blocks are presented in Table IX. A glance at the table reveals immediately that once again the subjects were strongly influenced by stimulus frequency independently of outcome probability. For example, on the test pair A_1 versus A_3, both having π values of .58 but differing in frequency, we find 76% choices of A_1; and in the A_2 versus A_4 pair, both members having had π values of .42 but differing in frequency, we observe 68% choice of A_4. But most spectacularly, when we consider the test pair A_3 versus A_4, in which A_3 had the higher π value but the lower frequency, we observe only 41% choices of A_3. It may be remarked, further, that these results almost certainly do not reflect incompleteness of learning, for similar analysis performed on only the last two test blocks reveals the same pattern with, for example, the "aberrant" choice proportion for the critical A_3 versus A_4 pair being even further accentuated (38% choices of A_3). And finally, we observe that with the entries in Table IX

TABLE IX

RESPONSES ON PAIRED-COMPARISON TESTS OF EXPERIMENT 5[a]

		A_1 28	A_4 20	A_3 14	A_2 10	Average
A_1	28	—	63	76	78	72
A_4	20	37	—	59	68	55
A_3	14	24	41	—	69	45
A_2	10	22	32	31	—	28

[a]Varying stimulus frequency and outcome probability with overlapping observation pairs.

ordered in terms of total win frequencies per 72-trial observation block, we obtain the same orderly pattern of values, increasing up the columns and across the rows, observed for the same analysis of Experiment 4, whereas the order would disappear if the alternatives were ordered only in terms of π values.

There seems no remaining doubt that the subjects do not perform like rational statisticians who construct subjective probability scales making the best use of available information, but rather perform on the basis of memory for frequencies of the events to which they have been attending during observation trials.

IV. Theoretical Interpretation of Probability Learning Series

The first-order results to be interpreted present a relatively clear picture. All of the conditions yield systematic choice behavior on transfer tests, and in all conditions when the observation pairs have been presented in random sequence (that is, all experiments except Experiment 1), choice behavior on transfer tests is fully as accurate for new pairs as for observation pairs.

Further, the obtained paired-comparison matrices take on a standard form in all cases, with the probability of a choice of any one stimulus over another generally increasing as a function of their separation with respect to the independent variable used to order the stimuli of the rows and columns of the matrix. However, we have found that the independent variable has to change with experimental conditions. The π value, that is the probability of a winning outcome on occurrences of an observation pair, suffices for Experiments 1, 2, and 3, but total frequency of winning outcomes over the observation series proves to be a more appropriate independent variable for Experiments 4 and 5.

With few exceptions differences in average paired-comparison values (the row means of Tables II, III, V, VIII, and IX) between different stimuli prove directly related to differences in π value or win frequency, as appropriate. One exception will be observed in the case of Experiment 1 (Table II) where a disproportionately large difference in average paired-comparison value appears between the stimuli with π values of .54 and .46. A second deviation occurs in Experiment 3 where the paired-comparison value for the CL is out of line with expectation on the basis either of π value or of overall win frequency. A third discrepancy is the deviation from monotonicity in Experiment 4, Condition 1 (that is the inversion of the fourth and fifth row averages in the upper matrix of Table VIII).

The idea of a single subjective scale underlying predictive behavior in all of the conditions studied here can be maintained only if we assume that the discrepancies all represent noise in the data. That interpretation would be a possibility; but should we facilely accept the conclusion that deviations from a preconceived idea of regularity necessarily represent noise? I shall instead entertain the view that the discrepancies as well as the regularities are real. Proceeding on this assumption, I can find no single independent variable that straightens out all of the paired-comparison functions. However, ideas developed elsewhere (Estes, 1976) regarding the interpretation of probability learning in terms of concepts of memory suggest the possibility that the irregularities arise because the data represent, in effect, a mixture of choice behaviors based on two or more different psychological scales.

The reason for anticipating a mixture is that, depending on instructions, experimental context, and previous experience, different subjects may attend selectively to different events. In related studies (Estes, 1976) we have found that variations in task orientation led to different tendencies on the part of subjects to attend to and encode winning as compared to losing outcomes in situations like those studied in the present experiments. Further, faced with a similar problem in relation to subjects' ability to generate linear orderings on the basis of frequency information, Humphreys (1975) arrived at a hypothesis of a mixture of attentional tendencies toward correct and incorrect outcomes of verbal discrimination trials. Consequently, I propose now to seek an interpretation of all of the trends in the present data, both the regularities and the deviations already noted, in terms of a model predicated on the idea that probability judgments are based on memory for relative frequencies of the events to which subjects selectively attend during an observation series.

A. THE ASSOCIATIVE CODING MODEL

As applied to the present situation, we would assume on the basis of this model that test performance is mediated by categorical memory for relative frequencies of stimulus-outcome combinations. We conceive that the learner encodes the principal event categories to which he attends under a given condition, in this case stimuli together with winning or losing outcomes, and stores memory trace vectors that incorporate these encoded representations of event combinations together with contextual cues common to the observation and test situations. A trace vector may be denoted T_{xAO}, where x refers to the context, A the stimulus alternative and O the outcome (W or L) of an observation trial. The contextual cues are assumed to vary in availability from trial to trial (as in standard stimulus sampling theory or encoding variability theory) so that, over a series of trials, the number of traces established that include particular event combinations will on the average be proportional to their relative frequencies of occurrence. Owing to different task orientations, subjects may vary from one experiment to another in their probabilities of attending to and encoding particular event categories, here winning or losing outcomes.

These ideas can be given a simple quantitative representation in the following way. When learning is complete, if the subject has been encoding only winning outcomes on observation trials, then the proportion of all memory trace vectors stored which are associated with winning outcomes for alternative A_i can be represented by a quantity α_i, where α_i equals $W_i/\Sigma W_k$. In this expression, W_k denotes the actual frequency of wins over the observation series for alternative A_k ($k = 1, 2, \ldots, N$, where N is the number of alternatives). Similarly, if the subject were encoding only losing outcomes, then the proportion of trace vectors associated with losing outcomes for alternative A_i would be $\beta_i = L_i/\Sigma L_k$, L_k denoting the actual frequency of losses for A_k over the observation series.

With regard to the way in which choices are generated on the basis of the information in memory, it is assumed that on any test trial, the subject scans the two test stimuli and attempts to recall their previously associated outcomes. On a test trial when, say, alternatives A_i and A_j are presented, we assume that the subject scans the alternatives, terminating with a choice when he finds a match between the pattern of a test stimulus plus available contextual cues and a memory trace stored on an observation trial when a particular type of outcome occurred. It can be shown that very simple expressions relate asymptotic choice probabilities to the quantities α_i and β_i defined above, the form of dependence depending on the type of outcome encoded (for details, see Estes, 1976).

Letting $P_{ij}(i)$ denote the probability of choosing alternative A_i when alternatives A_i and A_j are presented for choice, the predicted values of this choice probability are given by Eqs. (1), (2), and (3), respectively, according as the subject has attended only to winning outcomes, only to losing outcomes, or to both, on observation trials:

$$P_{ij}(i) = \frac{\alpha_i^2}{\alpha_i^2 + \alpha_j^2} \qquad (1)$$

$$P_{ij}(i) = \frac{\beta_j^2}{\beta_i^2 + \beta_j^2} \qquad (2)$$

or

$$P_{ij}(i) = \frac{\alpha_i \beta_j}{\alpha_i \beta_j + \alpha_j \beta_i} \qquad (3)$$

Since we do not in general know to what events subjects have been attending, and wish to allow for some mixture within a group of subjects, we introduce three parameters, w, x, and b, to represent the proportions of instances in which Eqs. (1), (2), and (3), respectively, are applicable in a given experiment. Then by evaluating these parameters from the data, we can hope to determine what mixture of modes of selective attention is represented in the behavior of the subjects. Further, we must allow for the possibility that under particular experimental conditions learning may not be complete; to this end we introduce also a parameter ϕ to represent the probability that learning has occurred in the case of any given subject and item (hence, with probability $1-\phi$ learning has not occurred and choices should be expected to conform to a chance probability of .5).

Combining these various terms we arrive at the following equation:

$$P_{ij}(i) = (1-\phi)(.5) + \phi[w\frac{\alpha_i^2}{\alpha_i^2 + \alpha_j^2} + x\frac{\beta_j^2}{\beta_i^2 + \beta_j^2} + b\frac{\alpha_i \beta_j}{\alpha_i \beta_j + \alpha_j \beta_i}] \qquad (4)$$

representing predicted choice probability in terms of a weighted combination of unlearned and learned states and, in the latter case, different proportions of instances in which winning outcomes, losing outcomes, or both have been attended to.

To evaluate the fruitfulness of this development in the present situation, I shall now proceed in two steps. The first is to determine the best fit of Eq. (4) to the data of each of Experiments 1–5; the second is to consider the bearing of the results on the question of the nature of the psychological scales underlying the observed choice behavior.

B. PARAMETER ESTIMATES AND PREDICTIONS OF CHOICE PROBABILITY

The first step was initiated by a computer search of possible combinations of parameter values to determine the best fit of Eq. (4) to the full paired-comparison matrices of Tables II, III, V, VIII, and IX according to the least-squares criterion. There are 15 independent observed proportions in the paired-comparison matrices for Experiments 1–4 and six in Experiment 5; hence, even though we have to estimate the values of four parameters, the number of degrees of freedom in the data substantially exceeds the number of parameters estimated. Further, since on a preliminary analysis the parameter x turned out to be near zero in all cases, x was set equal to zero, thus dropping the term $\beta_j^2/(\beta_i^2+\beta_j^2)$ from Eq. (4) and reducing the number of free parameters to three. It appears that under the conditions studied here, there is very little likelihood that subjects will attend only to losing outcomes. That result was, however, obtained in an experiment reported elsewhere in which subjects were instructed to pronounce the names only of losing alternatives on observation trials (Estes, 1976). As may be seen from the parameter estimates summarized in Table X, it turns out that for all of the experiments in which the observation pairs were nonoverlapping, we are dealing with essentially asymptotic data ($\phi=1$).

Now I shall comment briefly on the problems encountered in treating the data of each of the experiments in turn in terms of the model. To provide comparability across experiments I have averaged the values associated with each stimulus (that is the values across the rows of the observed and predicted paired-comparison matrices) and plotted these as a function of the proportion of W's (α_i in terms of the model) in Figs. 1–4.

1. The first attempts to fit the data of Experiment 1 failed to yield a reasonable result, owing to the large gap between the mean paired-comparison values for the lowest three and highest three stimulus alternatives. Consideration of the special features of this experiment in terms of memory factors suggested that the key to the difficulty might lie in the fact that in this experiment, only, the observation

TABLE X
PARAMETER ESTIMATES FOR PROBABILITY LEARNING EXPERIMENTS

Experiment	Learning rate (ϕ)	W's (w)	L's (x)	W's & L's (b)
		\multicolumn{3}{c}{Weight of component reflecting attention to:}

Experiment	Learning rate (ϕ)	W's (w)	L's (x)	W's & L's (b)
1	1.00	0	0	1.00[a]
2	1.00	0	0	1.00[a]
3 Group W	.50	.37	0	.63
3 Group A	.57	0	0	1.00
4 Cond. 1	1.00	.70	0	.30
4 Cond. 2	1.00	.80	0	.20
5	.95	.71	0	.29

[a] For Experiments 1 and 2 the theoretical asymptotes for attention to W or W & L are almost indistinguishable, so the estimates of the weights are arbitrary.

trials were blocked, so that a particular pair of alternatives appeared on one block of 24 consecutive trials within each 72-trial cycle. Under this condition, it might have been especially easy for subjects to notice that one member of each observation pair was the winner on the average and thus to encode the two members of each pair as "winner" (W) and "loser" (L) or the equivalent. Then on all test trials in which a winner was paired with a loser the subject would be expected to choose the winner without having to consult his memory for relative frequencies of previous occurrences. On the supposition that this type of encoding occurred half of the time and that in the remaining instances choice behavior was governed by the relative frequency model with the parameter values carried over from Experiment 2 (discussed below), we arrived at the theoretical function shown in Panel 1 of Fig. 1. We appear to have quite a good description of the observed paired-comparison function with only one free parameter (the proportion of W-L encodings) estimated from these data. A similar conception of performance reflecting a mixture of memory for frequency and outcome encoding has been found useful by Medin (1974) in the interpretation of verbal discrimination data.

2. Since the proportion of correct responses (that is, choices of the member of a test pair which had actually the higher π value) was

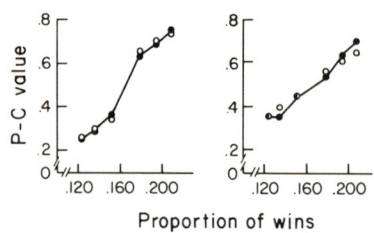

Fig. 1. The left and right panels, respectively, represent observed mean paired-comparison values for Experiments 1 and 2 (connected closed circles) together with predicted values (open circles) computed from the parameter estimates given in Table X.

virtually constant over successive test blocks, it was clear that the data of this experiment represent essentially asymptotic performance, so the parameter ϕ in Eq. (4) was set equal to 1. In evaluating the weighting parameters, w, and b, a small problem arose. The first two experiments were the only ones in this series conducted before the ideas embodied in the relative frequency model began to play a role in planning the experimental designs, and as a consequence it happens that for Experiments 1 and 2 the predicted asymptotic choice probabilities for Eq. (1) and (3) are virtually identical. Although the estimate of $b = 1$ was generated by the search procedure, a mixture of $w = .50$ and $b = .50$ yields an almost indistinguishable fit. The data for this experiment appear a bit noisy, owing no doubt to the very restricted range of π values, but nonetheless the correspondence between theoretical and observed values is fairly satisfactory (Panel 2 of Fig. 1).

3. In Experiment 3, which involved the pairing of each of four different candidates with a "common loser" during the observation series, we obtain rather peculiar looking paired-comparison functions (Fig. 2) owing to the fact that the stimulus alternative which was on the average a loser in each of the observation pairs yields mean paired-comparison values distinctly lower than would be expected solely on the basis of the total proportion of winning outcomes accrued to this alternative. The procedure of requiring the subjects to pronounce the name of the alternative paired with CL and also to state whether the alternative won or lost on each observation trial (used with Group A) yields distinctly faster learning than the standard procedure of requiring subjects only to pronounce the name of the winner (used with Group W); the difference in learning rate is manifest in the higher estimated value of ϕ for the former group (Table X) and the fact that the paired-comparison curve is elevated considerably, although similar in form. The parameter estimates

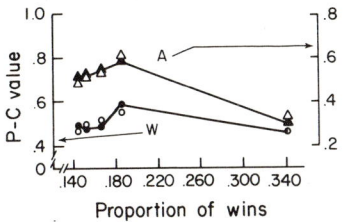

Fig. 2. Mean paired-comparison scale values (connected closed circles and closed triangles) for Experiment 3. The subjects in Group W pronounced the name of the winner on each observation trial, whereas the subjects in Group A pronounced the name of the candidate paired with the common loser and stated whether he won or lost. The open circles for Group W and open triangles for Group A represent predicted values from the model.

further reflect the difference in instructions in that the value of b is appreciably larger for Group A than for Group W. With these parameter values, the model has no difficulty in accounting for the curiously shaped paired-comparison functions of both groups.

4. Again for Experiment 4, the data appear to represent asymptotic performance, with ϕ equal to 1 for both Conditions 1 and 2. The estimation procedure yields the parameter values shown in Table X for each condition. As expected, since the subjects were instructed to pronounce only the names of winning alternatives on observation trials in this experiment, the parameter values showed that the subjects attended only to W's in the majority of instances. The theoretical functions computed using these parameter values and plotted in Fig. 3 provided rather good accounts of observed functions which otherwise might have seemed rather aberrant in form. In particular, both the drop in paired-comparison value from the second to the third point in Condition 1 and the very abrupt increases from

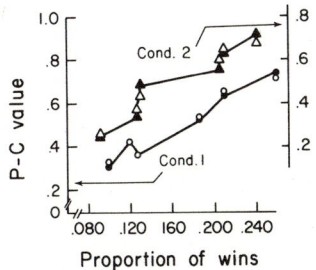

Fig. 3. Mean paired-comparison values (connected closed circles and closed triangles) for the two conditions of Experiment 4 together with predicted values (open circles and triangles, respectively).

the second to the third and fourth to the fifth points in Condition 2 are nicely handled by the model. The reason, in terms of the theory, for these deviations from smoothly increasing functions is that the independent variable in the figure is the proportion of winning outcomes associated with each stimulus alternative but the parameter estimates shown in Table X indicate that the subjects were on some occasions attending to both winning and losing outcomes. The third point for Condition 1 in Fig. 3 represents a stimulus alternative that had a higher proportion of winning outcomes than the one associated with the second point but also a disproportionally larger proportion of losing outcomes. Similarly, the sharp upturns in the curve for Condition 2 reflect points at which increases in proportion of winning outcomes were associated with substantial decreases in proportion of losing outcomes.

5. It will be recalled that in Experiment 5 the observation pairs were "connected" in the sense that for any two stimulus alternatives A_i and A_k which were not paired with each other during the observation series, each was paired with a common third alternative A_j. This design, together with instructions to pronounce only the names of winners on observation trials, yields an exceedingly orderly paired-comparison function and one closely described by the model (Fig. 4). As in the case of Experiment 4, the data appear to be asymptotic and the parameter estimates indicate that the subjects attended only to winning outcomes in a large majority of cases, but with a small admixture of instances in which they attended to both W's and L's.

Taking these results together, it appears that a model which assumes the basis of probability judgments to lie in memory for relative frequency information accounts both for the orderly scale-like choice performance that appears under optimal conditions and

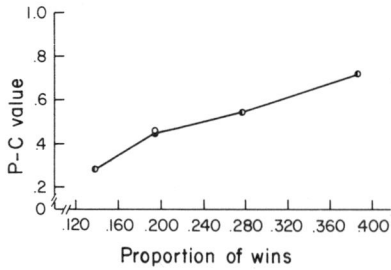

Fig. 4. Mean paired-comparison values for Experiment 5 (connected closed circles) together with predicted values (open circles).

also for the perturbations, sometimes large, that appear under various unusual circumstances.

C. SCALE PROPERTIES OF THE MODEL

Now to take the next step in our program of analysis and consider more formally the relation of the results to the conception of a psychological scale underlying choice, we return to Eqs. (1)–(3), which represent the asymptotic choice probabilities predicted by the model for the several pure cases of selective attention. We can convert these expressions to the form shown in Eqs. (5)–(7) by dividing the numerator and denominator of the right side of each equation by the numerator, obtaining

$$P_{ij}(i) = \frac{1}{1 + (\alpha_j^2/\alpha_i^2)} \qquad (5)$$

$$P_{ij}(i) = \frac{1}{1 + (\beta_i^2/\beta_j^2)} \qquad (6)$$

and

$$P_{ij}(i) = \frac{1}{1 + (\beta_i/\alpha_i)(\alpha_j/\beta_j)}. \qquad (7)$$

It will be noted that each of these turns out to be of the form

$$P_{ij}(i) = \frac{1}{1 + (v_j/v_i)} \qquad (8)$$

where $v_k = \alpha_k^2$, $1/\beta_k^2$, and α_k/β_k, for $k = i, j$, in the case of Eqs. (5)–(7), respectively. This common form will be recognized to be precisely that used to predict paired-comparison choices on the basis of a model assuming that the values of the alternatives fall on a ratio scale of some psychological magnitude (Luce, 1959).

Thus our result indicates that we can regard our subjects as making choices, at the asymptote of learning, on the basis of the relative positions of the stimulus alternatives on psychological scales which have their bases in memory representations of relative frequency information. The reason we could not have made sense of our data if we had started from a scaling approach is that we turn out to have a mixture of cases in which subjects have been selectively attending only to winning outcomes and thus are operating on one scale and cases in which they have been attending to both wins and losses and thus are operating on another.

Since a meticulous analysis of the situation in terms of concepts of memory has been necessary to bring order out of the data, one might ask what is added by introducing the notion of a psychological scale. The answer would seem to be that there is no immediate gain with regard to predictability of choice behavior in this situation. However, there may be some long-term benefits by way of bringing out communalities between choice behavior in learning situations and choice behavior as it has been dealt with traditionally in studies of preference in the scaling tradition. In particular, the concept of a scale may help to bring out communalities between probability learning and multiple choice learning, to which we turn in the next section.

V. Differential Reward Learning Relative to Values of Reward Sets

The preceding series of experiments shows clearly enough that in a probability learning situation subjects do develop a memory structure having properties of a psychological scale, though evidently the structure represents memory for relative frequencies of events rather than subjective probabilities as usually conceived. Now we wish to see whether a similar process operates in situations where the subject's problem is learning of relative reward magnitudes.

Much of our information concerning the functions of information and incentives in simple human learning comes from experiments that utilize variations on the standard multiple choice situation (see, for example, Estes, 1966; Keller, Cole, Burke, & Estes, 1965). Typically the task involves a list of items, each item comprising a pair of stimuli with associated reward values that are initially unknown to the subject. On a series of trials items occur in random order; as each item occurs, the two stimuli are presented, the subject makes a choice between them and then is given information either concerning the reward associated with each of the stimuli (full information condition) or only concerning the reward given for the alternative he chose (partial information condition).

The results of the studies just cited and others that I have reviewed elsewhere (Estes, 1969) lean heavily in favor of a cognitive interpretation of adult human learning in this type of situation. A simplified cognitive model would assume that the subject simply learns in paired-associate fashion the relations between stimuli and reward values and then bases his decisions on this information. However, studies by Allen (1972) and Allen and Estes (1972) have indicated that the full picture may not be quite so simple. Evidence was obtained that subjects often solve problems in the sense of meeting a criterion of 100% correct choices of the higher-valued alternative without being able to recall the explicit values when tested by means of a memory probe. A possible interpretation suggested was that, rather than attempting to learn explicit stimulus-reward associations, subjects may attempt to rehearse and encode labels for stimuli which they observe to be followed by high reward values. This differential rehearsal would, then, provide a possible mechanism for generating representations of relative frequency information in memory comparable to those inferred from the data of the probability learning experiments discussed in the previous sections of this chapter.

A. EXPERIMENT 6. VARIATION IN RANGE OF REWARD VALUES AND MEAN DIFFERENCES WITHIN ACQUISITION PAIRS UNDER A FULL INFORMATION CONDITION

If the frequency coding hypothesis is sound, then it should be possible for subjects to learn multiple-choice problems even under conditions so arranged that the learning of explicit stimulus-reward associations is impractical. In the present experiment, and those following in this series, an attempt was made to produce the desired conditions by using a design and procedure generally similar to those of previous multiple-choice experiments except that, in making up the problems, each stimulus was associated with a set of reward values rather than with a single value, and a probability distribution was defined over the set of possible values.

For example, in Problem 1 of the present experiment, one stimulus was associated with the reward values 6, 8, and 9 and a second stimulus with the values 4, 6, and 9. In each case the values were equiprobable so that if these two stimuli were presented for choice the subject would, on the average, obtain a larger reward by choosing the first stimulus over the second.

Four problems were constructed, each consisting of a set of five stimulus alternatives. We shall denote these A_i, but as displayed to the subjects they were represented by random sets of five letters of the alphabet, each stimulus being associated with a set of three reward values. All pairs that could be made up from the set of five stimuli were utilized in the course of a subject's experience on a given problem. The general idea was that a subset of four of these pairs would be presented during the acquisition phase; then the subject would be tested on all of the remaining pairs that could be made up from the given set of stimuli.

As illustrated in Table XI, Problems 1 and 2 were identical with respect to the average reward values of the five stimuli, as were Problems 3 and 4; and Problems 1 and 3 were identical with respect to the particular stimulus pairs presented on acquisition trials, as were Problems 2 and 4. As in the experiments on predictive behavior we wish to determine whether experience with a subset of the pairs that can be formed from a set of alternatives will permit the subject to generate a memory structure which can mediate correct performance on other test pairs in the manner that would be expected if his memory structure has the properties of a psychological scale. With the design illustrated in Table XI, we will be able to determine the way in which the acquisition of information reflects both the range of reward values and the mean reward differences within the stimulus pairs that are presented on the acquisition trials.

In the experimental situation the subject was seated in front of a teletypewriter which operated under the control of a PDP-8 I computer. Material could be typed out on the typewriter under the control of the computer, and when required control could be

TABLE XI
DESIGN OF EXPERIMENT 6[a]

	Training conditions			
	Av. reward values		Acq. pairs[b]	
Alternatives	Problems 1,2	Problems 3,4	Problems 1,3	Problems 2,4
A_1	7.7	6.3	x	x x
A_2	6.3	5.7	x x	x
A_3	5.0	5.0	x x	x x
A_4	3.7	4.3	x x	x
A_5	2.3	3.7	x	x x

[a] Varying mean reward differences with full information.
[b] x's in each column denote the alternatives of training pairs, e.g., for Problems 1,3 A_1 vs. A_2, A_2 vs. A_3, etc.

switched to the subject, who could communicate his responses back to the computer by typing them on the keyboard. The subject was told that he was to play a game against the computer, which operated according to certain specific rules. The game would consist of a series of trials on which he would be presented with pairs of stimuli and would be rewarded for his choices. The rewards would take the form of point values which at the end of the session would be converted into monetary payoffs. The specific rule under which the computer operated varied from experiment to experiment.

Subjects were run on one problem at a time. On each problem the acquisition series consisted of 60 trials, a block of 10 trials on each pair followed by a block of five trials on each pair. The transfer series consisted of a block of five trials on each of the six remaining pairs, the reward assignments and procedure being unchanged from acquisition to transfer trials. Each trial of the experiment began with presentation of two stimuli, for example:

$$\text{A or B?}$$

Then when the subject typed in his choice, say B in the example, the reward sets associated with the two stimuli were typed out by the teletypewriter below them on the display, which might now look as follows:

$$\begin{array}{cc} \text{A or} & \text{B ?} \\ \text{B 689} & 257 \end{array}$$

Finally, the reward which the subject received for his choice, 5 in the example and the cumulative total points received through the given trial were typed out.

$$\text{Reward} = 5 \quad \text{Total} = 61$$

After a delay of 1–2 sec the stimuli for the next trial were presented and so on.

The subjects were sixteen young adults all of whom were run on all four problems except for a few instances of incomplete sessions owing to apparatus or scheduling problems.

The first conspicuous result with this procedure is that even though the acquisition conditions made it impractical for the subjects to learn associations between stimuli and specific reward values, they did acquire information on the basis of experience with a limited number of stimulus pairs that permitted them to choose with substantially better than chance success on new test pairs. If we look only at the very first trial on which each test pair appeared, the average proportions of correct choices (that is, choices of the alternative with the higher average reward value) were .82, .66, .62, and .62 for Problems 1–4, respectively.

A better picture of the quantitative properties of test performance can be obtained by pooling data over the five transfer trials and assembling these choice percentages in paired-comparison tables for Problems 1 and 2 and for Problems 3 and 4 combined, as displayed in Table XII. It is apparent that, in spite of the smaller number of observations in the present experiment, the paired-comparison data yield the same orderly pattern that we saw repeatedly in the case of the experiments on predictive behavior. To obtain an adequate basis for comparing the effects of the variations in conditions that differentiated the four problems, I have combined the choice proportions for the terminal acquisition block on each problem and the full five test trials on each test pair into a single paired-comparison table and then determined a scale value for each stimulus by computing the proportion of times that it was chosen over all of the other stimuli of the set. This procedure yields values corresponding to the row averages in Table XII and other preceding paired-comparison tables [and essentially the equivalent of the scale values obtained by Thurstone's Case IV in classical paired comparison scaling (Thurstone, 1927)]. The values so obtained for the four problems are plotted in Fig. 5. The two striking features of this figure are the substantial difference between the first two and second two problems, reflecting the difference in range of reward values during acquisition, but the very close similarity between Problems 1 and 2 and between Problems 3 and 4, indicating that the memory structure developed by the subjects is quite independent of the particular subset of stimulus pairs with which they had experience during acquisition. The effect

TABLE XII

CHOICE PERCENTAGES OVER FIVE TRANSFER TRIALS OF EXPERIMENT 6

	Problems 1 and 2						Problems 3 and 4					
	A_1	A_2	A_3	A_4	A_5	Av.	A_1	A_2	A_3	A_4	A_5	Av.
A_1	—	75	83	89	90	84	—	69	65	77	81	73
A_2	25	—	79	83	89	69	31	—	50	77	84	60
A_3	17	21	—	65	77	45	35	50	—	70	72	57
A_4	11	17	35	—	74	34	23	23	30	—	72	37
A_5	10	11	23	26	—	18	19	16	28	28	—	23

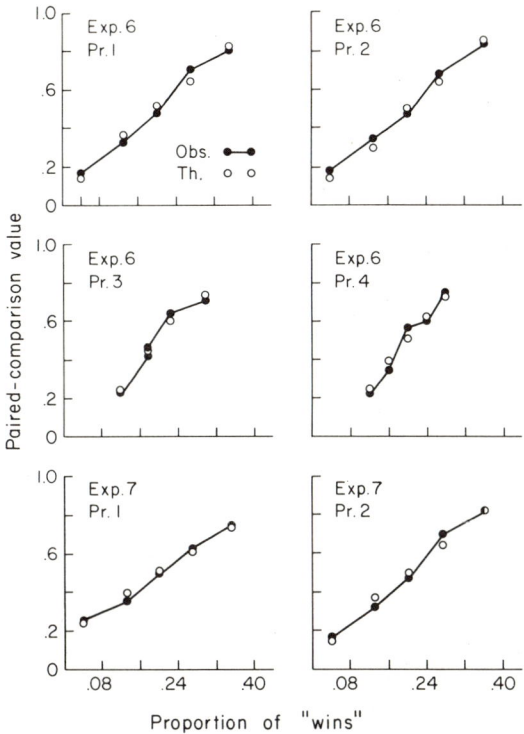

Fig. 5. Mean paired-comparison values for Experiments 6 and 7 (connected closed circles) together with predicted values (open circles).

of range of reward values during acquisition supports the impression gained from previous studies (e.g., Allen, 1972) that subjects do not master problems by learning relations between stimuli and numerical values in a paired-associate fashion.

B. EXPERIMENT 7. VARIATION IN MEAN REWARD DIFFERENCES WITHIN ACQUISITION PAIRS UNDER A PARTIAL INFORMATION CONDITION

The full information procedure of Experiment 6 leaves some doubt as to just what information the subjects were using from that displayed on each trial. Although a set of reward values was assigned to each alternative, some one member of the reward set being selected randomly on each trial when the subject chose the given alternative, nonetheless the full reward sets were displayed. It is possible that the subjects might, for example, have added up the values in each set and then responded on the basis of these recoded values rather than on the basis of the sequence of rewards actually received. In order to clarify this point, in the present experiment we utilize the same procedures as those of Experiment 6 in all respects except that the full reward sets are never displayed. At the end of the trial on which, for example, the alternatives are A and B, the printout in front of the subject might take the form

$$\text{A or B?}$$
$$\text{A}$$
$$\text{Reward} = 5 \quad \text{Total} = 61$$

Since the observation pairs of a given problem are presented at a rather rapid rate, and the subject sees on each trial only the single reward value that was selected by the computer from the appropriate reward set, it seems most unlikely that in a limited number of trials the subjects can possibly discover just what values belong to the various reward sets. Thus if the subjects are able under these circumstances to learn on the average to choose the higher paying alternative, they must do so by building up representations in memory of the relative positions of the stimulus alternatives on a reward scale. The task seems difficult, but not necessarily impossible since in earlier studies (Allen, 1972; Allen & Estes, 1972) it was found that even under simpler conditions when each alternative was associated with a single reward value the subjects did not always learn the exact values to the point of being able to verbalize them.

The stimuli and reward sets of the first two problems of Experiment 6 were used again, with a new group of eight subjects assigned to each. In view of the increased difficulty of the partial information procedure, 30 acquisition trials were given on each training pair before the administration of a five-trial test block on each of the test pairs.

In spite of the much increased difficulty of the task, rates of learning were not grossly different from those observed in Experiment 6. On Problem 1, with the relatively small differences in mean reward value within pairs, the subjects reached a terminal level of only 62% correct performance on the acquisition pairs by the end of the 30 training trials but on Problem 2, with the larger differences in reward values, learning was rapid and reached a terminal value of .92. On the critical first transfer trial, the subjects chose the higher valued alternatives 65% of the time on Problem 1 and 71% of the time on Problem 2.

To provide sufficiently stable data for quantitative comparison with the full information procedure, I have assembled in Table XIII

TABLE XIII

CHOICE PERCENTAGES OVER FINAL ACQUISITION BLOCKS AND FIVE TRANSFER TRIALS OF EXPERIMENT 7[a]

	Problem 1						Problem 2					
	A_1	A_2	A_3	A_4	A_5	Av.	A_1	A_2	A_3	A_4	A_5	Av.
A_1	–	61	85	75	80	75	–	62	86	86	92	82
A_2	39	–	52	80	82	63	38	–	78	75	90	70
A_3	15	48	–	62	75	50	14	22	–	70	88	48
A_4	25	20	38	–	59	36	14	25	30	–	58	32
A_5	20	18	25	41	–	26	8	10	12	42	–	18

[a]Varying mean reward differences with partial information.

paired-comparison tables for each problem in terms of the percentage of choices of the row over the column alternative for the final acquisition block in the case of the training pairs and the full five transfer trials in the case of the test pairs. On the whole, both tables exhibit the typical orderly paired-comparison pattern. Also, if we consider the average values in the right-hand columns, it may be noted that for Problem 1 these are only slightly constricted as compared with those of Problem 1 in Experiment 6 and in the case of Problem 2 the quantitative agreement with the corresponding values for Problem 2 of Experiment 6 is striking indeed. It seems clear that the shift from full to partial information has made no qualitative difference in the mode of information processing.

C. EXPERIMENT 8. MEAN REWARD DIFFERENCES WITHIN DISJOINT TRAINING PAIRS

In both of Experiments 6 and 7, the training pairs were connected, in the sense discussed in relation to Experiment 5. Thus it remains to be determined whether the systematic transfer behavior depends on this property in the multiple-choice situation. The present experiment was designed to check on this question, and also to ascertain whether performance on pairs of former "winners" or former "losers" would vary as a function of mean reward differential within training pairs when differentials within test pairs were equated. The design is summarized in Table XIV.

Procedures were the same as those of Experiment 7. One group of eight subjects was assigned to Problems 1 and 3 and a second group to Problems 2 and 4, in each case receiving 30 acquisition trials on each training pair and 10 test trials. The test pairs were A_1 versus A_3,

TABLE XIV
DESIGN OF EXPERIMENT 8 IN TERMS OF MEAN REWARD VALUES PER TRAINING STIMULUS

Training pairs	Problems			
	1	2	3	4
A_1 vs. A_2	7.7	7.7	7.7	7.0
	6.3	6.3	7.0	6.3
A_3 vs. A_4	5.0	6.3	5.0	5.7
	3.7	5.0	4.3	5.0
A_5 vs. A_6	2.3	5.0	2.3	4.3
	1.0	3.7	1.7	3.7

A_3 versus A_5, and A_1 versus A_5 for the first group, and A_2 versus A_4, A_4 versus A_6, and A_2 versus A_6 for the second. The special feature of the design is that in Problems 1 and 3 the mean reward values of the high members (winners) of the training pairs were matched while the lower members differed, and in the other two problems, the lower members (losers) were matched while the higher members differed.

The principal result is that choices of the higher valued stimulus on transfer pairs prove to be substantially above chance for both pairs of winners (Problems 1 and 3) and pairs of losers (Problems 2 and 4), and to be directly related to differences in mean reward value between the members of a transfer pair: For Problems 1 and 3, mean reward differences of 2.7 and 5.4 yielded mean correct choice proportions of 76 and 90, respectively, whereas for Problems 2 and 4, differences of 1.3 and 2.6 yielded proportions of 60 and 66, respectively. As in previous experiments, more was learned in the case of former winners than former losers.

If we look, rather, at mean reward differences within training pairs, we find virtually no effect, overall correct choice proportions for Problems 1 and 3, respectively, being 81 and 80, for Problems 2 and 4, 63 and 60.

VI. Theoretical Interpretation of the Differential Reward Series

Taking the results of the present series of experiments together with others previously reported, we can assemble an array of rather well-established facts that should sharply constrain the form of a model for acquisition and transfer in the multiple-choice situation.

1. In the case of two-choice problems, the rate of acquisition depends on the difference in reward value of the two alternatives when training is given with the partial information procedure but not with the full information procedure (Keller *et al.*, 1965).

2. Rate of acquisition is largely independent of the ease of associating stimuli with specific reward values being, for example, quite comparable when there is a single reward value assigned to each stimulus and when there is a reward set with a probability distribution assigned to each stimulus.

3. Memory probes given during multiple choice acquisition show that specific reward values most often are not recallable by subjects until they are well into the final criterion series of 100% correct responding (Allen & Estes, 1972).

4. Probe tests calling for recall of reward values associated with individual stimuli yield orderly generalization gradients around the correct reward value following training under a partial information procedure (Estes, 1966).

5. When training has been given on only a subset of the pairs that can be formed from a set of stimuli, choice behavior at the end of training is comparable on training pairs and new transfer pairs, in both cases depending on the difference in reward value between the members of the test pair (Experiments 6 and 7).

6. More is learned concerning reward values associated with winning than with losing members of training pairs. However, transfer performance appropriately reflects differences in mean reward value within test pairs of former winners or former losers.

7. Choice performance on transfer trials depends strongly on the range of reward values prevailing during training but not on the differences in reward value between members of training pairs (Experiments 6–8).

The most general conclusion from the present series of studies is that transfer behavior following differential reward training has the character that would be expected if subjects had, in effect, learned to place stimuli on a scale of relative reward values. A central theoretical problem now is to formulate a model to account for the way in which the scale properties develop and the basis for them in the memory system. A number of hypotheses concerning both of these aspects of the problem that might be suggested by previous research and theory can be rather clearly refuted on the basis of the findings listed above.

First, in view of items 5 and 6, it is clear that subjects do not simply learn to approach the higher and avoid the lower valued members of training pairs. Second, on the basis of items 1, 2, and 3, it seems equally clear that subjects do not in general associate specific numerical reward values with stimuli; and when they do so, at least in some cases this learning occurs too late to be importantly involved in the process of arriving at correct choice performance. Third, it does not appear that subjects master the problem by placing the stimulus alternatives on a preexisting scale of reward magnitudes; on such a hypothesis, we could account neither for item 1 nor for the fact that choice performance depends so strongly on the range of reward values involved in each specific problem of the series on which a given subject receives training (item 7).

This last observation implies that scale properties must be built up by some learning process that occurs independently on each problem of a series. What might be the nature of this process? One direction in which we might look for an answer is suggested by theoretical developments both in our previous analysis of probability learning and in the closely related area of verbal discrimination learning (Ekstrand, Wallace, & Underwood, 1966). Proceeding on analogy from those developments, one might speculate that, rather than rehearsing explicit reward values, subjects rehearse codes or labels for the stimulus alternatives, frequency of rehearsal being directly related to the placement of a stimulus in a range of possible values.

On this line of interpretation, the major question remaining is just how subjects achieve the result of rehearsing stimuli in proportion to their average reward values. A hypothesis considered by Medin (1972) requires the assumption of considerable long-term storage of reward information on the part of subjects. I shall proceed on a slightly different tack, allowing instead for a role of short-term memory.

Suppose we entertain the assumption that, following the appearance of the outcome on any trial, a representation in the form of an uncertainty distribution around the true reward value is entered in short-term memory, with some probability of being lost from memory (becoming unavailable) during each trial. In general, then, after the first few trials of an acquisition series, the subject will have available in short-term memory representations of the reward values associated with one or more stimuli. The critical assumption regarding rehearsal is that, once this state has been reached, when the subject observes the reward value given for the stimulus he chooses on a given trial, he compares this value with some one of the representations then active in short-term memory and rehearses a label for the chosen stimulus if its value is the larger. When more than one representation is in the active state, we assume that the one to be compared with the stimulus chosen on the given trial is sampled at random. The one exception is that, on a full information trial,[2] the comparison is made between the displayed reward values rather than between representations in memory.

In general, the probability that the reward value of the stimulus chosen on a trial is greater than that of the one with whose representation it is compared will be an increasing function of the value of the given stimulus and consequently this modified hypothesis fits all of the same facts as the original. The advantages are two. First, we have a reasonably simple interpretation of the way in which the subject achieves the result of giving more rehearsal to stimuli with higher reward values. Second, since with a full information procedure the reward value of the stimulus not chosen from the pair presented on a trial is actually present in the display, it will always be the one compared to the chosen stimulus. Whenever the stimulus chosen has the higher value of the two it will, then, receive rehearsal regardless of the absolute value, so in the full information case, rate of acquisition is predicted to be independent of reward value, in accord with the results of Allen (1972) and Keller et al. (1965).

To obtain some more specific evidence regarding the merits of the present rehearsal hypothesis, I have conducted an analysis suggested by the analogy between the multiple choice and probability learning paradigms. In the case of each problem employed in Experiments 6 and 7, I consulted the listing of reward sets and determined for each stimulus the proportion of instances when a randomly selected member of its reward set would be larger in magnitude than that of a randomly selected member drawn from the other reward sets of the given problem. The value so obtained was assumed to represent the proportion of cases in which the given stimulus would be a "winner" in the hypothesized memory comparison engaged in by subjects during differential reward training. The proportion of cases in which the stimulus would be a "loser" was similarly determined. Then these two proportions for each stimulus were entered as estimates of α_i and β_i in Eqs. (1)–(4), and the relative frequency model was applied to the data in the four paired-comparison matrices for Experiment 6 and the two for Experiment 7.

---

[2] This statement applies only to the standard full information procedure in which only one reward value is assigned to each stimulus alternative.

The results of this theoretical analysis are summarized in Fig. 5 in the same form used for those of the probability learning experiments in Figs. 1–4. Once again, the agreement of observed and theoretical paired-comparison values appears quite promising. The estimates of the parameters a and b indicate some mixture of attentional strategies, but the generally high values of b (near unity for both problems of Experiment 7) suggest that in most instances subjects were encoding both wins and losses when engaged in memory comparisons. As in the case of probability learning, a direct approach to these data in terms of scaling theory would have encountered difficulties in that the observed choice behavior evidently again reflects a mixture of scales.

It is worth noting the perhaps counterintuitive result that the slopes of the functions in Fig. 5 are somewhat steeper for Problems 3 and 4 of Experiment 6, the problems with the more restricted ranges of reward values, than for Problems 1 and 2. In terms of the model, estimates of ϕ are higher in the former case (.99 and 1.0 for Problems 3 and 4 versus .85 and .88 for Problems 1 and 2, respectively). However, it is a property of the model that differences in slopes of almost exactly the magnitude seen in the upper two panels of Fig. 5 would be predicted for the latter part of acquisition ($\phi = .50$ to $\phi = 1.0$) even if learning rates (ϕ values) were equal for all problems.

VII. General Discussion

For each of the two main types of tasks we have studied, probability learning and differential reward learning, we can find interpretations such that transfer behavior conforms to expectations on the assumption that the subject has placed the choice alternatives on a psychological scale and chooses from test pairs on the basis of scale values. The functional properties of the system yielding these scale properties provides economy of information storage and precision in transfer performance.

But the question remains whether the conception of a psychological scale should be regarded as a fundamental one for theoretical purposes or whether it is derivative to more basic theoretical ideas. We have seen that, in the case of probability learning, the scale does not agree with the traditional conception of probability in that it is not always monotonely related to objective probability. Further, in cases where the function is monotone, it does not generally prove to be linear. It is apparent from Eq. (8) that observed choice probability should be curvilinearly related to v_k. However, we can transform the equation into the form

$$\frac{1 - P_{ij}(i)}{P_{ij}(i)} = \frac{P_{ij}(j)}{P_{ij}(i)} = \frac{v_j}{v_i},$$

and, taking logarithms of both sides,

$$\log P_{ij}(j) - \log P_{ij}(i) = \log v_j - \log v_i. \qquad (9)$$

The quantity on the left can be directly estimated from the observed choice proportions, and the average value for alternative A_i should yield a linear function of $\log v_i$. With v_i taken to be α_i^2 for probability learning and β_i/α_i for multiple-choice learning, these plots (not reproduced here) prove to be linear in neither instance. In several cases, for both types of data, the functions appear to be better described by two straight lines of different slopes, possibly reflecting a mixture of two scales as suggested by our analysis in terms of the learning model. It would seem sensible to defer further pursuit of this analysis until experiments have been run under conditions which either yield homogeneity of attentional strategies for groups of subjects or provide adequate data for theoretical analysis of the choice behavior of individual subjects.

On the whole, the evidence from the present studies indicates that the psychological scales manifest in transfer performance do not represent preexisting structures that subjects learn to use in a given situation. Rather they appear to represent a type of organization of information in memory that takes form in the course of learning in a given task situation.

Consideration of the effects of various experimental manipulations leads to the conclusion that the psychological scales represent memory structures built up by differential rehearsal of stimulus codes. These structures have some of the properties of the frequency count assumed by Ekstrand *et al.* (1966) in their frequency theory of verbal discrimination learning, and come still closer to the notion of a relative frequency indicator (Estes, 1976) reflecting memory for relative frequencies of event categories. In the case of probability learning, the nature of the scale structure closely reflects the relative frequencies of outcomes to which subjects selectively attend. In the case of multiple-choice learning, the structure may well reflect the relative reward values that subjects come to expect as a consequence of their learning experience, but not necessarily the different amounts of reward received for alternative choices on past occasions. In both cases, close attention to conditions of selective attention, event coding in memory, and retrieval from long-term memory are necessary in order to specify the type of scale that will take form.

REFERENCES

Allen, G. A. Memory probes during two-choice differential reward problems. *Journal of Experimental Psychology,* 1972, **95**, 78–89.

Allen, G. A., & Estes, W. K. Acquisition of correct choices and value judgments in binary choice learning with differential rewards. *Psychonomic Science,* 1972, **27**, 68–72.

Buchwald, A. M. Effects of "right" and "wrong" on subsequent behavior: A new interpretation. *Psychological Review,* 1969, **76**, 132–143.

Cohen, J. *Behaviour in uncertainty.* New York: Basic Books, 1964.

Ekstrand, B. R., Wallace, W. P., & Underwood, B. J. A frequency theory of verbal discrimination learning. *Psychological Review,* 1966, **73**, 566–578.

Estes, W. K. Probability learning. In A. W. Melton (Ed.), *Categories of human learning.* New York: Academic Press, 1964. Pp. 89–128.

Estes, W. K. Transfer of verbal discriminations based on differential reward magnitudes. *Journal of Experimental Psychology,* 1966, **72**, 276–283.

Estes, W. K. Reinforcement in human learning. In J. Tapp (Ed.), *Reinforcement and behavior.* New York: Academic Press, 1969. Pp. 63–94.

Estes, W. K. The cognitive side of probability learning. *Psychological Review,* 1976, **83**, 37–64.

Humphreys, M. J. The derivation of endpoint and distance effects in linear orderings from frequency information. *Journal of Verbal Learning and Verbal Behavior,* 1975, **14**, 496–505.

Keller, L., Cole, M., Burke, C. J., & Estes, W. K. Reward and information values of trial outcomes in paired associate learning. *Psychological Monographs,* 1965, **79**, No. 12 (Whole No. 605).

Krantz, D. H., Luce, R. D., Suppes, P., & Tversky, A. *Foundations of measurement.* New York: Academic Press, 1971.

Luce, R. D. *Individual choice behavior. A theoretical analysis.* New York: Wiley, 1959.

Luce, R. D., & Suppes, P. Preference, utility, and subjective probability. In R. D. Luce, R. R. Bush, & E. Galanter (Eds.), *Handbook of mathematical psychology,* Vol. 3. New York: Wiley, 1965. PP. 249–410.

Medin, D. L. Partial information and choice behavior in differential reward magnitude learning. *Psychonomic Science,* 1972, **27**, 73–76.

Medin, D. L. Frequency and coding responses in verbal discrimination learning. *Memory & Cognition,* 1974, **2**, 11–13.

Myers, J. L. Probability learning and sequence learning. In W. K. Estes (Ed.), *Handbook of learning and cognitive processes,* Vol. 3. Hillsdale, N.J.: Erlbaum Associates, 1976.

Peterson, C. R., & Ulehla, Z. J. Sequential patterns and maximizing. *Journal of Experimental Psychology,* 1965, **69**, 1–8.

Reber, A. S., & Millward, R. B. Event observation in probability learning. *Journal of Experimental Psychology,* 1968, **77,** 317–327.

Rubinstein, I. Some factors in probability matching. *Journal of Experimental Psychology,* 1959, **57,** 413–416.

Thurstone, L. L. A law of comparative judgment. *Psychological Review,* 1927, **34,** 273–286.

Thurstone, L. L. *The measurement of values.* Chicago: University of Chicago Press, 1959.

REPETITION AND MEMORY[1]

Douglas L. Hintzman

UNIVERSITY OF OREGON, EUGENE, OREGON

I.	Introduction	47
II.	The Representation of Frequency	48
	A. Theories	49
	B. Evidence: Strength versus Multiple Traces	52
	C. Evidence: Multiple Traces versus Propositional Encoding	59
	D. Conclusions	64
III.	The Spacing Effect	65
	A. Definition and Generality	65
	B. Theories and Experimental Evidence	69
	C. Conclusions	80
IV.	Repetition and Retrieval	80
	A. Study-Phase Retrieval	80
	B. Coincidences	84
	C. Conclusions	87
	References	87

I. Introduction

Repetition is one of the most powerful variables affecting memory. Theoretical interpretations of the effects of repetition on memory have been remarkably varied; but the fact that repetition improves retention, established empirically in Ebbinghaus's experiments and in thousands of studies since, seems beyond dispute. Repetitive drill, once common in American schools, has been attacked as "unnatural" by progressivist educators; and Kvale (1975) has even denounced experiments on rote repetition as contrary to the teachings of Mao Tse-Tung. Yet, drill is still employed (apologetically) in our classroom instruction, and according to recent reports of travelers to the Peoples Republic of China, it is almost pervasive in schooling there.

---

[1] Preparation of this chapter was supported by a grant GB-40360 from the National Science Foundation. Special thanks are due to Michael J. Hacker and James V. Hinrichs for making their unpublished data available to the author.

Evidently, even strongly held views of educational philosophy and political ideology must yield to this basic psychological law.

Despite the obvious importance of repetition for memory theory, many questions about its mode of operation remain to be answered. The purpose of the present paper is to review research on effects of repetition which we have conducted in our laboratory over the last several years, and to tie our work in with relevant research by other investigators.

Many of the experiments to be discussed employ what may be called the "method of memory judgments." In this technique, a list of items is presented, and the subject is then presented with each test item and asked to judge from memory some aspect of its presentation in the list. Judgments of recency, frequency, exposure duration, list membership, input modality, spacing, and serial position have all been used, singly and in combination. Such judgments reveal much more about the richness of information encoded in memory than can be inferred from more traditional recall and recognition measures. They do not supplant recognition and recall, but rather complement them. Memory judgments have been particularly revealing where effects of repetition on memory are concerned.

The following discussion is divided into three parts. The first concerns how frequency or number of occurrences is represented in memory. The second reviews research on effects on memory of the spacing of repetitions. The third presents evidence on the role of repetitions as retrieval cues. The three sections are largely independent—the only common theme is a concern with repetition and memory.

II. The Representation of Frequency

The question, "How does repetition affect memory?" is probably too broad to be given a simple answer. Practicing a musical instrument, acquiring English grammar, becoming familiar with a particular chess opening, and learning to like martinis are all examples of effects of repetition on memory, and the underlying mechanisms in all these examples may not be the same. Rather than attempting to answer the broad question, therefore, the present discussion will focus on a restricted problem, "How is frequency represented in memory?" Conclusions drawn about the representation of frequency might be extrapolated to account for other effects of repetition on memory, but that will not be attempted here.

To make the problem of representation of frequency more concrete, consider a subject who studies a list of 300 words, presented one at a time, at a uniform rate. Different words occur in the list one, two, four, six, or ten times. Following presentation of the list, the subject is given a test form which includes, along with the words from the list, a few that did not occur. He is asked to write alongside each word the number of times he thinks it occurred in the list. Performance on a frequency judgment task such as this is fairly accurate (e.g., Hintzman, 1969); mean judged frequency increases monotonically with true frequency, and the function is roughly logarithmic in form. What is the underlying mnemonic representation upon which such judgments are based?

A. THEORIES

Three theories of the representation of frequency will be described briefly, and then relevant experimental evidence will be discussed. The three thories will be referred to as the strength, multiple-trace, and propositional encoding hypotheses.

1. Strength

The traditional view of learning held by classical animal learning theorists such as Thorndike, Pavlov, and Hull, was that reinforced repetition strengthens the memory trace, or associative bond. An important implication of this view is that the change in memory between presentation n (P_n) and P_{n+1} is strictly quantitative. That is, P_{n+1} simply strengthens the trace remaining after P_n; the two presentations have no qualitatively different effects.

The cumulative effect of repetition on strength provides a ready answer to the question of how frequency is represented in memory. One can assume that the subject is able to assess strength directly, and that he partitions the strength dimension into intervals which are mapped onto judged frequency in a suitable fashion.

The concept of strength has been related to effects of recency and exposure duration, in addition to effects of repetition. As will be shown, this is one source of difficulty for the hypothesis. Another source of difficulty is that in a cumulative strength representation of frequency, the contributions of individual presentations are not identifiable. The only effect of repetition is an increase in magnitude of the strength of the memory trace, and the effects of any given presentation of the item cannot be differentiated from the effects of any other.

2. Multiple Traces

What we shall call the multiple-trace hypothesis is directly related to Bernbach's (1970) "replica" theory and Bower's (1967) hypothesis of "multiplexing." The basic assumptions of the multiple-trace hypothesis are: (*a*) that each encoded presentation of an item leaves its own memory trace; (*b*) that traces of different presentations coexist with one another in memory; and (*c*) that traces of different presentations of the same item can carry different "attributes" (Hintzman & Block, 1971).

To account for frequency judgments, one can assume either (*a*) that the subject retrieves and counts the relevant traces of the test item, or (*b*) that he does not actually count relevant traces, but makes a crude estimate of how many there are. In the latter case, estimates could be adjusted upward or downward, depending upon what the appropriate range of values is thought to be. The most important fact differentiating the multiple-trace hypothesis from the strength hypothesis is that in the multiple-trace representation of frequency, the identifiability of individual presentations is preserved.

Two points should be made explicit about the multiple-trace hypothesis. First, acceptance of the multiple trace view does not commit a theorist to an all-or-none learning position; there is no particular reason that traces of individual presentations could not differ from one another in strength, depending upon degree of attention, exposure duration, recency, etc. Second, the multiple-trace hypothesis should not be confused with encoding variability theory, which emphasizes the fact that a verbal item could be given different semantic encodings on two different presentations. There is strong evidence that variable encoding cannot provide the basis for frequency judgments (see Section III, B, 1, a). The assumption made here is that while the traces resulting from different presentations of an item may differ in certain attributes (time and modality tags for example), ordinarily they will be semantically the same.

3. Propositional Encoding

A third hypothesis is that frequency information per se is accumulated in propositional form during study of the list. Anderson and

Bower (1974) have shown how subjects might form propositions about the to-be-remembered material which would mediate later memory test performance. This hypothesis could be extended to account for memory for frequency in at least two ways. One extension assumes that encodings of different presentations coexist in memory, and so is essentially the same as the multiple-trace hypothesis. The other extension assumes only one proposition, which is updated on each presentation and thus can include information about frequency.

Assume first, that on a given presentation the subject encodes a proposition about the presented item that includes whatever related information he thinks about at the time; and second, that one effect of presentation of an item is to retrieve the trace of the previous presentation. Then on presentation P_n, the proposition formed will typically include: (*a*) information about the occurrence of P_n; and (*b*) any retrieved information from P_{n-1} to which the subject attends. Other information from P_{n-1} is deleted—and since the last proposition always replaces previous ones, this information is permanently lost.

The degree to which the propositions formed contain information relevant to frequency should depend on what aspects of the presented material the subject attends to. In a typical frequency-judgment experiment in which the subject does not know beforehand exactly what his memory task is, the encoded frequency information may be rather imprecise. For example, if we could listen in on the subject's "stream of consciousness" during four presentations of a word, we might hear the following:

P_1: "Hmm . . . *cat*. Try to remember *cat*."
P_2: "*Cat*. I remember seeing that one before."
P_3: "*Cat*. That must be three or four times *cat* has occurred."
P_4: "There's *cat* again. I've seen *cat* several times already."

Confronted with the word *cat* on a frequency-judgment test, the subject would retrieve from memory the proposition encoded during P_4: "I have seen *cat* several times," and give a numerical frequency judgment that seems appropriate (e.g., one between 3 and 7).

A mechanism such as this, which would update the propositional encoding of an item on each presentation, seems intuitively plausible. And there is experimental evidence for one of the key assumptions: that P_n triggers retrieval of information stored about P_{n-1}. This evidence comes from experiments on the ability of subjects to judge the spacing of repetitions. The data linking judgments of the spacing of P_{n-1} and P_n with retrieval of the trace of P_{n-1} by P_n are reviewed later in this chapter (Section IV).

The propositional "counter" theory assumes that the frequency representation is cumulative, and in this way it is similar to strength. But unlike strength and like the multiple trace representation, it can preserve information about individual presentations. If a word is presented auditorily on P_1 and visually on P_2, for example, the propositional encodings might be as follows:

P_1: "*Cat*, spoken in a low monotone."
P_2: "*Cat*, presented visually. It occurred before, but I remember that last time I heard it."

The propositional encoding of P_2, retrieved on a later test, tells the subject that *cat* occurred both auditorily and visually, in that order.

The propositional encoding hypothesis is extremely flexible. Propositions are free for the asking, and can be embedded in one another and concatenated to any degree of complexity. If subjects are able to remember frequency, the theorist can assume that propositions about frequency were stored. If they also remember recency and mode of presentation, he can assume that this information was included, as well. But the flexibility of the hypothesis does not necessarily make it untestable. It results from the presumed flexibility of propositional encoding; and this may be the most testable characteristic of the hypothesis. The encoding of frequency information into memory should depend on the degree to which the subject attends to information relevant to frequency. Thus, by manipulating the "set" with which the subject approaches the task, one should be able to manipulate the quality of the information upon which frequency judgments are based.

B. EVIDENCE: STRENGTH VERSUS MULTIPLE TRACES

1. *Independence of Frequency Information*

A basic appeal of the strength construct is one of economy. Effects of recency, frequency, and exposure duration on the accuracy and latency of both recognition and recall can be assumed to be mediated by a single intervening variable. If strength is also the basis of judged frequency, then judged frequency should covary with recall and recognition measures in predictable ways. Such independent variables as recency, frequency, and duration should have the same effects on judgments of frequency as they have on the more traditional measures.

The relative independence of frequency information has been demonstrated in a variety of ways. Consider the relationship between recency and frequency. Hintzman (1969) presented 320 slides of words at a 3-sec rate, and then gave two tests. One was a frequency discrimination test, in which subjects were given pairs of words and asked to circle the more frequent member of each pair. The other was a numerical frequency judgment task in which words were judged individually. In neither of these tests, when data were analyzed according to position in the study list, was there any evidence of a recency effect. Over longer retention intervals, recency does affect memory for frequency—but while the ability to discriminate frequencies declines, overall mean judgments change very little (Underwood, Zimmerman, & Freund, 1971).

Peterson (1967) had subjects judge the recencies of words. Some words occurred two times and others occurred only once prior to the recency judgment test. Judged recency was affected only by the recency of the last presentation, and was independent of frequency. In this study, presentations of repeated words were widely spaced in time. Another study showed that when repetitions are close together, apparent recency is increased (Peterson, Johnson, & Coatney, 1969). The effect of massed repetition on judged recency can be explained without resorting to strength theory. We shall return to this point later.

Finally, Hintzman and Waters (1970) showed that the effects of recency and frequency on list discrimination are largely independent. Manipulating the frequency of items in List 2 apparently did not affect the subject's ability to use the relative recencies of items in List 1 as cues regarding which list an item was from.

Two studies (Hintzman, 1970; Hintzman, Summers, & Block, 1975b, Experiment III) have demonstrated independence of frequency and duration information. In the latter experiment, for example, pictures occurred one, two, or three times, with exposure duration (the same on each presentation) either 2.2, 5.2, or 8.2 sec. On the memory test, subjects give both frequency and duration judgments. Frequency accounted for 98% and duration for 1% of the variance among frequency judgment means. Among duration judgment means, by contrast, the contribution of frequency was 21% and that of duration was 76% of the variance. Apparently, the internal representations of frequency and exposure duration are largely independent.

That judged frequency and free recall do not covary exactly has been shown in investigations by Underwood (1969) and by Howell (1973b). Underwood found that the effects of primacy and recency, which are sizable when measured by free recall, are negligible where judged frequency is concerned. He also reported that there was little if any correlation between the recallability and judged frequency of individual words. Howell (1973b) reported that list length affected free recall, but had no effect on judged frequency. The type of test subjects expected was also manipulated. Like list length, this manipulation affected free recall performance but did not affect judged frequency.

The relationship between judged frequency and recognition memory was studied by Wells (1974). She had three conditions: a single presentation condition, a condition in which P_1 and P_2 were massed, and one in which P_1 and P_2 were spaced. To provide a wide range of performance levels, frequency judgments were taken at several retention intervals. Taking judged frequency greater than zero as equivalent to recognition, Wells plotted Pr(judged frequency = 2) against Pr(recognition). If judged frequency were based upon a single magnitude which increases with repetition and decreases over time, then one would expect such a plot to produce a single function. If an immediate test of a single presentation item and a delayed test of a repeated item give rise to the same value of Pr(recognition) for example, they should also give rise to equivalent values of Pr(judged frequency = 2). What Wells obtained, however, was three different functions—one for each presentation condition. Thus while recognition and judged frequency are affected similarly by manipulations of frequency, recency, and spacing, they do not covary in a way indicating that the underlying information is exactly the same.

Wells' result is consistent with the multiple-trace hypothesis. If Pr(recognition) depends upon retrieval of at least one trace of the item and Pr(judged frequency = 2) depends upon retrieval of two, then a manipulation affecting one measure is likely to affect the other. But a single- and a double-presentation condition giving rise to the same recognition performance would not produce the same likelihood of saying the item occurred twice; for in the latter condition it is likely that two traces were encoded originally, while in the former it is not.

2. Identifiability of Traces

In a strength representation of frequency, effects of individual presentations are not identifiable. In a multiple-trace representation they are. The most direct evidence in favor of the multiple-trace hypothesis, therefore, comes from studies demonstrating that information about individual presentations of a repeated item are preserved in memory. Such a demonstration requires that the encodings of repetitions differ from one another in some qualitative way, and that the experiment be designed specifically to reveal that difference. One could, of course, induce different modality tags in P_1 and P_2 by presenting words once auditorily and once visually (e.g., Hintzman, Block, & Summers, 1973); but whether one could legitimately generalize conclusions to situations in which repetitions are nominally identical events would be debatable.

Fortunately, it is not necessary to deliberately induce such encoding differences. Yntema and Trask (1963) showed that subjects can remember something about when an event last occurred. They referred to the stored information upon which this ability rests as the "time tag"—a conveniently neutral term that will be adopted here. Hintzman and Block (1971) tested the hypothesis that subjects might discriminate among traces of different presentations of an item on the basis of their time tags. Different presentations by definition take place at different times, and so it seems plausible that, if the multiple-trace hypothesis is true, such temporal information would provide a cue by which the effects on memory of different presentations could be distinguished.

Hintzman and Block (1971, Experiment II) divided positions in a 50-item word list into four critical zones. Labeled A, B, C, and D, respectively, the four zones included positions 3–8, 9–14, 15–20, and 43–48. Most words occurred only one time in the list; but interest centers on those that were presented twice. There were four repeated-word conditions, with P_1 occurring in zone A or B, and P_2 in zone C or D. Thus the positions of P_1 and P_2 (and presumably their time tags) were manipulated orthogonally. After presentation, the subjects were given an unexpected position judgment test. A 10-point scale was used, with the numbers from 1 to 10 referring to successive tenths of the list. If the subject remembered seeing a test word once, he was to give one position judgment. If he remembered seeing it twice, he was to give two. Two position judgments were given for about 56% of the repeated words. The mean P_1 and P_2 judgments for the four repetition conditions are shown in Table I. It is clear from the means that both judgments were primarily determined by the target position and were affected by the nontarget position little, if at all. Indeed, a computation of regression of judgment means on log position shows that 92% of the variance among P_1 means was accounted for by P_1 position, while 91% of the variance among P_2 means could be explained by P_2 position.

TABLE I

MEAN POSITION JUDGMENTS FOR
REPEATED WORDS THAT WERE GIVEN
TWO JUDGMENTS[a]

Condition	P_1 Judgment		P_2 Judgment	
	A	B	C	D
AC	2.18		7.16	
AD	2.39			8.04
BC		3.55	7.49	
BD		3.14		8.14

[a]Hintzman & Block, 1971, Experiment II.

An unpublished replication and extension of the Hintzman and Block experiment, using six different repetition conditions, has been conducted by Michael J. Hacker and James V. Hinrichs at the University of Iowa. Zones A, B, C, and D were defined in their study to include positions 5–12, 16–23, 28–35, and 39–46, respectively. The six repetition conditions involved all pairwise combinations of these four zones of the list. The judgment task was the same as in the original study. About 54% of the repeated words were given both P_1 and P_2 position judgments; the means are presented in Table II. Again, P_1 and P_2 judgments were determined almost exclusively by the position being judged. Target position accounted for 96% and 95% of the variance among P_1 and P_2 judgment means, respectively.

In both these studies, P_1 and P_2 position judgments were remarkably independent of one another. This was true despite the fact that the range of possible values of the subject's second judgment is restricted by the value he assigns the first—a restriction that could induce a spurious correlation between the two judgments. Even though there is this reason to expect some dependence between the judgments, there is little evidence of it in either Table I or Table II.

The data just presented show clearly that when P_2 occurs the individuality of the trace of P_1 is not lost. Independent P_1 and P_2 position judgments would be impossible if the sole effect of repetition were to increase the strength of a single, undifferentiated memory trace of the item.

Earlier, it was noted that judged recency of P_2 is not always independent of the recency of P_1. Peterson et al. (1969) compared judged recency of single-presentation words with that of words repeated at spacings of zero and four intervening items. When P_1–P_2 spacing was zero, the apparent recency of the word was enhanced.

TABLE II

MEAN POSITION JUDGMENTS FOR REPEATED WORDS THAT WERE GIVEN TWO JUDGMENTS[a]

Condition	P_1 judgment			P_2 judgment		
	A	B	C	B	C	D
AB	2.73			7.17		
AC	2.71				7.70	
AD	3.05					7.96
BC		3.64			7.78	
BD		3.69				8.21
CD			4.38			8.13

[a] Hacker & Hinrichs, unpublished.

When it was four, apparent recency was the same as in the single-presentation condition. Other investigators have also reported effects of repetition on judged recency (Flexser & Bower, 1974; Morton, 1968). A problem with the design of Morton's experiment is that subjects were not allowed to call an unrecognized item "new." It is likely, therefore, that the effect of repetition on judged recency in his study is at least partly an artifact, due to the effect of repetition on recognition memory. Flexser and Bower (1974) conditionalized on recognition to remove this artifact, and found a sizable residual effect of repetition on judged recency.

There is an apparent inconsistency between the results of Peterson et al. (1969) and those of Flexser and Bower (1974). In the former study, there was no effect of repetition on judged recency when P_1-P_2 spacing was four items. In the latter investigation, there was an effect when spacing was five items. This seeming discrepancy may be resolved by noting that retention intervals were also different. Recency discrimination has been shown to depend upon relative rather than absolute differences in recency (Yntema & Trask, 1963). In the Flexser and Bower (1974) experiment, the Morton (1968) study, and the massed condition of Peterson et al. (1969), the ratio of the P_1-P_2 and P_2-Test intervals was in each case less than .20. In the spaced repetition condition of Peterson et al. (the condition showing no repetition effect), the ratio was .50 and greater.

The apparent dependence of the repetition effect on the relative, rather than absolute, recencies of P_1 and P_2 suggests that it is not due to strength, but to overlap between the time tag distributions of P_1 and P_2. Shortening the P_1-P_2 interval and lengthening the P_2-Test interval both have the effect of increasing the degree of this overlap. The more overlap there is, the more likely it is that the apparent recency of P_1 will exceed that of P_2 and determine the subject's recency judgment.

Flexser and Bower (1974) have shown that a multiple-trace theory can account for the effect of repetition on judged recency in just this way. From single-presentation conditions, they were able to make good quantitative predictions of how much repeating an item would affect judgments of comparative recency. More important, they noted that the multiple-trace hypothesis predicts that repetition should have an effect on judgments of "distance" just the opposite of its effect on judgments of recency. That is, if subjects are asked to indicate how long ago an item first appeared, the apparent distance of a repeated item should be greater than that of an item that occurred only once. An experimental test of this hypothesis showed it to be correct. This phenomenon is not predicted by strength theory, and so adds support to the multiple-trace hypothesis.

The assumption that each occurrence of an event leaves its own memory trace, including a unique time tag, implies that remembered frequency is not absolute. That is, frequency must be defined relative to a particular "time window" and context. Thus, subjects easily discriminate the experimental frequency of a word from its preexperimental or "background" frequency. But in addition, they should be able to break down experimental frequency into components. How many times did *elk* occur in the first half of the experimental session? The last half? The middle two thirds? Answers to such questions, though far from perfect, should correlate with the actual target values if the multiple-trace hypothesis is correct.

To show that a word can have more than one remembered experimental frequency, Hintzman and Block (1971, Experiment III) presented two 104-item word lists, separated by 5 min on an unrelated task. Each word was assigned a List 1 frequency of 0, 2, or 5 and a List 2 frequency of 0, 2, or 5 in an orthogonal design. Following presentation of List 2, subjects were given an unexpected test on which they were asked to assign a List 1 and a List 2 frequency to each test word. The data showed that while frequency judgments were affected by frequency in the nontarget list, they were primarily determined by target list frequency. The variance among mean List 1 judgments was 89.6% explained by List 1 frequency, while that among List 2 judgments was 86.4% due to List 2 frequency. Apparently, as expected by the multiple-trace hypothesis, a word can simultaneously possess more than one remembered frequency within the experimental context.

If the critical cue by which subjects discriminate List 1 and List 2 frequencies is the time tag, then the greater the temporal separation of the two lists, the better should be the discrimination. In another experiment on the ability to assign frequencies to lists, Macey and Zechmeister (1975) used either 0- or 7-min separations between List 1 and List 2. The interlist generalization of frequency information, as predicted, was less with the long than with the short separation. Additional positive evidence comes from the verbal discrimination paradigm. Taking for granted the notion that verbal discrimination learning is primarily a matter of frequency discrimination (see Ekstrand, Wallace, & Underwood, 1966), Hintzman and Block (1971) predicted that negative transfer in verbal discrimination learning would decrease with an increase in the interlist interval. This prediction has been confirmed for at least one situation producing negative transfer (Pasko & Zechmeister, 1974).

C. EVIDENCE: MULTIPLE TRACES VERSUS PROPOSITIONAL ENCODING

There are two basic differences between the multiple-trace and propositional encoding explanations of memory for frequency. One is that the multiple-trace hypothesis assumes the subject determines frequency at the time of retrieval, while the propositional encoding hypothesis assumes that the subject encodes frequency information while studying the list. The other basic difference is that, since multiple traces are the inevitable result of multiple encodings, the multiple-trace hypothesis gives special status to frequency information. The propositional encoding hypothesis, by contrast, does not see frequency information as a fundamental property of memory. Frequency is just one of many kinds of information that may or may not be encoded into memory, depending upon how the subject approaches the task.

The following discussion will deal first with the question of whether frequency decisions are made during encoding or retrieval, and second with the question of whether frequency information has the fundamental status the multiple-trace hypothesis assumes.

1. Retrieval of Frequency Information

Are frequency judgments made implicitly during study of the list, or are they generated at the time of test? Howell (1973a) has suggested that response latencies might tell which hypothesis is correct. If subjects count memory traces, then response latency should increase with frequency; if they simply retrieve and output a preexisting judgment, then the function relating latency to frequency should be flat.

Unfortunately, the assumptions linking the multiple-trace and propositional-encoding hypotheses to these two predictions are somewhat arbitrary. Certainly, if subjects actually count memory traces to determine frequency, a monotonic (perhaps linear) increasing function should result. But in the classical "span of apprehension" experiment, in which subjects judge the number of dots presented visually, counting only occurs with long exposures and instructions emphasizing accuracy. Using brief exposures, Kaufman, Lord, Reese, and Volkmann (1949) identified two processes: subitizing—a fast, accurate, and confident process applied to numbers less than 6; and estimating—a slower, less accurate, and less confident process involved when numbers were greater than 6.

The parallel between the frequency judgment and span of apprehension tasks probably should not be taken too seriously, but the possibility that different processes may be involved at different frequencies deserves consideration.

In the frequency judgment task, judgments become more and more crude the greater the frequency is. Consider, for example, a new analysis of data from Experiment I of Hintzman (1969). In that experiment, words occurred at frequencies 1, 2, 3, 4, 6, and 10. Altogether, 9,720 frequency judgments were collected for all these frequencies combined. The distribution of frequency judgments, collapsed over frequency conditions, reveals that the values 0 through 5 were used about equally often; but beyond 5, two tendencies stand out: a strong preference for multiples of 5, and a somewhat weaker preference for even numbers. Both tendencies become more pronounced the higher the judged values become. To give just one example of the irregularities present: the judgement 15 was used more than five times as often as was 14, and nearly 29 times as often as 16.

Such data are only consistent with a counting hypothesis if one makes the peculiar assumption that the counting mechanism prefers to stop on certain values. Thus, it seems unlikely that subjects judge frequency by counting—at least for frequencies greater than 5—and it is not clear what kind of latency function the multiple-trace hypothesis predicts. Subjects may count at low frequencies and estimate at higher frequencies. One possibility, then, is that latencies may increase as a function of frequency up to a point, and then decline as the estimates become more and more haphazard.

Nor is it clear what kind of latency function the propositional encoding theory should predict. If the implicit frequency judgments encoded during study are exact, then the function should be approximately flat. But if the counter is imprecise, as has been assumed here (see Section II, A, 3), then the imprecise count must be translated into a particular numerical judgment before it is output. Again, a likely prediction is that latencies will increase over low frequencies, when the subject feels there is some chance of being correct, and then decline as frequency increases and "ball park" guesses take over.

Voss, Vereb, and Bisanz (1975) measured frequency judgment latencies, and found them to be an inverted U function of frequency. Such a finding, as the previous discussion suggests, does not discriminate between the multiple-trace and propositional encoding hypotheses. At best, it provides evidence against a version of the multiple-trace view that bases judged frequency strictly on a count of relevant traces, and against a "precise counter" version of the propositional encoding hypothesis. As is pointed out by Voss et al. (1975), the data simply show that the process whereby the retrieved information is transformed into a numerical frequency judgment may vary, depending upon whether frequency is high or low.

Perhaps more crucial to the question of whether frequency judgments are generated during the study or retrieval phase of the experiment are studies that vary the time window over which the frequency estimate is to be made. As was discussed previously (Section II, B, 2), the multiple-trace hypothesis implies that remembered frequency is relative rather than absolute. An item actually possesses several remembered frequencies simultaneously, because the set of time tags relevant to the frequency estimate varies, depending on the subject's task.

So far, it has been shown that subjects can judge frequencies in two lists with some independence (e.g., Hintzman & Block, 1971, Experiment III), but there seem to be no experiments showing how well subjects can remember local densities of repetition in arbitrarily defined parts of a single list. For example, how well could subjects remember that *elk* occurred three, zero, five, and two times, respectively, in successive quarters of a list, or (for the same list) three, four, and three times in successive thirds? Any appreciable ability of subjects to make such judgments would be damaging to the propositional encoding explanation of memory for frequency. The only ways to make the hypothesis compatible with such an ability would be to (a) assume that an absurd number and variety of propositions are encoded during study of the list, or (b) assume that the inferences are drawn from more basic information at the time of retrieval—a position nearly identical to the multiple-trace hypothesis.

2. The Status of Frequency Information

Does frequency have special status, as the multiple-trace hypothesis assumes, or is it just one of the many attributes that subjects can choose to encode or ignore at will? According to the propositional encoding hypothesis, directing the subject's attention toward other attributes of the stimulus material—through manipulation of instructions, previous experience, or saliency—should affect the ability to remember frequency of occurrence.

Howell (1973b) investigated the effects of instructions on memory for frequency. Half the subjects in his study were led to expect a free recall test and half to expect a frequency judgment test. In each instruction condition, half the subjects were then tested on free recall and the other half on frequency judgments. While free recall was affected by the instructional set, frequency judgments were not. This outcome suggests that frequency information is encoded regardless of the subject's strategy—a conclusion consistent with the multiple-trace hypothesis. Acceptance of the conclusion, however, should await confirmation in experiments using other instructions and orienting tasks.

A number of experiments have had subjects judge frequency when other salient attributes of the material were also manipulated. Of particular interest are cases where these manipulations provide information that is redundant with information about frequency. The propositional encoding hypothesis predicts that such redundant information will influence judgments of frequency. For example, if P_1 and P_2 of a word are in different modalities, and the subject remembers both modality tags, he should quickly infer that the item occurred at least two times. A word occurring twice in the same modality should not benefit from this redundant cue. The multiple-trace hypothesis, on the other hand, predicts that redundant information should have no effect. The similarity of the traces of P_1 and P_2 should not affect the subject's ability to tell there are two of them.

Hintzman et al. (1973) presented words either auditorily or visually, with P_1 and P_2 either in the same or in different modalities. In their Experiment I, mean judged frequency was 1.55 when the P_1

and P_2 modalities were different, and 1.54 when they were the same. In Experiment II, the spacing of repetitions was varied. Collapsed over spacings, mean judged frequency was 1.28 when the modalities were different and 1.24 when they were the same. Although very small, the latter difference was statistically significant. In another study manipulating P_1 and P_2 modalities, Madigan and Doherty (1972) had subjects free recall words and then give one or two modality judgments for each word they were able to recall. Mean judged frequency, derived from their published modality judgment data, was 1.81 when the two modalities were different, and 1.79 when they were the same. The difference appears too small to be statistically reliable. Rowe (1974) presented words up to six times. In one condition the type style was different on each presentation; in another condition it was always the same. This manipulation did not affect judged frequency. Taken together, these experiments provide little evidence that different modes of presentation, by providing a redundant cue, have any influence on memory for the number of times an item occurred.

Another memory attribute that might help subjects infer that an item occurred more than once is the time tag. The multiple-trace hypothesis assumes that each trace has its own time tag (see Section II, B, 2). But judged frequency is assumed to depend upon the number of retrieved traces, not on their similarity. Based upon the propositional encoding hypothesis, on the other hand, one might well expect temporal information to directly affect judged frequency. If the subject knows an item occurred near the beginning of the list and also near the end, he can infer that it occurred more than once. If he only knows it occurred near the end, he has no basis for such an inference. Thus the more discriminable the time tags of different presentations become, the more evidence they provide regarding frequency.

Do similar time tags lead to lower frequency judgments than dissimilar ones? The repetition conditions of the Hintzman and Block (1971) and Hacker and Hinrichs (unpublished) studies discussed earlier (Section II, B, 2) provide some relevant evidence. In the former experiment, separation of P_1 and P_2 of a word ranged from six items in Condition BC to 40 items in Condition AD. The correlation between P_1-P_2 separation and judged frequency (i.e., the number of position judgments given) was $-.44$. In the latter study, P_1-P_2 separations ranged from 11 items in Conditions AB and CD, to 34 items in Condition AD. The correlation of separation with judged frequency was −.20. Neither correlation was significantly different from zero, and in any case both were negative rather than positive.

When P_1-P_2 separations are quite short (less than 15 sec), the relationship between judged frequency and spacing is positive. This is one manifestation of the "spacing effect" (see Section III). The spacing effect typically asymptotes when P_1-P_2 spacing is about 15 sec. Since the similarity of time tags apparently does not asymptote at a 15-sec interitem interval (e.g., Yntema & Trask, 1963), it seems unlikely that the spacing effect itself is due to the use of temporal cues as supplemental information regarding frequency.

Another source of evidence regarding effects of redundant attributes on memory for frequency can be found in investigations of the ability to assign overall frequency of presentation of an item to two different lists. Macey and Zechmeister (1975) varied frequency of occurrence of words in two lists using both auditory and visual presentation. For half the words that occurred in both lists, input modality was the same in List 2 as it had been in List 1. For the other half, input modality was changed in List 2. The ability to discriminate List 1 and List 2 frequencies was not affected by this manipulation. Using a similar paradigm, Reichardt, Shaughnessy, and Zimmerman (1973) presented words either by massed or distributed practice. Method of study was the same in Lists 1 and 2 for half the words and different for the other half. The ability to assign frequencies to Lists 1 and 2 was not influenced by the switch in method of study. Again, there is little evidence that redundant information plays a role in memory for frequency.

D. CONCLUSIONS

How is frequency represented in memory? On the basis of the experiments reviewed here, the strength hypothesis can be rejected. While it would be improper to conclude that strength never plays a role in memory for frequency, the experimental evidence points overwhelmingly to the involvement of other mechanisms. The multiple-trace and propositional encoding hypotheses (or some combination of the two) are both viable candidates. The existing data on frequency judgment latency do not discriminate between them and appropriate experiments varying the time window over which frequency estimates are to be made apparently have not been done.

Evidence regarding the special status of frequency information is fairly consistent. One experiment found that instructional set had no effect on memory for frequency. And redundant information, which the propositional encoding hypothesis suggests should influence judged frequency, has little effect, if any. Thus at present there seems to be no strong evidence against the view that frequency information is an inevitable result of the encoding of repetitions, as the multiple-trace hypothesis maintains. In a comparison of the multiple-trace and propositional encoding explanations of memory for frequency, both parsimony and the experimental evidence appear to favor the former.

III. The Spacing Effect

A. DEFINITION AND GENERALITY

A puzzling fact about repetition of an item is that successive repetitions affect memory less than do repetitions that are spaced apart in time. This outcome has been obtained in a wide variety of memory tasks, using several dependent variables (for a review, see Hintzman, 1974).

Although such spacing effects occur in a variety of tasks, the form of the spacing function, plotting retention test performance as a function of the spacing between P_1 and P_2, can vary with the experimental task. The most typical findings is that performance increases as the P_1-P_2 interval increases from 0 to about 15 sec, and then levels off. This is the outcome almost always obtained with frequency judgments. It is sometimes obtained with free recall and paired associates as well. But in free recall the spacing function often continues to increase in a monotonic fashion far beyond the 15-sec spacing interval—a phenomenon sometimes called the "Melton" or "lag" effect—and in paired associates it frequently peaks somewhere past 15 sec and then turns downward, forming an inverted U.

The term "spacing effect" will be used here to refer to the increase in the function over short spacings—from 0 to about 15 sec—regardless of the experimental task. It will be assumed that the cause of this effect is the same in all tasks, and that the Melton lag effect found in free recall and the downward-turning functions found with paired associates reflect processes different from those that cause the spacing effect itself.

This assumption is not entirely arbitrary, as it has some empirical support. D'Agostino and DeRemer (1972, 1973) have shown that certain manipulations eliminate the Melton lag effect without diminishing the influence of short spacings on retention. This clearly implies that the effects of short and long P_1-P_2 spacings in free recall reflect different underlying processes. Similarly, Glenberg (1976) has shown that the inverted U spacing curve sometimes found with paired associates only occurs when the P_2–Test interval is relatively short. As the retention interval is lengthened, the peak of the function disappears. The peak may reflect the fact that when both the P_1-P_2 and P_2–Test intervals are short, P_1 is fairly recent. Any recency effect attributed to P_1 would necessarily decrease as the P_1-P_2 interval lengthens, causing the observed downturn in the spacing function. Whatever the cause of the peak of the function, Glenberg's data suggest that the peak is not due to the same process that procedures the spacing effect, since manipulation of the retention interval appears to eliminate one without affecting the other.

The generality of the spacing effect, as defined above, extends over a variety of to-be-remembered materials, as well as a variety of tasks. As indicated in a recent review (Hintzman, 1974), the spacing effect has been obtained using CCC trigrams, nonsense syllables, words, sentences, and pictures. With verbal materials, the effect is found with both auditory and visual presentation.

Typical effects of spacing on the judged frequency of pictures are shown in the left panel of Fig. 1. In this experiment (Hintzman & Rogers, 1973, Experiment I), subjects viewed 190 slides of vacation

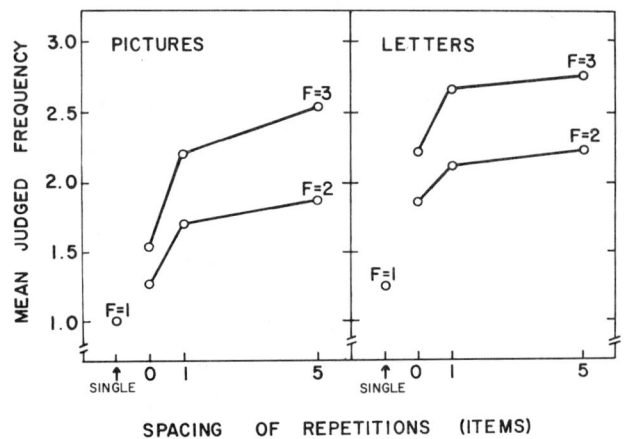

Fig. 1. Mean judged frequency as a function of frequence and the spacing of repetitions. Left panel: picture data. (Hintzman & Rogers, 1973, Experiment I.) Right panel: letter data. (Hintzman, unpublished.)

scenes, presented at a 3-sec rate. Each picture occurred with one of three frequencies (F = 1, 2, or 3). The spacing between presentations was either 0, 1, or 5 other items, and for F = 3 pictures, the P_1-P_2 and P_2-P_3 spacings were the same. Following presentation, subjects were shown the pictures one at a time and asked for frequency judgments. The mean judgments are shown in the figure.

Medin (1974) reported a failure to obtain the spacing effect with letters. However, a recent experiment conducted at Oregon fails to confirm this finding. The presentation rate, frequencies, and spacings were the same as in the picture study just described, but the list was shorter (61 items). Five rotations of letters among conditions were used, and there were 86 subjects altogether. Mean frequency judgments are presented in the right panel of Fig. 1. Letters are not remembered as well as pictures, and so the judged frequencies of letters were more variable. Nevertheless, the patterns displayed in the right and left panels of the figure are quite similar.

Words and single letters are familiar units or chunks, while CCC trigrams, nonsense syllables, and unfamiliar pictures are not. The generality of the spacing effect over these materials indicates that the effect is not peculiar to familiar or to unfamiliar items. The fact that it is obtained with pictures shows that it is not peculiar to verbal materials; and it is not peculiar to the visual modality, since with verbal materials auditory and visual presentation produce the effect equally well (Hintzman *et al.*, 1973).

Physical characteristics of the to-be-remembered item are of little importance compared with the semantic encoding provided by the subject. If a homograph is presented, accompanied by context words that bias different meanings on P_1 and P_2, the spacing effect may be attenuated or eliminated (e.g., D'Agostino & DeRemer, 1973; Madigan, 1969; Winograd & Raines, 1972). It may even be reversed, so that short spacings lead to better retention than do longer spacings (Hintzman, Summers, & Block, 1975a). A recent study by Elmes and Bjork (1975) found that when subjects were given "secondary rehearsal" instructions, encouraging them to elaborate upon and seek relationships among the presented words in various ways, the spacing effect was largely eliminated. The cause of this outcome is obscure, but it may have happened because the subjects were encouraged by the instructions to encode the items differently on P_1 and P_2.

An important fact about the spacing effect is that it occurs even in incidental learning situations (Rowe & Rose, 1974; Shaughnessy, in press). Equally important is the fact that a switch in the subject's orienting task from P_1 to P_2, if it does not encourage a different semantic interpretation of the word, does not eliminate the spacing effect. Shaughnessy (in press) had subjects rate words on semantic rating scales (imagery, pleasantness, and frequency) during presentation of a list, and then gave an unexpected free recall test. The spacing effect was just as pronounced under incidental as under intentional learning instructions; and in the incidental conditions it was just as great when P_1 and P_2 were rated on different scales as when they were rated on the same scale. The same finding obtained when effects of three different judgments were compared with effects of one judgment repeated three times.

Paivio (1975) has used the effects of such orienting tasks on free recall to investigate the independence of repetitions. If the effects of P_1 and P_2 are "additive" when the spacing is zero, according to Paivio, the two presentations have been given independent encodings. Like Shaughnessy, Paivio finds that a switch between P_1 and P_2 in the scale on which a word is rated has little effect on later recall. On the other hand, if P_1 is a word and P_2 is its corresponding picture (or vice versa), the effects of the two presentations are additive. Stated somewhat differently, there is no spacing effect with picture-word and word-picture repetitions, suggesting different underlying encodings of words and pictures. This conclusion is quite plausible in view of the evidence that verbal and pictorial retention can be interrupted independently by unilateral electroconvulsive shock. Left hemisphere shock disrupts verbal retention, while right hemisphere shock interferes with memory for pictures (Berent, Cohen, & Silverman, 1975).

Further evidence that the spacing effect in memory for words occurs at the semantic level is provided by experiments in which P_1 and P_2 are in different modalities. Hintzman *et al.* (1973) found that the effect of spacing on judged frequency was of the same magnitude when P_1 and P_2 were in different modalities as when they were in the same modality. A similar finding by Wells and Kirsner (1974) extends the conclusion to the free recall task. Input modality is typically encoded into memory, but modality attributes apparently do not play a part in the spacing effect.

If one considers the magnitude of the spacing effect to be an index of the commonality of the semantic encodings of P_1 and P_2, as Paivio has done, then pictures and words apparently involve separate encodings (Paivio, 1975), as do paraphrases of sentences (Gude & Zechmeister, 1975). With bilingual subjects, when P_2 is the translation of the P_1 word into the subject's other language, the spacing effect is attenuated (Glanzer & Duarte, 1971). This could reflect a degree of independence of the two language systems, or it may simply indicate that translations of words are not always equivalent. In a recent experiment conducted by Leonard Stern at Oregon, pictures were used as stimuli, and P_2 was the mirror-image reversal of P_1. The spacing effect was very small and not statistically significant. This may indicate that the difference between right and left is part of the "deep structure" encoding of pictures.

A difficulty with the use of a flat spacing curve as the baseline in such analyses is that related items sometimes produce a reverse spacing effect. This is true of associatively related words such as *spider* and *web* (Hintzman et al., 1975a; Jacoby & Hendricks, 1973), and may be true of homographs (Hintzman et al., 1975a) and even of corresponding words and pictures (see Paivio, 1974). Since identical encodings produce a rising spacing function and related encodings sometimes produce a falling function, a flat spacing curve could reflect some intermediate degree of similarity, rather than complete independence of the encodings used on P_1 and P_2.

B. THEORIES AND EXPERIMENTAL EVIDENCE

A number of different explanations of the spacing effect have been offered. Most of them can be classified under two main headings: encoding variability theories and deficient processing theories. In the following discussion, several of the more prominent hypotheses will be considered. More extensive discussions of some of the issues can be found in Hintzman (1974).

1. *Encoding Variability Theories*

a. Semantic Variability. Explanations of the spacing effect in terms of semantic variability focus on the fact that most verbal items can be interpreted in more ways than one. The spacing effect is explained by assuming that when the P_1-P_2 interval is short, the meaning assigned to the item on P_2 is likely to be the same as that given on P_1, while if it is long, the interpretation is likely to change. It is further assumed that the more different meanings of the item were originally encoded, the more ways there are to retrieve it. Thus the effect of spacing on recall or on recognition memory is explained.

This hypothesis enjoys considerable popularity but very little empirical support. In fact, there is a substantial amount of evidence against it.

The fact that biasing two different meanings of a homograph on P_1 and P_2 flattens the spacing curve (e.g., Madigan, 1969) simply shows that a homograph can function as two different words, depending on the context in which it occurs. Thus it cannot be considered strong evidence for encoding variability as an explanation of the spacing effect.

If one could demonstrate somehow that long P_1–P_2 spacings typically produce two different semantic interpretations of an item, while short spacings produce only one, the hypothesis would have strong support. However, no one seems to have presented such evidence. Martin (1972) has suggested that failure to recognize an item as "old" on P_2 might be taken as evidence that the P_1 and P_2 encodings are different. Bellezza, Winkler, and Adrasik (1975), however, found that pairs recognized on P_2 (therefore encoded in the same way) were better recalled on a final test than were those that were not recognized on P_2. And Johnston and Uhl (1976, Experiment II) found a negative correlation between recognition latency on P_2 and probability of free recall on a later test. If slow or erroneous recognition responses indicate multiple encodings, this evidence suggests that variable encoding harms recall rather than aiding it. In addition, Johnston and Uhl divided the words in each spacing condition into two categories—P_2 hits and P_2 misses—and found that the spacing effect occurred only on words that were P_2 hits. Thus recognition of the item as old at the time of P_2 may even be a prerequisite of the spacing effect, a conclusion completely contrary to the semantic variability hypothesis.

Attempts to manipulate the likelihood of different P_1 and P_2 interpretations of an item have had little influence on the magnitude of the spacing effect. Bellezza *et al.* (1975), for example, compared spacing curves for CCC-letter and CVC-letter pairs. Semantic encodings of low-meaningfulness CCC trigrams are, according to encoding variability theory, inherently more variable than those of high-meaningfulness CVC syllables (Martin, 1968). The two spacing functions, however, had virtually the same form. D'Agostino and DeRemer (1973, Experiment II) attempted to force subjects to use the same encoding on P_1 and P_2. Their manipulation made the Melton lag effect disappear, but the spacing effect remained, evidence that the lag effect may be due to variable semantic encodings but that the spacing effect is not.

A serious problem with the semantic variability hypothesis is its inability to deal with the effect of spacing on frequency judgments. If one supposes that subjects judge frequency by counting or estimating the number of meanings of the test item stored during the experiment, then one must assume that a test item is given several different interpretations at the same time, while a study item is given only one. The empirical evidence suggests that different semantic encodings of a repeated item lower judged frequency rather than raising it (Hintzman, 1974, p. 94; Rowe, 1973). Thus it appears to be consistent rather than variable semantic encoding that leads to high judgments of frequency.

b. Contextual Variability. A variable encoding hypothesis emphasizing contextual elements of the memory trace does not suffer from the drawbacks of the semantic variability hypothesis. Following Anderson and Bower (1972), one may assume that encoding involves the formation of associations between the meaning of the to-be-remembered item, on the one hand, and a bundle of contextual elements representing the momentary contents of the subject's stream of consciousness, on the other. Retrieved contextual associations enable the subject to decide that the item occurred during the experiment or in a particular list—crucial information in most memory tasks. The more relevant contextual associations there are, the more evidence there is that the item was presented previously; and the more different bundles of associations can be identified, the greater will by the item's subjective frequency. The spacing effect can be explained in the recognition memory, recall, and frequency judgment tasks by assuming that a spaced repetition is more likely to sample different contextual elements than is a massed repetition (Hintzman, 1974).

The most convincing evidence for the contextual variability hypothesis would be a clear demonstration that induced contextual variability eliminates or attenuates the spacing effect. What evidence there is on this point, however, is negative. As was already indicated, switching the input modality between P_1 and P_2 does not attenuate the spacing effect (Hintzman *et al.,* 1973; Wells & Kirsner, 1974). And in Experiment I of Hintzman, Summers, Eki, and Moore (1975), the spacing of repetitions of pictures was varied in two conditions: one in which P_1 and P_2 were both accompanied by silence, and one in which P_1 was accompanied by silence and P_2 by a tone used as an incentive signal. The tone was effective as an incentive signal, so it certainly was part of the cognitive context of P_2. The magnitude of the spacing effect was not altered by the presence of the tone. Finally, there is the incidental learning experiment by Shaughnessy (in press) in which the spacing effect was just as great when the orienting task was different on P_1 and P_2 as when it was the same.

The orienting task must have affected the cognitive context of the word, but it did not affect the magnitude of the spacing effect.

The failure of such manipulations to alter the form of the spacing function is a serious challenge to the contextual variability hypothesis. Neither this nor the semantic version of the encoding variability hypothesis can be said at present to have any strong empirical support.

2. Deficient Processing Theories

Previously proposed theories that attribute the spacing effect to deficient processing when the P_1-P_2 interval is short fall into four categories depending on (*a*) whether the locus of the critical processing is assumed to be between P_1 and P_2 or during P_2, and on (*b*) whether the critical processing is assumed to be autonomous or under the subject's voluntary control. Following Hintzman (1974), the four hypotheses will be called rehearsal, consolidation, attention, and habituation. The 2 × 2 classification of these hypotheses is shown in Table III.

a. Rehearsal. This hypothesis attributes the spacing effect to the fact that long P_1-P_2 intervals allow more voluntary rehearsal of the item prior to P_2 than do short intervals (Rundus, 1971). There is considerable evidence against rehearsal as a general explanation of the spacing effect. The essence of all this evidence is that manipulations that affect rehearsal do not have the effects on the spacing function that the hypothesis predicts. The recent finding that the spacing effect is as great in incidental learning, where the subject has no reason to rehearse, as it is in intentional learning is one example. Other evidence regarding the rehearsal hypothesis has been reviewed by Hintzman (1974), and need not be repeated here.

TABLE III

CLASSIFICATION OF DEFICIENT PROCESSING
THEORIES OF THE SPACING EFFECT

	Control of processing	
Locus of processing	Involuntary	Voluntary
Between P_1 and P_2	Consolidation	Rehearsal
During P_2	Habituation	Attention

b. Consolidation. The consolidation hypothesis (Landauer, 1969; Peterson, 1966) postulates an autonomous increase over time in the retrievability of the memory trace. The consolidation of P_1 and P_2 of the same item are assumed to use the same "pathway," thus the consolidation of P_1 can be interrupted by P_2. If P_2 occurs shortly after P_1, the degree of consolidation produced by both presentations together will be less than if P_2 is delayed until consolidation of P_1 is complete.

Consolidation is usually assumed to involve the transfer of information, over time, from a short-term state to a long-term state. Thus manipulations that interfere with the short-term retention of P_1 should disrupt consolidation, producing poor long-term retention. Contrary to this prediction (and to intuition), Bjork and Allen (1970) reported that a difficult task performed between P_1 and P_2 resulted in slightly better retention than did an easy task. A similar outcome was obtained by Tzeng (1973). Such evidence cannot be considered conclusive disproof of a consolidation hypothesis, however, because of the concept of consolidation does not necessarily entail the transfer of information from short-term to long-term memory. In the theory of Wickelgren and Berian (1971), for example, consolidation is the transformation of a potential memory trace into a retrievable trace. The transformation has nothing to do with a short-term store.

A second type of evidence that casts doubt on the consolidation hypothesis was presented by Hintzman *et al.* (1973). In order to learn which presentation was remembered better at long than at short spacings, P_1 and P_2 of words were presented in different modalities. On the final test, subjects were asked to give combined frequency and modality judgments. The modality judgments were consistent with the hypothesis that P_2 is the locus of the spacing effect—that is, that memory for P_2 increases with P_1–P_2 spacing, while memory for P_1 is unaffected. This conclusion appears contrary to the consolidation hypothesis. Again, however, there is no necessary contradiction, since the hypothesis can be modified to assume that ongoing consolidation of P_1 blocks the consolidation of P_2, rather than vice versa. The difficulty of the consolidation hypothesis is not negative evidence so much as it is the lack of evidence in its favor.

c. Habituation. The habituation-recovery hypothesis holds that the cause of the spacing effect is an inability of the nervous system to encode P_2 at full strength when it follows shortly after P_1. The process responsible for encoding the particular to-be-remembered item continues to habituate for as long as the subject devotes attention to P_1, and begins to recover when he ceases to do so. Thus, the spacing function, according to this hypothesis, traces out the time course of recovery from habituation.

One way to test this hypothesis is to try to manipulate the degree of habituation, seeking predictable effects on the spacing (i.e., recovery) function. Presumably, the greater the amount of habituation, the slower should be the recovery process. Hintzman et al. (1975b, Experiment I) attempted to control habituation by manipulating the exposure duration of P_1. Judged frequency was the dependent variable. As can be seen in Fig. 2, the spacing functions following P_1 durations 2.2, 5.2, and 8.2 sec were virtually identical. In Experiment II of the same paper, pictures were presented either one, two, or three times in close succession, followed by a variable spacing interval and then final presentation. The number of massed presentations preceding the spacing interval affected judged frequency, but its effect did not interact with the effect of spacing. Thus neither lengthening P_1 duration beyond 2.2 sec nor presenting an item several times in succession had the predicted effect on the spacing curve. If the habituation-recovery hypothesis is correct, the degree of habituation must reach a maximum in less than 2.2 sec study time.

d. Attention. According to the voluntary attention hypothesis, the subject chooses to pay less attention to P_2 when it closely follows P_1 than he does when the P_1-P_2 interval is longer. This explanation differs from the habituation-recovery hypothesis in two

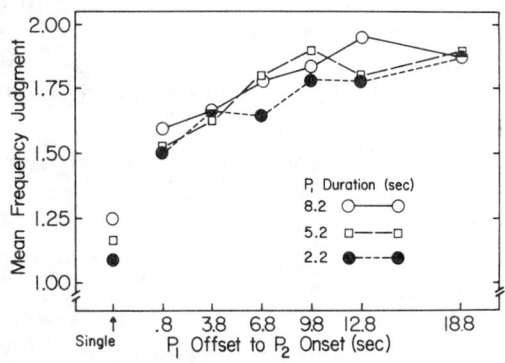

Fig. 2. The spacing effect as a function of duration of P_1. (From Hintzman, Summers, & Block, 1975b, Experiment I, reprinted with permission.)

ways. First, it assumes that the amount of processing given P_2 is under the subject's voluntary control, while habituation and recovery are assumed to be autonomous. Second, it implies a central mechanism whose processing effort can be allocated among stimuli in a flexible way, while habituation and recovery are assumed to be located only in the "pathway" activated by a particular item.

Experimental evidence bearing on the voluntary attention hypothesis is decidedly mixed. To clearly show that the spacing effect is due to a voluntary mechanism, one must demonstrate that appropriate manipulations of the subject's attention eliminate the effect. Hintzman et al. (1975, Experiment I) attempted to make subjects pay special attention to P_2 of a picture by accompanying it with an incentive signal that indicated a high payoff for remembering the picture on a later test. As was indicated above, the effect of spacing on judged frequency was just as great when P_2 was accompanied by the incentive signal as when it was not. This manipulation of attention was indirect, however, and subjects may have paid less attention to P_2 at short spacings than at long spacings even when the incentive tone was present.

Ciccone and Brelsford (1974) tested memory for three-digit numbers in a running recognition task. In their constant rehearsal condition, the subject was required to say the current number aloud four times, and thus had to attend to it on both P_1 and P_2. The resulting spacing function was flat. However, assuming that the spacing effect asymptotes at about 15 sec, the failure to obtain it in this case was a matter of single datum point (for 0 spacing). Experiment II of Hintzman et al. (1975) failed to confirm the Ciccone and Brelsford finding using different materials (words) and a different dependent variable (judged frequency). The spacing effect was just as great when subjects had to chant the current word aloud three times per presentation (once per second) as it was when they studied the words silently. It may be that the discrepancy between the two studies is due to the different materials, since rehearsing an unfamiliar three-digit number very likely requires more attention than does rehearsing a familiar word. Nevertheless, the failure of controlled rehearsal to produce the same result in these two studies is unsettling and derserves further investigation.

Free recall data of Elmes, Greener, and Wilkinson (1972) suggest that central processing capacity may be somehow involved in the spacing effect. They examined recall of words occurring immediately after massed and spaced repetitions of other items. Those occurring after massed repetitions were better recalled than those occurring after spaced repetitions, a finding which suggests that less effort is expended in processing a massed repetition.

More direct evidence that subjects may allocate processing effort to P_2 in the way the attention hypothesis assumes comes from work by Johnston and Uhl (1976) and by Zimmerman (1975). In their Experiment I, Johnston and Uhl required subjects to monitor and respond to weak audio signals, as a secondary task, while studying a word list for free recall. Words occurred four times, with repetitions either massed or spaced. Mean time to respond to the audio signals decreased monotonically over massed repetitions of a word, but did not decrease over spaced repetitions. The obtained decrease suggests that subjects paid less attention to massed than to spaced repetitions, and thus had more leftover processing capacity to devote to the secondary task.

A similar interpretation was given to the outcome of a study by Shaughnessy, Zimmerman, and Underwood (1972), in which presentation of words was self-paced and the amount of time a subject was exposed to each word was monitored. Less time was devoted to studying P_2 and P_3 when they were massed than when they were spaced. A more adequate investigation of this phenomenon has been carried out by Zimmerman (1975), and his data are particularly interesting.

In Zimmerman's experiment, there were three frequencies ($F = 1$, 2, and 3) and three degrees of spacing (0, 3–4, and 13–14 intervening items). The subject initiated each trial by pressing a button which advanced a memory drum. Zimmerman took the study time for a given item to be the time from the response initiating the presentation to the one terminating it and initiating the next one. If the recall performance of Zimmerman's subjects is plotted, for each condition, as a function of total study time, it is clear that recall of massed presentations suffered disproportionately. That is to say, the difference in study time between massed and spaced words was not great enough to account for the difference in recall. This was Zimmerman's conclusion, as well.

But is it valid to count the entire interval from one button press to the next as study time? One might suppose that there is a certain amount of "dead time," after the subject stops attending to one word and before he begins attending to the next, which should be subtracted from each value. Indeed, when dead time is treated as a free parameter to be estimated from the data, Zimmerman's results take on a quite different appearance.

In Fig. 3, Zimmerman's data have been reanalyzed. Proportion recalled is plotted as a function of "effective study time" (EST), which is given by:

$$\text{EST} = \text{TST} - F \times \text{DT} \qquad (1)$$

where TST is total study time as measured by Zimmerman, F is frequency or number of presentations, and DT is estimated dead time per presentation. The straight line fitted to the data accounts for 98.7% of the variance. All three frequencies fall on the same function. More importantly, for a given frequency the same $F \times \text{DT}$ value was subtracted regardless of spacing. Thus the effect of spacing on recall, while disproportionate to its effect on total study time, is not out of proportion to its effect on effective study time, determined in this way. (Incidentally, the intercept of the function is nearly zero, but in the absence of any theoretical justification for assuming a straight-line relationship between proportion recalled and study time, it is difficult to know what to make of this fact.)

If one accepts this reanalysis, the conclusion that the effect of spacing on study time cannot account for the effect of spacing on recall appears to be incorrect. It should be noted, however, that the value of DT (estimated by eye) was 4.0 sec, and this much dead time per presentation seems excessive. Still, in a self-paced task subjects may spend a considerable amount of time daydreaming, resting, or engaging in ineffective rehearsal. If one can accept the 4 sec figure, this reanalysis of Zimmerman's data seems to offer more support to

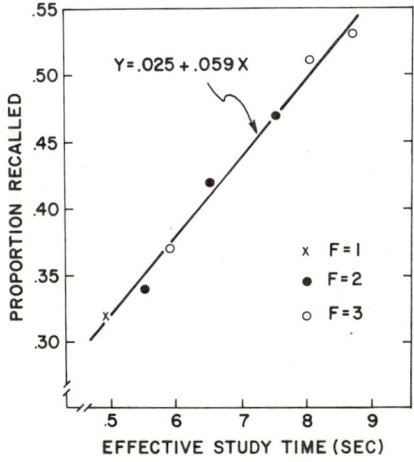

Fig. 3. Reanalysis of the free recall data of Zimmerman (1975). For explanation, see text.

the voluntary attention hypothesis than was given by the original analysis.

A third experiment, similar in intent to the two just described, failed to support the voluntary attention hypothesis. Hintzman *et al.* (1975, Experiment III) presented pictures at a 5-sec rate, and counted the number of eye fixations given to each one. Each picture occurred three times, in one of three spacing conditions. As Fig. 4 shows, the number of fixations dropped regularly from P_1 to P_2 to P_3, but was not affected by spacing.

It is not at all clear why this experiment failed to show the attenuation of attention to massed repetitions found by Johnston and Uhl (1976) and by Zimmerman (1975). This study used pictures instead of words. Also, the measure of attention used was "unobtrusive," while the other two studies measured responses that the subject viewed as part of his task (responding to audio signals in one case, and initiating presentation of the next item, in the other). One should keep in mind, in addition, that the positive evidence offered by these two studies is correlational only. Showing that the spacing of repetitions affects the attention given a secondary task or the time spent looking at a word is no substitute for a demonstration that appropriate manipulations of attention eliminate the effect of spacing on retention.

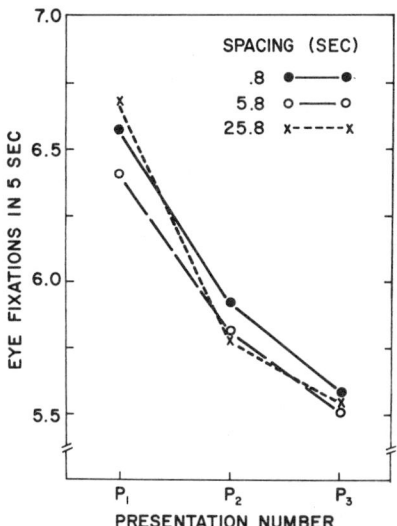

Fig. 4. Eye fixations of pictures, as a function of the spacing and number of presentations. (Hintzman, Summers, Eki, & Moore, 1975, Experiment III.)

The voluntary attention hypothesis is incomplete without the addition of an explanation of why the subject chooses to attend less to massed than to spaced repetitions. A plausible answer is that the decision is based on how well P_1 is remembered at the time P_2 occurs. Presumably, the subject chooses to study only items he feels he is likely to forget. If this is the case, the effect of spacing on memory for P_2 is an indirect manifestation of the effect of recency on memory for P_1.

As a test of this notion, Zechmeister and Shaughnessy (1974) had subjects rate how well they thought they would remember a word upon a single presentation, a massed repetition, or a spaced repetition. The mean ratings were: 3.25, 4.57, and 4.23, respectively. The difference between massed and spaced repetitions was in the appropriate direction, but was small and not statistically significant.

The finding that a difficult task interpolated between P_1 and P_2 leads to better retention than does an easy task (Bjork & Allen, 1970; Tzeng, 1973) lends support to the hypothesis that the forgetting of P_1 somehow determines the attention given P_2. But the findings of Bellezza et al. (1975) and Johnston and Uhl (1976, Experiment II), indicate that items for which P_1 is forgotten when P_2 occurs are more poorly remembered than are items for which P_1 is remembered (see Section III, B, 1, a). These analyses are undoubtedly influenced by item selection, but they cast some doubt on the notion that attention given to P_2 is directly related to forgetting of P_1.

The generality of the spacing effect over experimental materials also argues against its being related to forgetting of P_1. Pictures are remembered much better than letters, yet the spacing functions look much the same (see Fig. 1). CVC nonsense syllables are remembered better than CCC trigrams, but again, the spacing functions are nearly identical (Bellezza et al., 1975). Recency effects differ for auditory and visual presentation, but the spacing effects are indistinguishable (Hintzman et al., 1973; Wells & Kirsner, 1974). Likewise, exposure duration and number of prior presentations both affect retention, but neither appears to influence the form of the spacing curve (Hintzman et al., 1975b, Experiments I and II). In addition, there is the fact that forgetting curves (despite the popular myth) do not asymptote, but continue to decline indefinitely, while the spacing curve typically asymptotes at around a 15-sec P_1-P_2 interval.

Particularly damaging to the notion that the decision to attend to an item is based on the subject's assessment of how likely it is to be forgotten is the fact that the spacing effect occurs in incidental learning tasks (Rowe & Rose, 1974; Shaughnessy, in press). There is no reason for a subject to worry about fogetting an item when he does not expect a retention test, yet the spacing effect appears to be as great in incidental as it is in intentional learning.

C. CONCLUSIONS

Of the several theoretical explanations of the spacing effect considered here, only one—the voluntary attention hypothesis—has any real empirical support; and that support, at present, is somewhat limited. This hypothesis assumes a central processing capacity, under voluntary control, which is directed more toward spaced than toward massed repetitions. The evidence that central processing capacity is involved in the spacing effect is somewhat better than the evidence that it is under voluntary control. If it is under voluntary control, the rule subjects use to guide their direction of processing effort is remarkably resistant to experimental manipulation.

Vagueness about the nature of this rule is a particular weakness of the hypothesis. It seems unlikely that it has anything to do with the absolute forgetting of P_1. Perhaps the rule proposed by several two-process theorists (e.g., Glanzer, 1972)—that P_2 will not be entered into the short-term store if P_1 is still in that state—is basically correct. But this still leaves open the question of whether the decision is voluntary—in which case it should be modifiable through instructions—or beyond the subject's conscious control.

IV. Repetition and Retrieval

A. STUDY-PHASE RETRIEVAL

The fact that the study, retention, and test phases of a typical memory experiment roughly parallel the theoretical process of encoding, storage, and retrieval sometimes misleads investigators to implicitly assume that the relationship between experimental phases and theoretical processes is one-to-one. Among other effects of this assumption is that a repetition is viewed by the theorist in quite different ways, depending on whether it occurs during the study or test phase of the experiment. If P_2 of an item occurs on a memory test, interest focuses on its ability to retrieve the trace of P_1; if P_2

(like P_1) occurs during the study phase, its role as a possible retrieval cue for P_1 is usually ignored.

What evidence is there that would lead one to think of a study phase P_2, like a P_2 presented on a test, as a retrieval cue for P_1? Hintzman and Block (1973) interpreted the ability of subjects to judge spacing in these terms. They presented a list in which some words occurred twice, with P_1-P_2 spacings ranging from 0 to 25 items. On the test, subjects were given pairs of words and asked to judge their spacing in the list. The accuracy of such spacing judgments was found to depend upon the relationship between members of the pair. When the test pair consisted of unrelated words, the ability to judge spacing was very poor. But when the test pair represented P_1 and P_2 of the same word, spacing judgments increased regularly as a function of actual spacing (see Fig. 5).

Hintzman and Block (1973) explained this ability to judge the spacing of repetitions by assuming that P_2 retrieves the trace of P_1, including information about its recency, and that an implicit recency judgment is therefore encoded as part of the trace of P_2. Retrieval of the implicit recency judgment on the test provides the information needed to judge the previous P_1-P_2 spacing.

Support for the assumption that the encoding of spacing information depends on P_2 functioning as a retrieval cue comes from a study

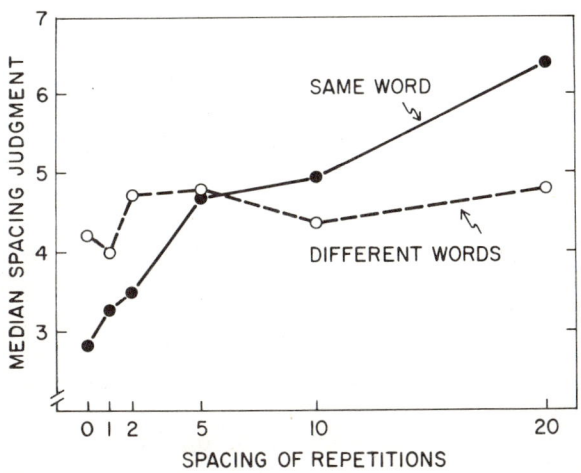

Fig. 5. Spacing judgments as a function of spacing for repeated words and unrelated words. (From Hintzman & Block, 1973. Copyright 1973 by the American Psychological Association. Reprinted by permission.)

in which subjects judged the spacing of associatively related words. Hintzman *et al.* (1975a, Experiment I) found that spacing judgments for associatively related pairs were as accurate as those for a repeated word.

There are other data indicating that presentation of a word during the study phase of an experiment can remind the subject of an associate that occurred earlier in the list. Rundus (1971), for example, noted that subjects instructed to rehearse aloud during study of a free recall list tended to rehearse related items together, even when this meant including in the "rehearsal set" a word that had dropped out of it some time previously. Gruneberg (1972) noted that subjects were able to detect associative relationships between widely spaced words—an experience one subject described as "like a bell ringing." And Shaughnessy and Underwood (1973) found that the enhancement of recognition memory taken as evidence for implicit associative responses (IAR's) was greater if the critical item occurred before its associate in the list than if it occurred afterward. Their explanation is compatible with the present one: If the associate occurs after the critical item, it is very likely to retrieve the critical item and initiate its rehearsal (i.e., an IAR).

What is suggested by the comparison of related-word and repeated-word spacing judgments is very plausible: that study-phase retrieval occurs with repetitions of the same item, just as it does with associatively related items.

The idea that repetition triggers study-phase retrieval is not new, so much as it is neglected. The associative interference manifested in negative transfer in an A-B, A-C paired-associate learning paradigm was explained by classical interference theory as due to the implicit occurrence of B responses during the learning of the A-C list. Stated differently, it was assumed that the repetition of A in List 2 triggered retrieval of the A-B association from List 1, interfering with A-C acquisition. Although interference theory did not do so, one can think of this occurrence of A-B during study of A-C as a rehearsal. Indeed, A-B rehearsals during A-C learning play a key role in a recent theory of retroactive interference (Petrich, 1975).

Evidence for A-B rehearsal during A-C acquisition can be found in studies of retroactive facilitation, using the A-B, A-C paradigm. Ordinarily, subjects may attempt to inhibit retrieval and rehearsal of A-B during the study of A-C. But if they know that they are likely to be tested on A-B later, and feel that they do not know it very well, they may use the retrieval triggered by repetition of A as an opportunity to rehearse. Bruce and Weaver (1973) and Robbins and

Bray (1974) both found retroactive facilitation in a minimal paired-associate learning task under these conditions.

Retrieval and deliberate rehearsal of A-B during A-C learning might also account for an otherwise puzzling finding of Tulving and Watkins (1974) regarding negative transfer in the A-B, A-C paradigm. They reported several experiments in which the learning of A-C was influenced by whether or not A-B was given an immediate test, prior to A-C acquisition. If no immediate test was given on A-B, negative transfer was considerably greater than it was when an immediate A-B test was given. The immediate A-B test improved later recall of B, so the test on A-B was evidently an effective learning experience, as well as a test trial. It seems likely that subjects who did not have the benefit of such a test trial deliberately rehearsed A-B during A-C presentation, and therefore learned List 2 less well than the subjects who had been given the immediate A-B test.

The degree to which memory retrieval is automatic as opposed to voluntary is an important problem that only recently has begun to receive the attention it deserves (e.g., Posner & Snyder, 1975). The evidence indicates that memory retrieval is automatic, at least in the case of word meanings. In the Stroop color naming task, for example, the response of naming the color of ink is interfered with when the stimulus printed in that color is a conflicting color name. It would be to the subject's advantage to inhibit retrieval of the word meanings, if he could do so; but the generality and persistence of the interference suggest that he cannot. Warren (1974) has used a variant of the Stroop task to show that when a word is presented its associates are retrieved or activated. Interference with color naming was obtained when the test word or carrier of the color was a forward associate of a preceding stimulus, but not when it was a backward associate. Apparently, words may be activated or retrieved without even entering consciousness. Corteen and Wood (1972) conditioned the GSR to certain words by pairing them with shock, and then presented those words interspersed with others in the unattended channel in a dichotic listening task. The GSR occurred when shock-associated words were presented, even though the subject was not aware (or could not recall being aware) of them.

Other evidence that retrieval of word meanings is automatic comes from studies using homographs and homophones as stimuli. In an experiment by Ogden (1917), observers heard a word, stopped a clock as soon as they became aware of its meaning, and then gave a retrospective report of the contents of consciousness during the retrieval interval. They frequently reported ambiguous words such as *felt* and *bark* as eliciting more than one meaning nearly simultaneously. Recent investigations using the Stroop task (Conrad, 1974) and the release from PI paradigm (Warren & Warren, 1975) indicate that more than one meaning of a homograph is retrieved even when the subject is "set" by the context to think of only one. Spacing judgment data, also, are consistent with the notion that multiple meanings are retrieved. Hintzman *et al.* (1975a, Experiment II) presented homographs, along with context words chosen to bias particular interpretations. The homographs occurred twice. In one condition, the context word was the same on P_1 and P_2; in another it was different but biased the same meaning (e.g., *flower-bulb, tulip-bulb*); and in a third it biased a different meaning (e.g., *flower-bulb, light-bulb*). Spacing judgments increased with spacing equally in all three conditions, suggesting that the ability of P_2 to retrieve the trace of P_1 was not affected by the difference in semantic context.

This is not to deny that voluntary processes often play a part in the retrieval of information from memory—but the emphasis in recent years on the role of "control processes" in effortful memory search has exaggerated the extent to which retrieval is independent of external stimuli. Effortful retrieval is the exception, rather than the rule. In everyday life, most memory retrieval is triggered by encounters with cues in the environment and involves no conscious attempt to remember.

B. COINCIDENCES

The notion that chance encounters with appropriate stimuli can retrieve traces of relatively recent events and provide an opportunity for their rehearsal may help explain a striking phenomenon that has convinced many persons that they (or others) possess precognition—the ability to foresee the future. Whenever a dream, an imagining, or a prediction "comes true"—as when you dream about Uncle Mo and the next day learn that he has been in an automobile accident—a skeptic can call it a coincidence and point out that such occurrences are probably no more common that would be expected by chance. Logically, this argument seems sound, but intuitively, it is often not convincing.

The reason may be that our intuitive estimates of the base rates of the predictor events are too low. How often, for example, do you dream about Uncle Mo? How often do you dream at all? Most of us remember few of our dreams, and most dreams that we do recall may survive in memory only because of a chance encounter with an appropriate retrieval cue during the day following the dream. The retrieval cue, being related to the content of the dream, may appear to be an event predicted by the dream. Since dreams that "predict" such cues will tend to be remembered while those that do not will be forgotten, our dreams may appear to be far more closely related to future events than one would attribute to chance. The same basic argument, of course, can be applied to prophesies and coincidences of other kinds.

To provide evidence relevant to this argument, we conducted an experiment attempting to simulate the hypothesized predictor-retrieval cue interaction in the laboratory. As an undergraduate thesis project, Steve Asher puts subjects through a five-phase experiment. In the first phase, subjects rated the objects named by 21 concrete nouns on two 7-point rating scales: small to large, and ugly to beautiful. These words were to be recalled at the end of the experiment, but the subjects were not told this at the time. In the second phase, the subjects were given a 9-min filler task involving memory for letters. In the third phase, they were shown 18 pictures of objects and were asked to estimate, for each one, how often they came into contact with or used the pictured object. Seven of the 18 pictures depicted objects corresponding to words rated in the first phase of the experiment; but the subjects were told nothing about this relationship. In the fourth phase, another filler task was given, involving memory for two-digit numbers. This task lasted about 6 min. Finally, in the fifth phase, the subjects were asked to free recall the words from the initial rating task.

Of the 14 control words, which did not correspond to pictures presented in the third phase, 46.6% were recalled. Of the seven experimental words which did, 62.9% were recalled. Intrusion of other picture names in word recall was very rare. As expected, presentation of related pictures during the retention interval aided later free recall of the words.

A number of explanations of this finding could be given. One is that the picture, providing a retrieval cue, leads to implicit rehearsal of the corresponding word. On a questionnaire given at the end of the experiment, 58% of the subjects reported noticing that some of the pictures corresponded to previously rated words, and this is evidence for such retrieval. However, even the subjects who did not report noticing the relationship recalled more experimental than control words. Another hypothesis is that subjects mediated word recall by retrieving the pictures and using them, in turn, as retrieval cues for the words. But asked on the questionnaire whether they had used this strategy, 54% of the subjects said "no," 25% said "sometimes," and only 21% replied "yes." Still a third hypothesis is that the retrieval, when it occurs, serves somehow to emphasize both the predictor and the retrieving event, enhancing their retention.

According to the rehearsal hypothesis, the order of the two related events is critical. If P_2 retrieves and provides rehearsal for P_1, memory for P_1 should be enhanced, while that for P_2 should not be. Indeed, to the extent that rehearsal of P_1 precludes attending to P_2, memory for P_2 might be impaired. To test this prediction, a second experiment was done. The design was exactly the same as that of the experiment conducted by Asher, except that the picture rating task was given in the first phase and the word rating task in the third. The final test, as before, required free recall of the words. Recall of the experimental words, which corresponded to pictures rated in the first phase, was 63%. That for control words was 54%. This difference is smaller than the one found in the Asher study, but is statistically significant.

In these experiments, word recall was enhanced by a corresponding picture, whether the picture occurred after the word or before it. But the effect was greater in the first experiment, where the picture occurred during the retention interval of the word. A tentative explanation for these results is that the enhanced memory for coincidences involves two factors: (*a*) rehearsal of the predictor event when the retrieval cue occurs; and (*b*) an emphasis of both the predictor and the retrieval cue, making both events more memorable.

The second of these factors can be likened to the von Restorff effect. When a stimulus retrieves the trace of a recent, related event from memory, the relationship itself may increase the saliency of both events. There is other support for this hypothesis. Chapman (1967), for example, found that the rate of co-occurrence of related words in a list of word pairs was overestimated. He labeled this phenomenon "illusory correlation," and suggested that it might underlie various common but erroneous beliefs about causal relationships. Other studies have shown that when related words occur in close proximity in a list, they are remembered better than when they are spaced further apart. Glanzer (1969), for example, reported this result in a free recall task, and both Jacoby and Hendricks (1973) and Hintzman *et al.* (1975a) obtained it using recognition memory. The findings may all reflect the high subjective saliency of coincidental events.

C. CONCLUSIONS

The tendency for a stimulus to automatically retrieve related information from memory, even when the subject is not consciously attempting to remember, has been overshadowed in recent years by a theoretical emphasis on control processes. A renewed appreciation of the fact that a stimulus may automatically retrieve from memory recent traces of the same item or related items may help explain a number of experimental phenomena, including the ability of subjects to judge the spacing of repetitions, transfer and retroaction effects in paired-associate learning, the clustering of related words in free recall, and the effect of the spacing of related words on their recall and recognition. In addition, it may help us understand certain puzzling phenomena occurring outside the laboratory—particularly the fact that some kinds of coincidences, such as dreams that appear to be related to subsequent events, seem to occur too frequently to be attributed to chance. Our experiments show that the apparent high rate of occurrence of coincidences may be at least partly due to the selective effect that retrieval, triggered by repeated or related events, has on retention.

REFERENCES

Anderson, J. R., & Bower, G. H. Recognition and retrieval processes in free recall. *Psychological Review,* 1972, **79,** 97–123.

Anderson, J. R., & Bower, G. H. A propositional theory of recognition memory. *Memory & Cognition,* 1974, **2,** 406–412.

Bellezza, F. S., Winkler, H. B., & Andrasik, F., Jr. Encoding processes and the spacing effect. *Memory & Cognition,* 1975, **3,** 451–457.

Berent, S., Cohen, B. D., & Silverman, A. J. Changes in verbal and nonverbal learning following a single left or right unilateral electroconvulsive treatment. *Biological Psychiatry,* 1975, **10,** 95–100.

Bernbach, H. A multiple-copy model for post-perceptual memory. In D. A. Norman (Ed.), *Models of human memory.* New York: Academic Press, 1970.

Bjork, R. A., & Allen, T. W. The spacing effect: Consolidation or differential encoding? *Journal of Verbal Learning and Verbal Behavior,* 1970, **9,** 567–572.

Bower, G. H. A multicomponent theory of the memory trace. In K. W. Spence & J. T. Spence (Eds.), *The psychology of learning and motivation.* Vol. 1. New York: Academic Press, 1967.

Bruce, D., & Weaver, G. E. Retroactive facilitation in short-term retention of minimally learned paired associates. *Journal of Experimental Psychology,* 1973, **100,** 9–17.

Chapman, L. J. Illusory correlation in observational report. *Journal of Verbal Learning and Verbal Behavior,* 1967, **6,** 151–155.

Ciccone, D. S., & Brelsford, J. W. Interpresentation lag and rehearsal mode in recognition memory. *Journal of Experimental Psychology*, 1974, **103**, 900–906.

Conrad, C. Context effects in sentence comprehension: A study of the subjective lexicon. *Memory & Cognition*, 1974, **2**, 130–138.

Corteen, R. S., & Wood, B. Autonomic responses to shock-associated words in an unattended channel. *Journal of Experimental Psychology*, 1972, **94**, 308–313.

D'Agostino, P. R., & DeRemer, P. Item repetition in free and cued recall. *Journal of Verbal Learning and Verbal Behavior*, 1972, **11**, 54–58.

D'Agostino, P. R., & DeRemer, P. Repetition effects as a function of rehearsal and encoding variability. *Journal of Verbal Learning and Verbal Behavior*, 1973, **12**, 108–113.

Ekstrand, B. R., Wallace, W. P., & Underwood, B. J. A frequency theory of verbal-discrimination learning. *Psychological Review*, 1966, **73**, 566–578.

Elmes, D. G., & Bjork, R. A. The interaction of encoding and rehearsal processes in the recall of repeated and nonrepeated items. *Journal of Verbal Learning and Verbal Behavior*, 1975, **14**, 30–42.

Elmes, D. G., Greener, W. I., & Wilkinson, W. C. Free recall of items presented after massed- and distributed-practice items. *American Journal of Psychology*, 1972, **85**, 237–240.

Flexser, A. J., & Bower, G. H. How frequency affects recency judgments: A model for recency discrimination. *Journal of Experimental Psychology*, 1974, **103**, 706–716.

Glanzer, M. Distance between related words in free recall: Trace of the STS. *Journal of Verbal Learning and Verbal Behavior*, 1969, **8**, 105–111.

Glanzer, M. Storage mechanisms in recall. In G. H. Bower (Ed.), *The psychology of learning and motivation*. Vol. 5. New York: Academic Press, 1972.

Glanzer, M., & Duarte, A. Repetition between and within languages in free recall. *Journal of Verbal Learning and Verbal Behavior*, 1971, **10**, 625–630.

Glenberg, A. M. Monotonic and nonmonotonic lag effects in paired-associate and recognition memory. *Journal of Verbal Learning and Verbal Behavior*, 1976, **15**, 1–16.

Gruneberg, M. M. The effect of distance between related words on the identification of semantic relationships. *Acta Psychologica*, 1972, **36**, 275–279.

Gude, C., & Zechmeister, E. B. Frequency judgments for the "gist" of sentence meaning. *American Journal of Psychology*, 1975, **88**, 385–396.

Hintzman, D. L. Apparent frequency as a function of frequency and the spacing of repetitions. *Journal of Experimental Psychology*, 1969, **80**, 139–145.

Hintzman, D. L. Effects of repetition and exposure duration on memory. *Journal of Experimental Psychology*, 1970, **83**, 435–444.

Hintzman, D. L. Theoretical implications of the spacing effect. In R. L. Solso (Ed.), *Theories in cognitive psychology: The Loyola Symposium*. Potomac, Md.: Erlbaum Associates, 1974.

Hintzman, D. L., & Block, R. A. Repetition and memory: Evidence for a multiple-trace hypothesis. *Journal of Experimental Psychology*, 1971, **88**, 297–306.

Hintzman, D. L., & Block, R. A. Memory for the spacing of repetition. *Journal of Experimental Psychology*, 1973, **99**, 70–74.

Hintzman, D. L., Block, R. A. & Summers, J. J. Modality tags and memory for repetitions: Locus of the spacing effect. *Journal of Verbal Learning and Verbal Behavior*, 1973, **12**, 229–239.

Hintzman, D. L., & Rogers, M. K. Spacing effects in picture memory. *Memory & Cognition*, 1973, **1**, 430–434.

Hintzman, D. L., Summers, J. J., & Block, R. A. Spacing judgments as an index of study-phase retrieval. *Journal of Experimental Psychology: Human Learning and Memory*, 1975, **1**, 31–40. (a)

Hintzman, D. L., Summers, J. J., & Block, R. A. What causes the spacing effect? Some effects of repetition, duration, and spacing on memory for pictures. *Memory & Cognition,* 1975, **3,** 287–294. (b)

Hintzman, D. L., Summers, J. J., Eki, N. T., & Moore, M. D. Voluntary attention and the spacing effect. *Memory & Cognition,* 1975, **3,** 576–580.

Hintzman, D. L., & Waters, R. M. Recency and frequency as factors in list discrimination. *Journal of Verbal Learning and Verbal Behavior,* 1970, **9,** 218–221.

Howell, W. C. Representation of frequency in memory. *Psychological Bulletin,* 1973, **80,** 44–53. (a)

Howell, W. C. Storage of events and event frequencies: A comparison of two paradigms in memory. *Journal of Experimental Psychology,* 1973, **98,** 260–263. (b)

Jacoby, L. L., & Hendricks, R. L. Recognition effects of study organization and test context. *Journal of Experimental Psychology,* 1973, **100,** 73–82.

Johnston, W. A., & Uhl, C. N. The contributions of encoding effort and variability to the spacing effect on free recall. *Journal of Experimental Psychology: Human Learning and Memory,* 1976, **2,** 153–160.

Kaufman, E. L., Lord, M. W., Reese, T. W., & Volkmann, J. The discrimination of visual number. *American Journal of Psychology,* 1949, **62,** 498–525.

Kvale, S. Memory and dialects: Some reflections on Ebbinghaus and Mao Tse-Tung. *Human Development,* 1975, **18,** 205–222.

Landauer, T. K. Reinforcement as consolidation. *Psychological Review,* 1969, **76,** 82–96.

Macey, W. H., & Zechmeister, E. B. Test of the multiple-trace hypothesis: The effects of temporal separation and presentation modality. *Journal of Experimental Psychology: Human Learning and Memory,* 1975, **1,** 459–465.

Madigan, S. A. Intraserial repetition and coding processes in free recall. *Journal of Verbal Learning and Verbal Behavior,* 1969, **8,** 828–835.

Madigan, S., & Doherty, L. Retention of item attributes in free recall. *Psychonomic Science,* 1972, **27,** 233–235.

Martin, E. Stimulus meaningfulness and paired-associate transfer: An encoding-variability hypothesis. *Psychological Review,* 1968, **75,** 421–441.

Martin, E. Stimulus encoding in learning and transfer. In A. W. Melton & E. Martin (Eds.), *Coding processes in human memory.* Washington, D.C.: Winston, 1972.

Medin, D. L. Repetition effects and memory theories. Paper presented at the annual Mathematical Psychology Meetings, Ann Arbor, Michigan, August, 1974.

Morton, J. Repeated items and decay in memory. *Psychonomic Science,* 1968, **10,** 219–220.

Ogden, R. M. Some experiments on the consciousness of meaning. In *Studies of psychology: Titchener commemorative volume.* Worchester, Mass.: Louis N. Wilson, 1917.

Paivio, A. Spacing of repetitions in the incidental and intentional free recall of pictures and words. *Journal of Verbal Learning and Verbal Behavior,* 1974, **13,** 497–511.

Paivio, A. Coding distinctions and repetition effects in memory. In G. H. Bower (Ed.), *The psychology of learning and motivation.* Vol. 9. New York: Academic Press, 1975.

Pasko, S. J., & Zechmeister, E. B. Temporal separation in verbal discrimination transfer. *Journal of Experimental Psychology,* 1974, **102,** 525–528.

Peterson, L. R. Short-term verbal memory and learning. *Psychological Review,* 1966, **73,** 193–207.

Peterson, L. R. Search and judgment in memory. In B. Kleinmuntz (Ed.), *Concepts and the structure of memory.* New York: Wiley, 1967.

Peterson, L. R., Johnson, S. T., & Coatney, R. The effect of repeated occurrences on judgments of recency. *Journal of Verbal Learning and Verbal Behavior,* 1969, **8**, 591–596.

Petrich, J. A. Storage and retrieval processes in unlearning. *Memory & Cognition,* 1975, **3**, 63–74.

Posner, M. I., & Synder, C. R. R. Attention and cognitive control. In R. Solso (Ed.), *Information processing and cognition: The Loyola Symposium.* Potomac, Md.: Erlbaum Associates, 1975.

Reichardt, C. S., Shaughnessy, J. J., & Zimmerman, J. On the independence of judged frequencies for items presented in successive lists. *Memory & Cognition,* 1973, **1**, 149–156.

Robbins, D., & Bray, J. F. The spacing effect and the A-B, A-C paradigm: Evidence for retroactive facilitation. *Journal of Experimental Psychology,* 1974, **103**, 420–425.

Rowe, E. J. Frequency judgments and recognition of homonyms. *Journal of Verbal Learning and Verbal Behavior,* 1973, **12**, 440–447.

Rowe, E. J. Depth of processing in a frequency judgment task. *Journal of Verbal Learning and Verbal Behavior,* 1974, **13**, 638–643.

Rowe, E. J., & Rose, R. J. Instructional and spacing effects in judgment of frequency. Paper presented at the annual meeting of the Canadian Psychological Association, June, 1974.

Rundus, D. Analysis of rehearsal processes in free recall. *Journal of Experimental Psychology,* 1971, **89**, 63–77.

Shaughnessy, J. J. Persistence of the spacing effect in free recall under varying incidental learning conditions. *Memory & Cognition,* in press.

Shaughnessy, J. J., & Underwood, B. J. The retention of frequency information for categorized lists. *Journal of Verbal Learning and Verbal Behavior,* 1973, **12**, 99–107.

Shaughnessy, J. J., Zimmerman, J., & Underwood, B. J. Further evidence on the MP-DP effect in free recall learning. *Journal of Verbal Learning and Verbal Behavior,* 1972, **11**, 1–12.

Tulving, E. & Watkins, M. J. On negative transfer: Effects of testing one list on the recall of another. *Journal of Verbal Learning and Verbal Behavior,* 1974, **13**, 181–193.

Tzeng, O. J. L. Stimulus meaningfulness, encoding variability, and the spacing effect. *Journal of Experimental Psychology,* 1973, **99**, 162–166.

Underwood, B. J. Some correlates of item repetitions in free-recall learning. *Journal of Verbal Learning and Verbal Behavior,* 1969, **8**, 83–94.

Underwood, B. J., Zimmerman, J., & Freund, J. S. Retention of frequency information with observations on recognition and recall. *Journal of Experimental Psychology,* 1971, **87**, 149–162.

Voss, J. F., Vereb, C., & Bisanz, G. Stimulus frequency judgments and latency of stimulus frequency judgments as a function of constant and variable response conditions. *Journal of Experimental Psychology: Human Learning and Memory,* 1975, **1**, 337–350.

Warren, R. E. Association, directionality, and stimulus encoding. *Journal of Experimental Psychology,* 1974, **102**, 151–158.

Warren, R. E., & Warren, N. T. Dual encoding of homographs embedded in context. Paper read at the meeting of the Psychonomic Society, St. Louis, November, 1975.

Wells, J. E. Strength theory and judgments of recency and frequency. *Journal of Verbal Learning and Verbal Behavior,* 1974, **13**, 378–392.

Wells, E., & Kirsner, K. Repetition between and within modalities in free recall. *Bulletin of the Psychonomic Society,* 1974, **2**, 395–397.

Wickelgren, W. A., & Berian, K. M. Dual trace theory and consolidation of long-term memory. *Journal of Mathematical Psychology,* 1971, **8**, 404–417.

Winograd, E., & Raines, S. R. Semantic and temporal variation in recognition memory. *Journal of Verbal Learning and Verbal Behavior,* 1972, **11,** 114–119.

Yntema, D. B., & Trask, F. Recall as a search process. *Journal of Verbal Learning and Verbal Behavior,* 1963, **2,** 65–74.

Zechmeister, E. B., & Shaughnessy, J. J. What you know that you know and when you think that you know but you don't. Paper presented at the meeting on the Psychonomic Society, Boston, November, 1974.

Zimmerman, J. J. Free recall after self-paced study: A test of the attention explanation of the spacing effect. *American Journal of Psychology,* 1975, **88,** 277–291.

TOWARD A FRAMEWORK FOR UNDERSTANDING LEARNING[1]

John D. Bransford and Jeffery J. Franks

VANDERBILT UNIVERSITY, NASHVILLE, TENNESSEE

I. The Place of Novelty	94
A. Problems of Novelty and the Memory Metaphor	95
B. Memory Metaphor Responses to Problems of Novelty	96
C. Summary	101
II. Toward a Stage Setting Metaphor of the Effects of Past Experiences	102
A. Further Examples of the Stage Setting Function of Knowledge	104
B. Linguistic Comprehension and the Uniqueness of Understood Meanings	107
C. Summary	111
III. Stage Setting and the Problem of Learning	112
A. On Shaping and Clarifying Knowledge Through Its Use	113
B. Processes of Decontextualization	114
C. Further Examples of Decontextualization	115
D. Decontextualization and the Advantages of the Abstract	118
E. More on the Value of Abstraction	119
IV. Overall Summary and Conclusions	121
References	125

The purpose of this chapter is to examine certain aspects of the phenomena of comprehending and learning. The focus revolves around problems of novelty and creativity. It will be argued that novelty and creativity are inherent aspects of the phenomena of

---

[1] This chapter was supported in part by grant NE-6-00-3-0026 to J. D. Bransford and J. J. Franks. Many of the concepts discussed were developed in conjunction with Nancy McCarrell and Kathy Nitsch, and are introduced in previous papers (e.g., Bransford, McCarrell, & Nitsch, in press; Bransford, McCarrell, Franks, & Nitsch, in press). Aspects of the present chapter mirror portions of these papers quite closely. We wish to thank McCarrell and Nitsch for their valuable comments on the present chapter. Kathy Nitsch has spent an extraordinary amount of time reviewing this manuscript. We are extremely grateful to her. However, misconceptions and errors in the particular arguments presented are the responsibility of the present authors.

comprehending and learning, and that any proposed account of these phenomena must come to grips with the problems that novelty and creativity pose. The major portion of this chapter is devoted to sketching an approach which acknowledges the role of novelty and creativity and may provide a fruitful metaphor for deeper understanding of comprehending and learning. Prior to developing this approach, we briefly consider current conceptualizations of cognitive processes and try to indicate some of their inadequacies for dealing with these domains.

I. The Place of Novelty

Instances of both comprehending and learning seem to have two facets. First, it seems clear that whenever we comprehend an event (whether perceptual, linguistic, etc.) what we comprehend is related to what we already know. This is also true of learning; when we learn something from experiencing an event, what we learn is related to what we already know. Second, it seems equally obvious that when we learn something from experiencing an event, aspects of what we learn are novel. Learning is essentially coming to know something we did not previously know. Similarly, novelty is inherently involved in the process of comprehending. At an abstract level we can probably all agree with Heraclitus and with William James (1890) that every event we experience is in some sense novel, i.e., different from any previously experienced event. The fact that we can recognize that every event is in some sense novel implies that acts of comprehension can involve novelty, i.e., the comprehension of information we did not already know.

To summarize, instances of learning and comprehending can be seen as involving two aspects. What is learned and comprehended is both (a) related to what was already known and (b) novel with respect to what was already known. The point to be developed in the next section is that most current approaches to cognitive and perceptual processes do not provide fruitful perspectives for examining the phenomena of learning and comprehension due to their preoccupation with the first aspect (i.e., what was already known) and their neglect of second (i.e., novelty). An alternative way to express this is that current approaches tend to focus on memory—the storage and manipulation of representations of previous experiences in long-term or semantic memory. We shall use the term *memory metaphor* to refer to the perspective of these approaches.

A. PROBLEMS OF NOVELTY AND THE MEMORY METAPHOR

Most of the recent work on cognitive processes (and also most of the more traditional work on learning, perception, etc.) falls within the perspective of the memory metaphor. This is most obviously shown by the pervasive interest in recent years in the phenomena of memory per se. We will not deal with problems of episodic memory in this chapter although we feel that many of the concerns developed here also apply to investigations of remembering (for further discussion of this point see Bransford, McCarrell, Franks, & Nitsch, in press). Our present concern is with the possible limitations the memory metaphor places on our understanding of comprehension and learning. Recent work on models of semantic memory can be used to illustrate these potential limitations.

Experimental investigations in the area of semantic memory generally involve some aspect of comprehension (e.g., Collins & Quillian, 1969; Freedman & Loftus, 1971; Loftus & Freedman, 1972; Meyer & Ellis, 1970; Meyer & Schvaneveldt, 1971; Rips, Shoben, & Smith, 1973; Smith, Shoben, & Rips, 1974; and other work by these and other researchers). Presupposed in all this work is the assumption that performance on various tasks involves contact with some representation of the input that is available in semantic memory. The structure of semantic memory and its effects on comprehension activities are the issues of basic concern. The work in semantic memory therefore falls within the perspective of the memory metaphor. The comprehension of inputs is accounted for in terms of what is already known, where what is already known may be variously characterized in terms of networks of relations (e.g., Collins & Quillian, 1969), sets of features (e.g., Rips, Shoben, & Smith, 1973), category membership (e.g., Meyer & Ellis, 1970), etc. As an example, data from Meyer and Ellis (1970) indicate that the verification time for determining "churches are buildings" is faster than for "churches are structures." They assume that the class of possible "structures" is larger than the class of "buildings." Since semantic decisions were assumed to involve search through the stored words in a semantic category, the larger the category the slower should be the response. Thus, at the basis of such accounts is the notion that verification (comprehension) involves finding stored (i.e., already known) information that can represent the input sentences.

As discussed above, an important aspect of comprehension *does* involve the relation between what is presently comprehended and what was already known (i.e., the focus of semantic memory models). However, it is equally important to consider the novel aspects of what is comprehended. In a series of recent articles (e.g., Barclay, Bransford, Franks, McCarrell, & Nitsch, 1974; Bransford & McCarrell, 1974; Bransford, McCarrell, & Nitsch, in press) we have demonstrated the potential importance of taking novelty into account when characterizing the nature of comprehension processes. This work showed that what is comprehended is a function of the context in which the item to be comprehended occurs. As we shall discuss in Section II, the importance of these demonstrations of flexibility as a function of context becomes more apparent when one realizes that there does not seem to be any limit on the number different contexts within which a given item (e.g., a word) can occur. Each of these different contexts can lead to differences (represented perhaps in terms of properties, relations, etc.) in what is comprehended. Novelty is inherently involved in comprehending since presumably no one could have previously experienced all the unlimited potential contexts.

From the memory metaphor perspective of semantic memory models, these differences in comprehension are accounted for by assuming that in each case contact is made with different relations, features, or senses stored in memory. For example, consider the cases investigated by Meyer and Ellis (1970) mentioned above. To verify that something is a "structure," it is assumed that our memory representation of the concept "structure" contains a listing of everything that can be a structure. The problem is that in order to account for comprehension within the memory metaphor, one must assume that in every instance the features, relations, or senses that are comprehended are already available (i.e., stored in memory). However, if the features or relations that are comprehended are a function of the context of occurrence and there appears to be an unlimited set of such possible contexts for any given item, two questions become apparent. (*a*) Is it reasonable to postulate the unlimited capacity memory system necessitated by the memory metaphor? (*b*) Even if this seems reasonable, how did this unlimited stored information initially get into memory?

B. MEMORY METAPHOR RESPONSES TO PROBLEMS OF NOVELTY

At this point, a proponent of the memory metaphor might argue that the problem as we have posed it is really a pseudoproblem. More specifically, it might be argued that our statement of the problem might hold for a theoretical position based on some simple episodic or specific trace notion of memory, but not for more sophisticated notions of semantic memory involving systems of concepts and relations and rules for inference or manipulation of the concepts and relations. That is, our hypothetical memory metaphor proponent might agree that a view of comprehension that attempted to account for the flexibility of understood meaning in terms of stored traces specifically representing each possible difference is indeed an *impossibly* complex theoretical position. However, one might further argue that the very purpose for proposing the more sophisticated semantic memory models is to go beyond such notions of specific memory traces in order to capture more general aspects of knowledge. It could be argued that flexibility in comprehension does not pose a problem for systems conceptualized along these lines. This flexibility might be accounted for by stored structures which represent general properties of, and relations among, concepts and by rules which can "use" these structures to make inferences by manipulating and transforming these structures.

As an illustration of this point, Collins and Quillian's (1969) notion of "economy of storage" is related to the issue of the potential unlimited flexibility in comprehension. In their model it is not necessary to have all the different potentially comprehensible properties and relations concerning a concept explicitly stored in memory with that concept. Rather, many relations and properties of a concept can be inferred from the general relational network of concepts by using inference rules. For example, the property "has wings" need not be explicitly stored with the concept "canary" in order to verify (comprehend) that "canaries have wings." Verification can be based on the explicitly stored information that "canaries are birds" and "birds have wings" and on an inference rule which combines this information. In general, all semantic memory models handle the problem posed by flexibility of comprehension in similar ways; that is, by storing a structure containing general properties and relations and postulating rules for using this structure to compute new inferences. In essence the basic approach is to treat novelty as a recombination of already available information. Can this approach solve the problems posed by novelty and thus provide an adequate basis within the memory metaphor for developing further understanding of the phenomena of comprehension and learning? We think the answer is "no." We believe novelty remains a problem even for these more sophisticated semantic memory models.

One way to state the problem is that these models are too logical. This may seem to be a strange criticism since, of course, one wants and indeed expects models to be logical. However, in attempting to account for the novelty inherent in comprehending and learning, we encounter a problem. In general logical models are fine, but a comprehender is also required to use the models for furthering his understanding of the phenomena being modeled. In our present case, however, the comprehender is the phenomenon being modeled. More precisely, this represents a problem since one of the primary roles of the user (comprehender) of a model is to introduce or take into account the novel aspects of the phenomena being modeled. The user provides interpretations for, and resolves any ambiguity in, the application of the terms and relations in the model to characteristics of the phenomena being modeled (i.e., he is the correspondence rules, e.g., see Kuhn, 1970, 1974). The user decides how the terms, relations, and manipulation rules of the model are to be applied in any given instance in order to derive the particular representation of the case which is of interest at the moment. In short, novelty in application is handled by the user. The user of the model may also note aspects of the phenomena of interest which are discrepant or anomalous with respect to the model. The user may then modify the old model or invent a new model to more adequately account for the phenomena. It is the user who provides the growth or learning, not the model per se.

By analogy, one can apply this thinking to the phenomena of present interest, i.e., to semantic memory models and more generally to any memory metaphor perspective. The concepts, relations, and rules in memory are like the terms, relations, and rules in a formal model. They capture aspects of phenomena common to a set of past experiences or events. They focus on repetition or recurrence of information, but not on novel or unique aspects of an experience which are inherent in comprehending and provide the basis for learning. By analogy with formal models, a user of the memory is necessary in order to permit comprehending and learning. Memory metaphor approaches have therefore introduced the problem of novelty through the back door without accounting for (or even explicitly acknowledging) this problem.

Is there any alternative left to the memory metaphor that eliminated this problem of needing a comprehender as an intrinsic part of one's theory of comprehension? There does appear to be an available alternative, but we find this alternative unacceptable (i.e., lacking in fruitfulness for further understanding). Further, this alternative appears to be contrary to basic metatheoretical assumptions held by typical proponents of views within the memory metaphor. This alternative is essentially the alternative of preformism (e.g., see discussion at various points in Piaget, 1971). The essence of this position is that we already know everything we can ever know; that all potentially knowable information is built into the system. This is obviously a very strong version of the memory metaphor. Under this assumption, novelty (meaning comprehending or coming to know something new) is no longer a problem since there is no novelty. Every experience or act is merely an instance of memory.

By making this basic preformist assumption, semantic memory models of the general form discussed above could be a *logically* viable approach to the phenomena of comprehension and learning. (Of course, these models would then simply be cases of memory.) What this would mean is that every difference in meaning that we could possibly experience would have to be preformed. All potential differences would have to be built into the semantic model, in terms, relations, or rules. Given this assumption, what is comprehended would be a representation generated by this semantic memory system and thus comprehension (and likewise learning) would fall under the memory metaphor perspective.

Two points might clarify what is implied by such a preformist-oriented semantic memory model. The first point is that this semantic memory system (consisting of terms, relations, and rules) is a closed system and *is* the comprehender. There is no outside agent or comprehender-homunculus who uses the system. The second point is that another way to characterize the general nature of this view is to see it as an element composition theory; i.e., knowledge consists of a set of basic elements, rules for composing these elements into more complex structures, and rules for transforming these structures. At first glance, noting that the proposed preformed semantic memory system is just an element composition position may seem to make the preformist assumption more palatable since much of the work to be done by the system can be given over to general combinatory functions, inference rules, etc. This might seemingly simplify what it means to already know everything one can potentially know, since all one would have to have in memory would be the set of basic elements and the set of the general functions. But given the first point above, this seeming simplification is actually misleading.

Since the system is closed with no outside comprehender-user, there exists no comprehender to supply or interpret the values for all the cover symbols or variables in the functions. Therefore, each of these values (representing say a distinctive feature of meaning or a different meaning sense) must be explicitly spelled out in the model, i.e., must also be explicitly represented in memory. It must further be assumed that there exists such a finite set of meaning atoms or elements despite arguments that such a set probably does not exist (e.g., see Bolinger, 1965, and Section II below). In addition, one must spell out constraints on the combinations and relations among these features and senses. As Cassirer (1923) (citing Lotze) points out, not just any combination or structure of features constitutes a "natural class" or "psychological valid" concept. Therefore, the set of functions in the system must be explicitly constructed so as to constrain the possible structures or combinations of features that can be generated. But explicitly building these conditions into the system means building in a constraint for each structure or feature that represents a potentially comprehensible meaning difference. This proliferation of constraints, necessitated by allowing no outside comprehender, obviates the seeming simplicity of the element composition approach. To accept the preformist alternative is to accept the position that everything we can know is built into the system explicitly and in detail.[2]

Finally, consider the possibility that in rejecting this preformism, a proponent of the memory metaphor might argue that all the conditions and values need not be explicitly built into the system but instead can be provided by the environment at input. It should be obvious that this is no solution. If one remains within the memory metaphor, it must be assumed that there are knowledge or memory structures (for example, "feature detectors") that enable one to detect and comprehend this information from the environment. This means that once again the conditions and values are built into the system. Indeed, most approaches to perception fall within the memory metaphor. For example, Gregory (1972) asserts: "Perceptions are constructed by complex brain processes from fleeting fragmentary scaps of data signaled by the senses and drawn from the brain's memory banks [p. 707]." Just as was the case with the semantic memory models, comprehension of meaningful aspects or relations in the input is assumed to be based on previously available memory traces. Once again all the points made above apply—in this case to perceptual models. This is also true for models of pattern

---

[2] It might be argued that recursion can provide a simplification for the present situation in a manner analogous to the simplification it offers in Chomsky's approach to grammar. Even if it is assumed that recursion plays a part in generating the feature structures representing meaning differences, without a comprehender to tell the recursion to stop, the particular constraints on stopping would also have to be explicitly spelled out for each particular case. (See Franks, 1974, for another discussion on possible limits on the value of recursion in dealing with the problem of comprehension.)

recognition (e.g., Neisser, 1967; Uhr, 1966) where performance of the system is based on representing the input in terms of features and relations among features (or more general frames as proposed by Minsky, 1975, although aspects of this latter development bear some resemblances to the alternate metaphor we will discuss in the next section). There is no explicit provision in these views for the introduction of novelty, of new information into the system. Thus passing the buck of novelty to perceptual processes is no solution for the memory metaphor perspective. This tactic merely ignores the problem.

C. SUMMARY

We have argued that instances of comprehension and learning involve both a relation to what is already known and an aspect of novelty. We have further tried to show possible inadequacies of most approaches to cognitive (and perceptual) processes for dealing with comprehension and learning due to these approaches lying in the domain of the memory metaphor. The memory metaphor attempts to account for what is comprehended or what is learned in terms of information already available (i.e., stored in memory). It emphasizes what is already known to the exclusion of the novelty inherent in comprehending and learning.

It is important to note that there are ways to conceptualize novelty that are congruent with the memory metaphor perspective. However, these conceptualizations do not involve novelty in the sense in which we are using the term. For example, one could program a computer to add and present it with a new combination of numbers. The particular output would be novel, but the rules of addition would not. Similarly, a robot could be programmed to walk into a room and pick up a block; and it may be able to do this in an unbounded number of situations. Again the particular behaviors might be novel but not the rules. A set of recursive rules that generate all and only the infinite set of grammatical sentences (e.g., Chomsky, 1965) also permit novel output. The rules, however, remain the same. None of the preceding examples constitute novelty in the sense that we use it in this chapter. Our use of novelty involves changes in the significances or meaning of individual elements, terms, relations, etc., rather than the novel recombination of old information. It is this latter sense of novelty that leaves the proponent of the memory metaphor facing a dilemma. It seems one must either accept the Scylla of preformism (a seemingly uncomfortable position for modern experimental psychology) or the Charybdis of an unaccounted-for comprehender who can make use of previously available information but who introduces novelty. This alternative merely ignores the problems of concern by tacitly assuming the very phenomenon of interest without explicitly acknowledging it.

In the next section we sketch an alternative to the memory metaphor that we hope will prove more fruitful for deepening our understanding of comprehending and learning. Our major purpose is to provide a direction for future inquiry rather than to present a theory per se. Indeed, our alternative metaphor is couched in terms that also presupposes a comprehender whose knowledge sets the stage for future discoveries. Our intent is to make this presupposition explicit rather than tacit. We attempt to illustrate why knowing cannot simply be equated with "contacting" stored representations, and why an explicit concern with novelty is necessary for adequately understanding learning and comprehending.

II. Toward a Stage Setting Metaphor of the Effects of Past Experiences

We have argued that learning and comprehending intrinsically involve the articulation of novel information. The problem is that any theoretical account which relies solely upon the storage and retrieval of traces (whether "semantic" or "episodic") deals only with old, previously articulated information. Perhaps memory traces can provide a basis for dealing with the "sameness" of the present experience with previous experiences, but the memory metaphor has no mechanisms for dealing with novel information. This suggests that a different, more comprehensive metaphor might be more fruitful.

As a first step toward such an alternative, consider the possibility that a major role of past experience is to provide "boundary constraints" that *set the stage* for articulating the uniqueness as well as sameness of information. And contrast this "stage setting" metaphor with the assumption that previous experience merely provides an accumulation of memories that are responsible for meaningful interpretations of subsequent events. In our opinion, the stage setting metaphor is both plausible and important. For example, Gibson and Gibson (1955) argue that perceptual learning involves a process of *differentiation* rather than *enrichment* by previously accumulated memories. The ability to differentiate an input from others presupposes that one can detect its uniqueness (relative to a set of alternatives) as well as its sameness (i.e., the invariant information across past and present experiences). Experience with a set of items sets the stage by providing boundary constraints that specify invariances relative to past experience, *but the present experience goes beyond these boundaries.* Unique aspects of the present situation are articulated as well.

An emphasis on stage setting suggests that the nature of one's present experience *depends upon* previous experiences but cannot be *reduced to* memories of such experiences. Perception is direct *given* the attunement that previous experiences provide. As an example, consider someone who usually drives a pickup truck and then drives a car. The smoothness of the car's ride is very noticeable. Past experiences with pickup trucks appears to set the stage for articulating the distinctiveness of a car's movement, but the perception of the latter cannot simply be reduced to previous memories of experiences with driving a truck. Garner (1974) provides additional examples of the stage setting effects of other information (see especially pp. 179–186). He illustrates how the articulation of novel features can be determined by the contrast set to which inputs are assumed to belong.

Note that the stage setting metaphor assumes that meaningful recognition can be direct *given* the appropriate level of stage setting or organismic attunement (see also, Gibson, in press). It is therefore assumed that meaningful recognition need not be mediated by "contact" with previously stored memories. As Gibson (1966) states: "Recognition does not have to be the successful matching of a new percept with the trace of an old one. If it did, novelty would have to be the failure to match a new percept with any trace of an old one after an exhaustive search of the memory store, and this is absurd [p. 278]." It seems useful to note that others (e.g., Norman, 1969) have also pointed toward the absurdity of assuming an exhaustive search of memory in order to know that something is novel (e.g., that "mantiness" is a novel word). Yet the "solution" to this problem has frequently been conceptualized within the framework of the memory metaphor; namely, that one automatically knows "where to look" for the item and finds that there is nothing stored in that "place." Such a solution may seem adequate for explaining how someone knows that he has no information about something. But how can such an explanation account for the fact that the attuned perceiver can frequently articulate aspects of the nature of the newness? Such an act involves something more than the mere realization that one has no information about the event. For example, how can the truck driver articulate the relative uniqueness of a car's ride instead of merely perceiving that the experience is unlike anything experienced before (assuming, of course, the truck driver never rode in a car before)?

Even if one assumes that an organism can "find" a trace and determine that it is similar but not identical to the new experience, there still remains a problem of accounting for the possibility of recognizing the *nature* of the difference. At some point, the detection of novel information seems to be a necessary assumption. The stage setting metaphor attempts to make this assumption explicit. The role of past experience is viewed as establishing boundary constraints that attune the organism and allow the articulation of unique aspects of a situation. Past experience is not viewed as simply providing memory traces that must be found and matched or compared to inputs.

A. FURTHER EXAMPLES OF THE STAGE SETTING FUNCTION OF KNOWLEDGE

Consider a more general example of the stage setting effects of past experience. Assume that an expert has acquired knowledge of a theory. In what sense does this knowledge set the stage for articulating and clarifying subsequent experiences? Dewey (1933) reports a segment from Charles Darwin's autobiography that helps clarify this question.

Darwin writes that, as a youth, he once found a seashell in a certain gravel pit. He mentioned his discovery to the geologist Sidgwich. Sidgwich's immediate response was something like "That's impossible." He then clarified his statement by noting that the shell must have been put there by someone. If it had actually been lodged there for centuries it would have upset all that was believed about the geological formation of that particular area. For Darwin, finding a seashell was finding a seashell. From Sidgwich's perspective, the same event had the potential for being an extremely significant (and different kind of) fact.

It is easy to miss the significance of the Darwin—Sidgwich example. It seems obvious that an expert can understand an event in a different manner from a nonexpert. One might assume that the expert can simply note that the event constitutes a fact which fails to "match" certain predictions from his theory. But consider this example in more detail. What did Sidgwich's knowledge of geological theory allow him to do?

The event "finding a seashell in a gravel pit" seems concrete and simple. Yet the simplicity is illusory. Assume, for example, that Sidgwich believed the shell had *not* simply been placed there and hence that it constituted crucial evidence against current geological theory. Which aspects of the event would make it a significant fact from Sidgwich's point of view? Would it matter where the gravel pit was located? It presumably had to be located within some geographically defined area in order to make it relevant, but would particular locations within this general area count? Would it matter precisely where the shell was located in the gravel pit? Presumably it would. Would the type of seashell matter? Would its shape, composition, color, etc., count? Would it matter whether Darwin had touched the shell with his hands rather than held it with a cloth? Without knowing Sidgwich's theoretical framework, it is difficult for us to determine the answers to these questions. Appropriate knowledge allows one to clarify new experiences; to determine *whether* and *in what way* (e.g., because of what "pattern of features") certain events are significant. Appropriate knowledge also sets the stage for knowing what further needs to be known in order to adequately understand a particular event. In the absence of a theoretical framework, it is even difficult to know *whether* further questions need to be asked.

Now assume that Darwin had reported his discovery to a detective rather than Sidgwich. Assume further that the detective was investigating a case where someone was murdered in the gravel pit, and there was a suspect who had a fetish for collecting tropical shells. Under these conditions, different "features" of the event would presumably be relevant. For example, the exact time at which the shell was found would presumably be more relevant to the detective than to Sidgwich. Precisely where it was found might have more significance (but a different kind) for the detective. In addition, whether Darwin had picked up the shell with his hands or a cloth would undoubtedly be significant for the detective. In short, the same events (and "features" of these events) assume different significances depending on the abstract framework from which one views them. This example illustrates the "conceptual nature of facts" (e.g., see Kuhn, 1970). In addition, it illustrates how knowledge sets the stage for clarifying experiences or situations. For example, a theoretical framework guides the search for new information that seems necessary to insure an adequate understanding of a particular event.

A simple study conducted by the present authors illustrates the use of previous knowledge to articulate and clarify subsequent inputs. The study investigated concept formation with inputs like those illustrated in Fig. 1. All subjects saw the same configurations, and these were presented successively. The task was to learn which configurations were A's and which were B's.

Two groups were tested in the study. They differed only in terms of the initial instructions they received. Group I was shown pictures of the individual elements in the configurations and told that these would occur in different organizations on each stimulus. Group II was told that all stimuli had to do with baseball: The circle was a ball, the square was a glove, and the line represented the trajectory of the ball. Both groups saw the identical set of 24 stimuli for five study-test trials. On study trials subjects were simply told whether each successively presented configuration was an A or a B. Order of presentation was changed for each trial.

The results were as clear-cut as they are obvious. None of the subjects in Group I learned to sort the stimuli correctly. All of the subjects in Group II learned to sort them, usually by the second or third trial. Through the use of "baseball knowledge" to structure stood meanings (significances) are simply the result of new combina- each configuration, certain dynamic "features" became relevant to

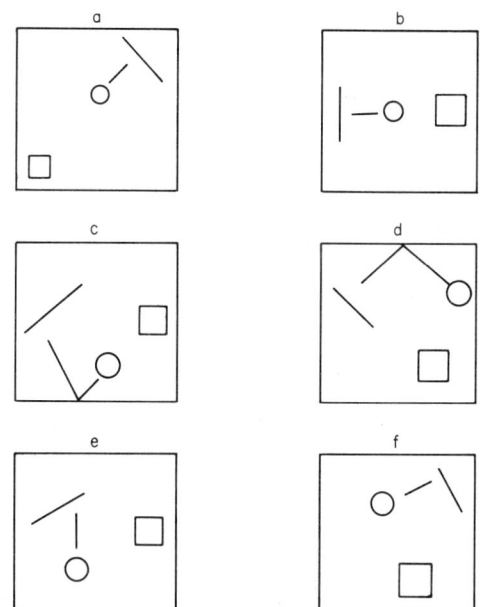

Fig. 1. Examples of stimuli for a concept formation task.

Group II subjects that made the solution easy. Subjects realized that for all A stimuli, the ball was proceeding in a direction (sometimes after a bounce) that would permit it to be caught by the glove. In all B stimuli, the ball missed the glove.

The baseball study is related to the Darwin—Sidgwich example discussed previously. On the basis of past knowledge, all subjects in the baseball study were potential experts (relatively speaking). The instructions simply served to manipulate the activation of this knowledge so that Group II subjects would be functional experts and Group I subjects would not. For Group II subjects, the activation of relevant knowledge permitted an articulation of relevant "features" and hence an ability to discount irrelevant "features." Like de Groot's chess masters (see de Groot, 1965; Chase & Simon, 1973) as compared to nonmasters, the Group II subjects were better able to see the problem and hence start at a "higher place." Knowledge of baseball set the stage for structuring and clarifying the input stimuli, but these articulated structures could not be *reduced* to past knowledge of baseball. More important, knowledge of baseball helped Group II subjects focus on what they needed to know in order to solve the problem that the experimenters posed.

B. LINGUISTIC COMPREHENSION AND THE UNIQUENESS OF UNDERSTOOD MEANINGS

The stage setting metaphor also has implications for conceptualizing questions about linguistic comprehension. For example, relatively short-term effects of past experience can be equated with the effects of context on comprehension. Elsewhere (e.g., Bransford & McCarrell, 1974; Bransford, McCarrell, & Nitsch, in press) it has been argued that the *understood meaning* or *significance* of utterances is uniquely specified as a function of the contextually induced attunement of the listener. The argument is that linguistic comprehension cannot simply be equated with "finding," "selecting," and "amalgamating" previously stored "meaning elements" (e.g., see Katz & Fodor, 1963, for a discussion of linguistic "selection" restrictions).

Note that finding, selecting, and amalgamating assumptions lie within the domain of the memory metaphor, where the meaning elements are basically stored traces. It is difficult to see how such assumptions imply anything other than the notion that novel understood meanings (significances) are simply the result of new combinations of old "meaning elements" that were already represented in memory.[3] A memory metaphor approach to linguistic comprehension neglects the problems discussed previously. At some point "old" "meaning elements" were "new" or "novel," and the memory metaphor fails to provide a basis for articulating new information. In contrast, the stage setting metaphor suggests that if one assumes the existence of "meaning elements," then the significances of these individual "elements" also change as a function of organismic attunement. From a stage setting perspective, the role of past experience is not simply to provide a repertoire of stored meanings (or senses) that can be retrieved and novelly recombined in terms of syntactic rule structures and selection restrictions. Instead the role of past experience is to provide the organism with relatively abstract tools that set the stage for articulating novel significances that a speaker or writer intends.

In order to clarify the stage setting function of language, it is important to distinguish between two different uses of the term "meaning." One use of "meaning" involves contrasts between letter strings such as *gex* and *paper.* English speakers know the meaning of *paper* but not *gex*. There is a second usage of the term meaning, however, that is potentially more important. This usage is illustrated by the problem of understanding what a speaker means (i.e., intends) by any utterance (e.g., by the utterance "paper"). This is a problem of grasping the *significance* (i.e., intended meaning) of an utterance. Bransford, McCarrell, and Nitsch (in press) report a number of experiments in which subjects knew what was said (e.g., the experimenter said "paper," "Bill has a red car," etc.) yet failed to grasp the intended meaning or significance of the utterances. The subjects were unable to understand what the speaker meant. The characterization of linguistic knowledge as tools that set the stage for understanding the significance of utterances is also suggested by Fillmore's (1971) arguments regarding linguistic semantics. We quote:

> The difficulties I have mentioned exist, it seems to me, because linguistic semanticists, like the philosophers and psychologists whose work they were echoing, have found it relevant to ask, not *What do I need to know in order to*

---

[3] Of course, some elaborations of input information might arise from deductive inference. However, the nature of one's deductions is a function of how one initially comprehends the input information (e.g., see de Groot, 1965; Katona, 1940; Staudenmayer, in press). Hence, one must still face the problem of accounting for differential interpretations of individual "meaning elements" as a function of the contextually induced level of attunement of the comprehender.

use this form appropriately and to understand other people when they use it?, but rather, *What is the meaning of this form?* And having asked that, linguists have sought to discover the external signs of meanings, the reflexes of meanings in the speech situation, and the inner structure of meanings. It is apparent that the wrong question has been asked [p. 274; italics his].

A stage setting approach to language suggests that linguistic knowledge per se may not always be sufficient to adequately comprehend utterances. For example, most listeners have difficulty understanding the significance of an utterance like *The haystack was important because the cloth ripped* (cf. Bransford & Johnson, 1973; Bransford & McCarrell, 1974). A cue like "parachute" helps listeners more adequately understand. From the present perspective, this cue does not aid comprehension simply by providing a referent for the word "cloth." Instead, it provides constraints that help subjects discover what they must further *assume* or *invent* in order to make the sentence meaningful. For example, one must assume that the parachute was *above* the haystack when it ripped.

Bransford and Johnson (1973) report a study designed to manipulate subjects' abilities to understand the significance of an utterance. More important, the study yielded data indicating what subjects *do* in order to understand. All subjects heard the following passage. For Group I subjects, the title was "A Trip to an Inhabited Planet."

> The view was breathtaking. From the window one could see the crowd below. Everything looked extremely small from such a distance, but the colorful costumes could still be seen. Everyone seemed to be moving in one direction in an orderly fashion and there seemed to be little children as well as adults. The landing was gentle, and luckily the atmosphere was such that no special suits had to be worn. At first there was a great deal of activity. Later, when the speeches started, the crowd quieted down. The man with the television camera took many shots of the setting and the crowd. Everyone was very friendly and seemed glad when the music started.

The preceding paragraph includes a target sentence that was the object of investigation. The target sentence was: *Luckily the landing was gentle, and the atmosphere was such that no special suits had to be worn.* Group I subjects had no trouble understanding the "landing" sentence. They showed excellent memory for it in both free and cued recall. A second group of subjects heard the identical passage, but they believed the title to be "Watching a Peace March from the 40th Floor." Most of these subjects were unable to understand the significance of the landing sentence and exhibited lower recall scores for the target sentence in both free and cued recall.

From our present perspective, the interesting data come from those few subjects in the second group who were able to understand the "landing" sentence. What did they have to do in order to make the sentence make sense? Consider one creative listener: She quickly "moved" the whole peace march from the downtown of a city to the airport, created a helicopter that landed with a famous person who was to be a speaker, and assumed that atmosphere referred to the aura of peacefulness so that no "anti-mace suits" had to be worn. In short, the process of comprehension involved a reorganization of the listener's cognitive framework in order to assimilate the "landing" sentence. Here the description "comprehension as invention" seems particularly appropriate.

Problems of invention and novelty are also revealed by the semantic flexibility studies reported in Barclay *et al.* (1974). For example, they found that subjects presented with the sentence *The girl hid behind the ball* were more effectively cued by the probe "large and round" than were subjects who heard the sentence *The girl hit the ball.* It was argued that these differential interpretations trancended the bounds of linguistic selection restrictions. However, if we assume that linguistic knowledge of the noun *ball* sets the stage for *inventing* a situation where hiding behind one is meaningful, this flexibility of interpretation makes more sense.

A study reported in Bransford, McCarrell, and Nitsch (in press) is also relevant. A retrieval cue like "home" was more effective for prompting subjects' memory of *oak* if they had heard *The racoon lived in the hole in the oak* than if they had simply heard the word *oak.* The sentential event led to the articulation of information that was not considered when *oak* was presented alone. It was further suggested that one could never exhaust the potential significances of any noun (e.g., in terms of potential category memberships). A clever speaker could always generate a context that prompted subjects to articulate certain significances of entities that they would not necessarily have realized if left to their own devices. Contextual information can therefore provide "hints" to invention in a manner analogous to hints in a problem-solving task (e.g., that a pliers is a weight; see Maier, 1930).

As a paradigmatic instance of "prods to invention," consider the following example. Assume that a speaker wants a listener to experience the utterance "Go buy some" as being extremely funny. What would he have to do to produce such an effect? Clearly, the speaker would have to create some contextual support that provided a framework for experiencing a certain significance of this utterance.

The context or framework provides a level of attunement that sets the stage for the nature of the experience afforded by a linguistic event. Could one ever exhaust the potential significances of an utterance? This seems unlikely. It seems more plausible to assume that a clever speaker could always specify some framework that permitted a unique articulation of information that the listener never considered before.

C. SUMMARY

We have suggested that notions of memory (e.g., "semantic" memory) underlie assumptions about the effects of past experiences on subsequent interactions with the environment. Yet one can assume that past experiences affect subsequent experiences without necessarily assuming that mere "contact" with previously accumulated memories is responsible for such effects. One alternative is that past knowledge "sets the stage" for subsequent experiencing. From this perspective, present experience *depends upon* past experiences, but it cannot be *reduced to* contact with "stored traces" of past experiences. A strength of the stage setting metaphor is its emphasis on the capacity for appreciating unique aspects of information never explicitly articulated before.

Note that the stage setting metaphor assigns an important role to past experiences (e.g., discovery *does* favor a "prepared mind"), but it does not attempt to reduce "knowing" to the act of merely contacting previously stored structures or representations. At this level, the metaphor is congruent with aspects of Piagetian theory:

> The meaning of a representation is found in its relation to ... knowing activity, and the vital factor of knowledge resides in that relation between knowing and the symbol and not in the symbol or representation as such [Furth, 1969, p. 20].

From the present perspective, to "know" is not to contact a representation. Instead, a representation can set the stage for knowing. One can represent a geographical area, for example, by drawing a map. But the map itself does not clarify one's present location. If the map eventually becomes "memorized" or "internalized" so that we now call it a "cognitive map," the latter still only sets the stage for knowing. Representations are invaluable aids to knowing, but "contact with stored representations" cannot be *equated* with knowing. One simple but important consequence of this view is that one can *revise* a representation (e.g., a cognitive map) in the process of using it to clarify subsequent situations. By tacitly assuming that knowing is equivalent to "contacting previously formed representations," most psychological accounts of knowing (e.g., the literature on "semantic memory") have little to say about processes of revising or shaping knowledge, i.e., about the problems of growth or learning. Aspects of these problems are discussed below.

III. Stage Setting and the Problem of Learning

The stage setting metaphor suggests an orientation toward the growth of knowledge, toward the general problem of learning. How is knowledge shaped into forms that set the stage for clarifying subsequent experiences (i.e., for promoting transfer and new discoveries)? It seems clear that knowledge of definitions, concepts, principles, theories, etc., can be shaped into forms that set the stage for remembering. However, knowledge in a form that permits remembering is not necessarily in a form where it can best set the stage for subsequent insights and discoveries. From the present perspective, growth and learning do not simply involve an expansion of some body of interconnected facts, concepts, etc. Learning involves a change in the form of one's knowledge so that it can set the stage for new discoveries.

As a general learning principle we assume that the current form of one's knowledge sets the stage for subsequent experiencing (e.g., Sidgwich's knowledge is in a form that permits him to grasp the potential significance of certain events). More important, we assume that knowledge can set the stage for the articulation of novel information heretofore unknown to the comprehender. This process can therefore lead to a clarification and reshaping of that knowledge itself. We shall focus on the processes by which knowledge becomes shaped into optimally usable forms as a function of its use in clarifying situations. This will lead to an argument for the *value of abstractness* of knowledge. Few would argue with the general assumption that abstractness can be valuable, yet there appear to be conceptual inconsistencies with respect to such assumptions. For example, models of semantic memory imply that one "adds" knowledge to the system by simply forming more connections between labels for concepts, properties, other concepts, etc. It will be argued that these models are therefore more like paraphrases of the *objects of our knowing activities* than they are models of the *tools* or *instruments* that set the stage for knowing.

A. ON SHAPING AND CLARIFYING KNOWLEDGE THROUGH ITS USE

We have argued that knowledge sets the stage for clarifying subsequent experiences. The form of one's knowledge determines the applications that can be made of it. Similarly, the application of knowledge to certain domains can result in the articulation of novel information and hence reshape the form of that knowledge itself. This postulated relationship between the form and applications of knowledge can be clarified by considering one of the most intuitively obvious techniques for promoting the growth of knowledge, namely, the use of examples. Why are appropriate examples so beneficial? What is it that they do?

At first glance, examples seem beneficial simply because they are concrete and hence easily understood and remembered. It appears easier to understand and remember concrete examples than abstract definitions of concepts or verbal descriptions of some theory. Note, however, that this latter type of "explanation" ignores the discussion of the preceding section. Certain frameworks or forms of knowledge set the stage for understanding even concrete experiences (cf. the Sidgwich example). Examples are usually presented in the context of some framework. That is, the presentation of an example *presupposes* that the listener realizes that the example is supposed to be an example of *something*. The listener's knowledge of that something (even though initially cursory) should affect his understanding of the significance of the presented example. At the same time, one's momentary knowledge of the "something" (i.e., of the definition, concept, principle, or theory that the example is supposed to be an example of) becomes shaped or clarified as a function of using it to understand the example. In short, knowledge is shaped through its use in clarifying subsequent experiences (where the experiences may be represented by examples). In Piagetian terms this process represents the mutual interplay between assimilation and accommodation. One assimilates the example to momentary knowledge of the concept, and at the same time accommodates his knowledge of the concept to the example. Through this process, knowledge can become shaped into optimally usable forms.

As an example, assume that subjects are presented with a set of sentences such as the following:

(a) Jean was not very attractive and couldn't get much attention from men, so she bought a dog and became very attached to it.

(b) Jim, who had been punished for sucking his thumb, began chewing his fingernails.

(c) Pat was really angry at his boss, but since showing this anger would get him fired, he became very short tempered at home and yelled at his roommate.

It is one thing to understand these sentences as descriptions of possible event sequences. It is another thing to understand them as examples of some concept—in this case, the concept of displacement. Even cursory knowledge about displacement can set the stage for understanding the significance of the example sentences; and in the process of understanding their significance, knowledge of the concept itself is shaped.[4]

B. PROCESSES OF DECONTEXTUALIZATION

We consider further the problem of shaping knowledge through its use in clarifying subsequent experiences. How might one begin to characterize the processes by which information becomes shaped into forms that set the stage for knowing? Note that, at one level, this question could be viewed as equivalent to how one moves from "episodic" to "semantic" memory (e.g., see Tulving, 1972). In our opinion, however, it is more fruitful to ask how one gradually moves from specific experiences to general knowledge, where the latter more readily sets the stage for understanding many subsequent domains.

At a general level, the shaping of knowledge into more usable forms involves a process of decontextualization. In a learning situation, it is initially difficult to separate conceptual knowledge (e.g., knowledge of a concept, principle, or theoretical perspective) from the contextual situation in which it was originally exemplified. Consider an hypothetical student's initial understanding of a principle like "Skinnerian principles of behavioral shaping." Initially, most students' knowledge seems to be closely tied to the concrete exemplary situation through which the principle was originally learned. In asking for a definition of "shaping," one frequently gets answers

---

[4] Kathy Nitsch is currently conducting studies to assess some of the differential consequences of processing inputs as descriptions of events versus as examples.

like the following: "It's like when you want a rat to press a bar and you give him food for first orienting to the bar, then gradually approaching it," etc. At this initial stage of acquisition, one would expect that students' identification of novel examples is based on the relatively "concrete" similarity of such examples to old ones previously learned.

Gradually, students' knowledge of a concept or principle begins to transcend any enumeration of its potential exemplars. One's knowledge is becoming decontextualized. In fact, one can "forget" the particular exemplary situations and still retain information about "what the examples were examples of." We suspect (and are designing studies to show) that in certain instances, the process of decontextualization can "hurt" specific remembering and yet help shape knowledge into forms that readily permit transfer. If true, this conjecture suggests some important pedagogical implications. For example, many educational tests tap abilities to remember specific facts or paraphrases of facts. If the initial acquisition activities that promote relatively specific remembering differ from those that permit information to be shaped into more usable forms, then the use of such tests may be promoting less usable forms of knowledge acquisition. Students who study for the purpose of passing such exams may therefore fail to acquire knowledge in a form that sets the stage for further articulation and discovery.

C. FURTHER EXAMPLES OF DECONTEXTUALIZATION

It seems fruitful to consider the proces of decontextualization from a different perspective. Consider attempts to characterize one's "knowledge of his native language" (e.g., Chomsky, 1965). The attempt is to articulate a *competence* model of an ideal speaker-hearer's *linguistic* knowledge: To account for our intuitive knowledge that *The boy hit the ball* is a grammatical sentence but *Boy the hit ball the* is not; that the sentence *John is eager to please* has a different syntactic deep structure than *John is easy to please;* that *John hit Mary* is essentially a paraphrase of *Mary was hit by John,* etc. It is customary to assume, for example, that the latter two sentences share similar linguistic deep structures. A linguistic characterization of relationships between deep and surface structures is assumed to account for the "knowledge of language" that an ideal speaker–hearer has acquired.

Note that a competence model of knowledge (in this case, "linguistic" knowledge) does not tell one much about the growth of this knowledge. It seems probable that children, for example, do not initially have a "knowledge of their language" that is distinct from other knowledge (for example, their knowledge of concrete settings, of the speaker's identity, of gestures, etc.). It is a gradual process by which knowledge of a language becomes decontextualized, i.e., begins to have a "life of its own."

Consider a study reported by Olson (1974). He investigated children's abilities to detect paraphrases of sentences by presenting them with inputs such as *John hit Mary* and then asking them whether these were equivalent to sentences like *Mary was hit by John.* Olson found that young children were very poor at identifying such equivalences. However, by increasing the extent to which the sentences were presented in rich contextual settings, Olson found a significant increase in children's abilities to detect accurate paraphrases. Performance was lowest in the case where arbitrary names (e.g., John, Mary) were used, but it was improved by simply including known characters even though the events remained arbitrary. The addition of a story context in which both characters and their relations were nonarbitrary further facilitated the children's abilities to make correct identifications of meaning equivalences.

Olson's study indicates that it is easier for children to detect paraphrases when input sentences are comprehended within a relevant contextual setting than in the absence of such a context. Indeed, it is in the presence of rich contextual settings that early language acquisition occurs (e.g., see MacNamara, 1972; Nelson, 1974). Olson's study further suggests that children do not first comprehend sentences at some linguistic deep structural level and then proceed to understand their significance as a function of context. His results suggest that the children's responses were based on their ability to understand the cognitive significances of input sentences and to see that they were equivalent to other significances. In short, their knowledge of language was not in a form that allowed them to recognize paraphrases on the basis of linguistic knowledge alone.

Adults, of course, can recognize the linguistic equivalence of sentences like *John hit Mary* and *Mary was hit by John.* However, such abilities seem to be the *result* of processes of decontextualization. Only gradually does our knowledge of language become decontextualized from support provided by everyday social settings. Only gradually do we explicitly learn words' meanings, and learn to understand a speaker's or writer's "explicit" or "literal" meanings. Gradually, our knowledge of language does take on a "life of its own." It seems doubtful, however, that even adults ever achieve ideal levels of decontextualized linguistic knowledge. For example, many words (especially relatively "abstract" words) are understandable even to adults only when they are used in certain specific or familiar contextual situations. In addition, the definitional "properties" of many words can only be articulated through their use. Maratsos (in press) provides an example. He asked people (including graduate students) whether the verb *convince* (as in *John convinced Mary to go to the party*) necessarily implied that the recipient (i.e., Mary) would carry out the action. Many of his respondents said "yes." Maratsos then asked whether someone could convince Mary (for example) to go to a party and then have her be unable to go (e.g., through sickness, death, etc.). In this situation, all of his respondents said "yes." This example indicates that people cannot simple "retrieve" the critical definitional "features" of a word and "read them off from memory." In the context of using the word, however, they may articulate which features do and do not count.

Processes of decontextualization are also related to progressions from "live" to "dead" metaphor. In present society, a phrase like "the legs of a chair" is understood relatively literally (i.e., it is a "dead" metaphor). Verbrugge (in press) notes that such a description was not always understood in a literal sense. In Victorian England, for example, chair legs were seen as *analogous* to people's legs, especially women's legs. The metaphor was "live." It was so live, in fact, that given the puritanical standards of Victorian England, chair "legs" were decent only if covered by a "skirt."

Examples of analogy and metaphor illustrate once again the stage setting function of knowledge. The latter permits the articulation and clarification of some subsequent experience or domain. Indeed, some philosophers (e.g., Hesse, 1966) have argued that all explanation is of the nature of *metaphoric redescription.* One learns to see domain Y from the perspective of domain X. Gradually, one eliminates the need to "mediate" interpretations in terms of domain Y; he begins to apprehend X relatively directly. Thus, the metaphor gradually becomes "dead." Note that this metaphorical function of previous knowledge is the rule rather than the exception. In the processes of understanding some new event from a familiar perspective, one can shape and even reject the validity of the metaphor from which the understanding began.

The preceding discussion suggests an important caveat with respect to understanding the nature of metaphor. One could compare the time to understand metaphorical versus literal descriptions of the same situation. If the form of someone's knowledge has been shaped (through its use) so that a literal statement can adequately describe a situation (i.e., if the organism has become "tuned" in a certain manner), then it should not be at all surprising that this attunement can result in faster comprehension. Under these conditions, a metaphorical statement is simply a more roundabout way to say the same thing. The important issue with respect to metaphor, however, seems to be the degree to which one can communicate novel information that *could not be communicated literally* (i.e., given the listener's present level of "literal" attunement). Metaphor encourages listeners to restructure their articulations of domain Y from the perspective of domain X. For example, if a speaker says *New York City is in Iowa* while viewing the activity of a small Iowa town on a Saturday night, the listener can preceive and understand the scene in a unique manner rather than merely reject the statement as false.

D. DECONTEXTUALIZATION AND THE ADVANTAGES OF THE ABSTRACT

We consider in more detail some of the advantages of decontextualized knowledge. One way to phrase questions about decontextualization is to ask about the advantages of moving from more concrete to more abstract forms to knowledge. *What value does abstraction afford?*

It is important to note that questions about the value of abstraction are not equivalent to questions about the ease of learning and remembering "abstract" versus "concrete" materials (e.g., see Paivio, 1971). Studies such as the latter are concerned with the *objects* of knowing. Our present concern is with the *tools* or *instruments* that set the stage for understanding particular inputs. As a simple example of differences between objects and tools of knowing, consider the words *cup* versus *structure.* As an object of knowing, *cup* is clearly more concrete than is *structure.* As a tool that sets the stage for communicating one's intentions, however, *structure* can be equally precise or perhaps even more precise than *cup.* For example, one can point to a cup and say "cup." Alternatively one can point to the cup as an example of some structure and say "structure." If one's intention is to induce the listener to explicitly notice the cup's particular structure, the utterance "structure" can be a much more precise indicant of this intention than the utterance "cup."

The preceding discussion assumes that listeners have already acquired relevant information about the lexical items *cup* versus *structure.* In considering the value of abstraction, we are assuming that a particular abstraction has been formed through a process of decontextualization. One's concept or knowledge has become abstract by virtue of its *use* in clarifying a number of situations. Simply telling a listener the *products* that result from one's personal processes of decontextualization (e.g., simply telling someone a verbal definition of an abstract concept) could not provide the quality of information available to a learner who, through using his knowledge, gradually shaped it into more abstract forms. To paraphrase Cassirer (1946), abstract conceptualizations are characterized by the fact that, through them " . . . a thousand connections are forged by one stroke [p. 28]."

From the present perspective, abstractions formed through processes of decontextualization are not defined by their vagueness relative to "concrete" experiences. We do not subscribe to a substractive theory of abstraction (e.g., see Cassirer, 1923; Bransford, 1970; Franks, 1970). As an alternative to equating "abstractness" with "vagueness," we assume that the intuitive notion of "abstract" refers to the greater diversity of circumstances to which one may apply a concept (see Cassirer, 1923; Dewey, 1933). In addition, it seems clear that knowledge in an abstract form can be extremely precise. Mathematics is a prime example of an abstract yet extremely precise form of knowledge. It is a powerful tool that can be used to clarify a large number of conceptual domains.

For instance, Hanson (1970) discusses the gradual evolution of abstract mathematical theories of aerodynamics. Knowledge of the current theory allows one to understand more precisely *how* and *why* certain structures afford flying. Consider the task of examining birds' wings in order to isolate and understand those invariant patterns that afford flying versus non-flying. One cannot blindly compare and contrast such wings in order to determine the common "features" that permit flying. What counts as a "feature" depends on one's framework (cf. the "baseball" study). In addition, it is certain *patterns* that afford a particular activity (e.g., flying), not the superficial identity of "concrete" features per se. For example, a "better mousetrap" can differ greatly (in terms of "concrete" features) from previous mousetraps. Despite this, one may still recognize what this new invention affords. (See Gibson, in press; Shaw & Pittenger, in press; on the concept of affordances.)

E. MORE ON THE VALUE OF ABSTRACTION

The value of abstraction is closely tied to the stage setting function of knowledge. Knowledge sets the stage for clarifying subsequent experiences. From this perspective, one advantage of abstract decontextualized knowledge becomes readily apparent. Decontextualized knowledge is in a form that frees it from particular superficialities. It is in a form in which it can set the stage for clarifying many subsequent domains. Katona (1940) provides an excellent illustration of this function. He taught two groups of students a card trick. Group 1 memorized the procedure for performing the card trick. The subjects in Group 2 were helped to understand a more abstract principle underlying the particular procedure. These latter subjects were then able to use that principle to understand and perform subsequent card tricks in which superficial aspects of the situations were changed.

The value of abstraction can also be illustrated from a different perspective. Assume that a person has a huge "stockpile" of knowledge. How does he selectively activate the knowledge that is appropriate for clarifying a particular situation at hand? It seems clear that an appropriately tuned organism does not have to exhaustively "search" the entire contents of his knowledge system in order to decide what is relevant in a particular situation. There is a great deal of flexible *selectivity* in activating just that knowledge which is potentially relevant to a particular task. Consider de Groot's (1965) studies of chess masters. Upon being presented with a chessboard, they seem to "find" the best move (or a very good one) extremely quickly (see also Chase & Simon, 1973). In contrast, players with less expertise frequently spend a great deal of time evaluating unfruitful possibilities. Their level of attunement is not as precise and selective as an expert's in the field.[5]

The process of shaping knowledge into abstract forms can permit an expert to be optimally *selective* in his thoughts and hypotheses. A simple way to conceptualize this value of abstraction is to consider a "stockpile of knowledge" experiment. Here, subjects learn a list of words (where "learning" means perfect recall) and then have to decide if any of the words can be used to perform a subsequent task (e.g., whether they can fit into a particular sentence frame like *The woman drank the* _____). Assume that subjects hear the latter test frame and that nothing in their particular "stockpile" is

---

[5] Notions of specificity (e.g., "encoding specificity") have often been equated with "rigidity" and opposed to "flexibility" (e.g., see Santa & Lamwers, 1974, p. 412). However, specificity can also involve precision, and appropriately attuned organisms can be flexibly precise. Relationships between flexibility and specificity are dealt with more fully elsewhere (Bransford & Franks, 1975).

appropriate. Our pilot data indicate a great deal of cumbersome, conscious "search" through the list before realizing that nothing in the stockpile is relevant to the test. Assume, however, that a different group of subjects have acquired a stockpile composed solely of furniture exemplars (e.g., couch, chair, table, etc.). Due to their past knowledge they will have an abstract characterization of the list (i.e., all are furniture). Such a characterization permits them to quickly reject the *total set* of items as being appropriate for a frame like *The woman drank the* _____. Categorization provides a simple illustration of abstract characterizations of certain domains of knowledge. In general, the ability to formulate increasingly abstract (and, ideally, precise) characterizations of certain domains greatly facilitates the ease with which one can reject whole areas of knowledge as being relevant to a particular task.

As a further example of the value of abstraction, assume that subjects memorize 20 schematic illustrations of birds' wings that all permit flying. Following acquisition, they are shown new schematic illustrations and asked to decide whether each of them is a structure that could fly. If they have not been taught through a process that gradually shaped their knowledge into an abstract decontextualized form, their only recourse is to compare each new bird wing to the "concrete" similarity of each "stored" bird wing. Their judgments will thus be cumbersome and slow (in addition to being frequently wrong). An expert, however, will not necessarily have to activate and compare each instance, but instead can respond on the basis of an abstract specification of structures that afford flying. The decision should therefore be relatively fast. It seems obvious that there are some situations in which a person may have to resort to the activation of concrete paradigmatic examples in order to make decisions. The important point is that the decontextualization of knowledge into relatively abstract structures greatly facilitates the ease with which one can understand and know.

IV. Overall Summary and Conclusions

In concluding this chapter, it appears useful to compare the present perspective to others—for example, ones that concentrate exclusively on either "episodic" or "semantic" memory. Are certain problems ignored by these latter perspectives? More significantly, does an emphasis on the stage setting effects of past experiences have any implications for such perspectives? We have argued that the stage setting function of knowledge can lead to the articulation of novel information, which in turn can lead to a modification of one's knowledge. This raised questions about the processes which shape knowledge into abstract, decontextualized tools or instruments that set the stage for knowing. To what extent might this emphasis on the function and growth of knowledge be useful in clarifying thinking about "episodic" and "semantic" memory domains?

In our opinion, the present perspective helps clarify why research on "episodic memory" (cf. Tulving, 1972) does not necessarily provide insights into the problems of knowing or the acquisition of knowledge. Information in a form that permits optimal remembering is not necessarily in a decontextualized form that permits it to set the stage for clarifying and understanding subsequent experiences. Moreover, a host of variables determining remembering seem to involve the manner in which subjects' previous knowledge has set the stage for organizing and making sense of to-be-learned materials (e.g., see the research on encoding; e.g., Melton & Martin, 1972; "levels of processing"; e.g., Craik & Lockhart, 1972; Jenkins, 1974, etc.). The memory literature provides an indication of the *effects* of previous knowledge, but it neither characterizes this knowledge nor accounts for its acquisition. Consequently, memory theories encompass only a limited domain.

What is the domain of theories of remembering? From the present perspective, their domain involves the abstract, invariant constraints that govern the *effects* of using previous knowledge to structure and clarify inputs. For example, there seem to be constraints on the "optimal number of items" that should be categorized as examples of some concept in order to produce optimal remembering (e.g., see Mandler, 1967). Phrased another way, there seem to be constraints on the number of inputs that can be effectively "retrieved" by a particular retrieval cue. One way to view the domain of theories of remembering is therefore to suggest that such theories should ultimately be expected to specify how and why certain structurings of inputs can result in optimal remembering. An orientation toward this question that is consistent with the present emphasis on stage setting has been presented elsewhere (Bransford, McCarrell, Franks, & Nitsch, in press).

The present orientation also has implications for defining the domain of theories of semantic memory. Like episodic theories, semantic memory theories do not attempt to characterize the acquisition of "semantic knowledge." Instead they purport to explain how the structure of one's current "semantic memory" determines the accuracy and speed with which decisions can be made (e.g., Is a robin a bird?). We have noted problems with the memory metaphor assumptions underlying theories of semantic memory. The memory metaphor fails to provide mechanisms for learning or understanding *novel* information. We have therefore stressed the importance of developing a stage setting metaphor that might eventually lead to more precise theories of growth and learning. However, most current theories of semantic memory are not intended to be growth theories. It therefore becomes useful to ask a further question: To what extent do such theories adequately characterize the products of previous learning? That is, does an emphasis on the process of forming abstract, decontextualized characterizations of experiences have any implications for these theories of semantic memory?

It might be argued that the present emphasis on problems of growth or learning has few or even no implications for extant theories of semantic memory. For example, investigations of the processes by which people decide that "A robin is a bird" are conducted on people who *already know* a great deal about robins and birds. Perhaps theories of semantic memory can tell us about the *end products* of decontextualized abstraction. That is, given *that* someone already knows something, perhaps such theories can tell us *what* is known and how this information is utilized to make a response.

In our opinion, however, the present perspective does have implications for theories of "semantic memory." These implications revolve around the stage setting function of knowledge and the value of abstraction. Consider models that represent knowledge as "links" between concepts (e.g., *furniture* may be represented as a node with links to *chair, couch,* etc.; Loftus, 1975). Such models fail to incorporate the necessary information and operations which would reflect the value of abstraction. For example, these models define one's knowledge of furniture *only* in terms of the concept labels and properties linked to the node furniture. One's knowledge of a concept is therefore defined solely in terms of a list of its exemplars. There appear to be important limitations of this type of approach.

Assume that a group of subjects learns a list comprised solely of furniture exemplars (e.g., *couch, chair,* etc.). They are then asked to determine whether any of the words they have learned can be used for some subsequent activity. For example, could any be used to appropriately complete the sentence *The woman drank the* _____? We have discussed pilot data indicating that subjects can easily reject the total set of furniture items as being relevant to the sentence frame. Given the previously noted models, however, how could people reject the total set without searching through all possible exemplars attached to the node "furniture"? Since the model provides no characterization of knowledge about furniture other than a list of exemplars, activation of these exemplars would seem to be a prerequisite for making a response.

Similar problems confront "feature" models. For example, it might seem reasonable to characterize the concept of furniture as + moveable, etc. But what does one know about a feature like + moveable? Doesn't one need a list of possible exemplars that define what a feature may or may not include? It seems unreasonable to assume that one's concept of "furniture" includes features like "not drinkable." Such an assumption would allow one to maintain a "feature matching" explanation for subjects' abilities to reject the total set of furniture items as being relevant to the previously mentioned test sentence. Yet the concept of "furniture" would ultimately have to be explicitly marked with features such as "not persuadable," "not tickleable," etc. (see also Bolinger, 1965). Even if one assumes that a host of negative features could be encompassed by a higher order feature (e.g., "not human"), there are still difficulties. How could one know what was included under the feature "not human" without running through all the features of "humanness" before making a response?

The preceding arguments return us to the discussion in Section I of this chapter. To what extent do our models and theories of comprehension presuppose a comprehender? As comprehenders of some model or theory, we can *assume* that people understand a concept or feature and hence are able to "cut off search" at a higher conceptual or feature level. Yet the models themselves do not necessarily predict or explain such behavior. Instead, it is *our interpretations* of such models that allow us to understand and predict. In short, models and theories are tools that set the stage for clarifying and understanding situations. Yet they are frequently viewed as explanations of understanding per se.

It seems useful to note that the problem of building a model or theory that explains psychological understanding is extremely different from problems faced by any previous science. Einstein's theory is a tool that sets the stage for understanding physics. Similarily, Darwin's theory of evolution is a tool. All scientific theories to date have presupposed both a creator and a comprehender. Our basic argument is that all extant theories of learning and understanding tacitly presuppose a creator and comprehender as well.

Is there an alternative to presupposing a creator and comprehender in one's theory of learning and comprehending? At least for the present, the answer seems to be "no." But this does not mean that we therefore accept current theories, for example of semantic memory, just because as comprehenders we can interpret them to mean what we want. A theory is fruitful to the extent that it is nonambiguous, i.e., to the extent that it sets the stage for more precise understanding of a phenomenon. We have argued that theoretical perspectives within the memory metaphor are limited in their potential for setting the stage for understanding the phenomena of comprehending and learning. This limitation includes the virtual equating of "knowing" with "contacting previous knowledge," the ignoring of problems posed by novelty, and the lack of explicit acknowledgment of the role of a comprehender. We have proposed a stage setting metaphor that attempts to explicitly acknowledge the problems posed by novelty and the need for a comprehender. Hopefully, this metaphor will set the stage for more precise understanding of the phenomena of learning and comprehending, and maybe eventually of the comprehender per se.

REFERENCES

Barclay, J. R., Bransford, J. D., Franks, J. J., McCarrell, N. S., & Nitsch, K. Comprehension and semantic flexibility. *Journal of Verbal Learning and Verbal Behavior*, 1974, 13, 471–481.

Bolinger, D. The atomization of meaning. *Language*, 1965, 41, 553–573.

Bransford, J. D. The problem of conceptual abstraction: Implications for theories of learning and memory. Special examination paper, University of Minnesota Archives, 1970.

Bransford, J. D., & Franks, J. J. Encoding specificity and flexibility: A theoretical note. Prepublication manuscript, 1975.

Bransford, J. D., & Johnson, M. K. Consideration of some problems of comprehension. In W. Chase (Ed.), *Visual information processing*. New York: Academic Press, 1973.

Bransford, J. D., & McCarrell, N. S. A sketch of a cognitive approach to comprehension. In W. Weimer and D. Palermo (Eds.), *Cognition and the symbolic processes*. Hillsdale, N.J.: Erlbaum Associates, 1974.

Bransford, J. D., McCarrell, N. S., Franks, J. J., & Nitsch, K. E. Toward unexplaining memory. In R. E. Shaw and J. D. Bransford (Eds.), *Perceiving, acting and knowing: Toward an ecological psychology*. Hillsdale, N.J.: Erlbaum Associates, in press.

Bransford, J. D., McCarrell, N. S., & Nitsch, K. E. Context, comprehension, and semantic flexibility. *Bulletin de Psychologie*, in press.

Cassirer, E. *Substance and function*. Chicago: Open Court Publ., 1923.

Cassirer, E. *Language and myth*. New York: Dover, 1946.

Chase, W. G., & Simon, H. A. The mind's eye in chess. In W. G. Chase (Ed.), *Visual information processing*. New York: Academic Press, 1973.

Chomsky, N. *Aspects of a theory of syntax*. Cambridge, Mass.: M.I.T. Press, 1965.

Collins, A. M., & Quillian, M. R. Retrieval time from semantic memory. *Journal of Verbal Learning and Verbal Behavior*, 1969, **8**, 240–247.

Craik, F. I. M., & Lockhart, R. S. Levels of processing: A framework for memory research. *Journal of Verbal Learning and Verbal Behavior*, 1972, **11**, 671–684.

de Groot, A. B. *Thought and choice in chess*. The Hague: Mouton, 1965.

Dewey, J. *How we think*. (Rev. ed.). Boston: D. C. Heath, 1933.

Fillmore, C. J. Verbs of judging: An exercise in semantic description. In C. J. Fillmore and D. T. Langendoen (Eds.), *Studies in linguistic semantics*. New York: Holt, 1971.

Franks, J. J. Toward a psychological theory of knowledge. Special examination paper, University of Minnesota Archives, 1970.

Franks, J. J. Toward understanding understanding. In W. Weimer and D. Palermo (Eds.), *Cognition and the symbolic processes*. Hillsdale, N.J.: Erlbaum Associates, 1974.

Freedman, J. L., & Loftus, E. F. Retrieval of words from long-term memory. *Journal of Verbal Learning and Verbal Behavior*, 1971, **10**, 107–115.

Furth, H. G. *Piaget and knowledge: Theoretical foundations*. Englewood Cliffs, N.J.: Prentice-Hall, 1969.

Garner, W. R. *The processing of information and structure*. Potomac, Md.: Erlbaum Associates, 1974.

Gibson, J. J. *The senses considered as perceptual systems*. Boston: Houghton, 1966.

Gibson, J. J. The theory of affordances. In R. E. Shaw and J. D. Bransford (Eds.), *Perceiving, acting and knowing: Toward an ecological psychology*. Hillsdale, N.J.: Erlbaum Associates, in press.

Gibson, J. J., & Gibson, E. J. Perceptual learning: Differentiation or enrichment. *Psychological Review*, 1955, **62**, 32–41.

Gregory, R. L. Seeing as thinking: An active theory of perception. *The Times Literary Supplement*, June 23, 1972, 707–708.

Hanson, N. R. A picture theory of theory meaning. In R. G. Colodny (Ed.), *The nature and function of scientific theories*. Pittsburgh: University of Pittsburgh Press, 1970.

Hesse, M. B. *Models and analogies in science*. South Bend, Indiana: University of Notre Dame Press, 1966.

James, W. *The principles of psychology*. New York: Henry Holt, 1890.

Jenkins, J. J. Remember that old theory of memory? Well forget it! *American Psychologist*, 1974, **29**, 785–795. Also reprinted in R. E. Shaw and J. D. Bransford (Eds.), *Perceiving, acting and knowing: Toward an ecological psychology*. Hillsdale, N.J.: Erlbaum Associates, in press.

Katona, G. *Organizing and memorizing*. New York: Columbia University Press, 1940.

Katz, J. J., & Fodor, J. The structure of a semantic theory. *Language*, 1963, **39**, 170–210.

Kuhn, T. S. *The structure of scientific revolutions*, 2nd Ed., enlarged. Chicago: University of Chicago Press, 1970.

Kuhn, T. S. Second thoughts on paradigms. In F. Suppe (Ed.), *The structure of scientific theories*. Urbana, Ill.: University of Illinois Press, 1974.

Loftus, E. F. Spreading activation within semantic categories: Comments on Rosch's "Cognitive representations of semantic categories." *Journal of Experimental Psychology: General*, 1975, **104**, 234–240.

Loftus, E. F., & Freedman, J. L. Effect of category-name frequency on the speed of naming an instance of a category. *Journal of Verbal Learning and Verbal Behavior*, 1972, **11**, 343–347.

MacNamara, J. Cognitive basis of language learning in infants. *Psychological Review*, 1972, **79**, 1–13.

Maier, N. R. F. Reasoning in humans. I. On direction. *Journal of Comparative Psychology*, 1930, **10**, 115–143.

Mandler, G. Organization and memory. In K. W. Spence and J. T. Spence (Eds.), *The psychology of learning and motivation, Vol 1*. New York: Academic Press, 1967.

Maratsos, M. P. Disorganization in thought and word. In R. E. Shaw and J. D. Bransford (Eds.), *Perceiving, acting and knowing: Toward an ecological psychology*. Hillsdale, N.J.: Erlbaum Associates, in press.

Melton, A. W., & Martin, E. (Eds.), *Coding processes in human memory*. Washington, D.C.: Winston, 1972.

Meyer, D. E., & Ellis, G. B. Parallel processes in word recognition. Paper presented at the meeting of the Psychonomic Society, San Antonio, November, 1970.

Meyer, D. E., & Schavaneveldt, R. W. Facilitation in recognizing pairs of words: Evidence of a dependence between retrieval operations. *Journal of Experimental Psychology*, 1971, **90**, 227–234.

Minsky, M. A framework for representing knowledge. In P. H. Winston (Ed.), *The psychology of computer vision*. New York: McGraw-Hill, 1975.

Neisser, U. *Cognitive psychology*. New York: Appleton-Century-Crofts, 1967.

Nelson, K. Concept, word, and sentence: Interrelations in acquisition and development. *Psychological Review*, 1974, **81**, 267–285.

Norman, D. A. *Memory and attention*. New York: Wiley, 1969.

Olson, D. R. Towards a theory of instructional means. Invited address presented to the American Educational Research Association, Chicago, April, 1974.

Paivio, A. *Imagery and verbal processes*. New York: Holt, 1971.

Piaget, J. *Biology and knowledge: An essay on the relations between organic regulations and cognitive processes*. Chicago: University of Chicago Press, 1971.

Rips, L. J., Shoben, E. J., & Smith, E. E. Semantic distances and the verification of semantic relations. *Journal of Verbal Learning and Verbal Behavior*, 1973, **12**, 1–20.

Santa, J. L., & Lamwers, L. L. Encoding specificity: Fact or artifact. *Journal of Verbal Learning and Verbal Behavior*, 1974, **13**, 412–423.

Shaw, R. E., & Pittenger, J. Perceiving the face of change in changing faces: Implications for a theory of object perception. In R. E. Shaw and J. D. Bransford (Eds.), *Perceiving, acting and knowing: Toward an ecological psychology*. Hillsdale, N.J.: Erlbaum Associates, in press.

Smith, E. E., Shoben, E. J., & Rips, L. J. Structure and process in semantic memory: A feature model for semantic decisions. *Psychological Review*, 1974, **81**, 214–241.

Staudenmayer, H. Understanding conditional reasoning with meaningful propositions. In R. Falmagne (Ed.), *Psychological studies of logic and its development*. Hillsdale, N.J.: Erlbaum Associates, in press.

Tulving, E. Episodic and semantic memory. In E. Tulving and W. Donaldson (Eds.), *Organization of memory*, New York: Academic Press, 1972.

Uhr, L. (Ed.), *Pattern recognition*. New York: Wiley, 1966.

Verbrugge, R. R. Resemblances in languages and perception. In R. E. Shaw and J. D. Bransford (Eds.), *Perceiving, acting and knowing: Toward an ecological psychology*. Hillsdale, N.J.: Erlbaum Associates, in press.

ECONOMIC DEMAND THEORY AND PSYCHOLOGICAL STUDIES OF CHOICE[1]

Howard Rachlin

STATE UNIVERSITY OF NEW YORK AT STONY BROOK,
STONY BROOK, NEW YORK

Leonard Green

WASHINGTON UNIVERSITY, ST. LOUIS, MISSOURI

John H. Kagel and Raymond C. Battalio

TEXAS A & M UNIVERSITY, COLLEGE STATION, TEXAS

I. Introduction	129
Demand Theory	130
II. The Purpose of the Experiments	135
III. Experiments on Substitutability: Procedure and Results	136
IV. Experiments on Substitutability: Discussion	141
A. Effort as a Commodity	141
B. The Place of Psychology in Economic Demand Theory	142
C. The Place of Economic Demand Theory In Psychology	143
V. Summary	152
References	152

I. Introduction

In operant experiments, objects of choice have usually been various parameters—rates, amounts, delays, etc.—of a single com-

---

[1] The chapter was jointly written by H. Rachlin and L. Green; the experiments described were done in collaboration with J. H. Kagel and R. C. Battalio. The work was partially supported by an NSF grant to H. Rachlin, NIH Fellowship to L. Green, and NSF grant to J. H. Kagel and R. C. Battalio. We are grateful to Dr. Peter Henderson who developed the computer program.

modity. Matching of parameters of reinforcement to parameters of responding (Herrnstein, 1970) and other quantitative expressions of choice developed by operant researchers (Catania, 1963; Squires & Fantino, 1971) can be applied only with difficulty when the objects of choice are qualitatively dissimilar. For instance, Hollard and Davison (1971) found that pigeons' choices between electrical brain stimulation and food conformed to Herrnstein's matching law only when a new parameter (q) representing unmeasured differences between the rewards was introduced. It is unlikely that even this tactic, the introduction of new parameters into the matching equation, would suffice for choices between such commodities as food and water where complex biological interactions play a major part.

The purpose of this chapter is to introduce a framework borrowed from economics within which choices between different commodities may be studied in a consistent manner. This framework is *demand theory* and the particular concept within demand theory that most directly applies to studies of choice is that of *substitutability*.

DEMAND THEORY

The modern version of the theory of demand has common roots with psychological theories of choice. The axiomatization of psychological choice theory (Luce, 1959) and demand theory (Newman, 1965) both begin with the analysis of behavior under uncertainty of von Neumann and Morgenstern (1947). Because none of the conclusions of the theory are counterintuitive and since some are as reasonable to assume as the axioms themselves, we will present aspects of the theory here, without deriving them. Our main concern is their application to psychological data.

The axes of Fig. 1A define a space consisting of combinations of various amounts of two commodities, a and b. Thus, a point in the upper right part of the space represents a package containing large quantities of a and b. A point near the origin represents small quantities of a and b, etc. Now suppose an individual starts out at point M. He might be willing to trade a fairly large amount of a which he has a fair amount of, for a small amount of b, which he has none of. This would put him, say, at point X. Now, having some b he would be willing to part with less a than before for the same amount of b. The more b he acquires, the less each new unit of b is worth in terms of a. A series of such trades might take him all the way to point N. The curve from M to N is called an indifference function. If his choices were transitive, an individual would be willing to exchange any package of commodities on that line for any other package on the line.[2] The slope of the indifference line at any point is called the personal rate of substitution. The commodity space is assumed to contain an infinite number of indifference lines, none of them crossing. An indifference line such as M'-N' higher in the space is more valuable than any lower indifference line. This is because movement to a higher indifference line is always equivalent to a trade such as X' for X whereby more of one commodity is obtained without sacrificing any of the other commodity. One of the axioms of demand theory is that any package containing more of either commodity (and no less of the other) is preferred to a package containing less of that commodity.

The shape of the indifference functions is determined by the degree to which the two commodities can be substituted for each other in actual use. The concept of substitutability is easiest understood by considering the extreme cases. Let us first consider the extreme of complete substitutability. Suppose a and b have some common element which is of value to the individual and that all other dimensions of a and b, the dimensions along which they differ, are of no value. Then, the indifference functions would look like those of Fig. 1B. The diagonal lines represent constant amounts of the common element. If a had more of the element per unit than b the lines would be steeply sloped (a little a is worth a lot of b). If b had more of the element per unit than a, the lines would be shallow. The case of complete substitutability is actually the case most studied in operant experiments where choice is between various rates and amounts of a single commodity. For instance, the b axis might represent food obtained by a pigeon by pecking the left key and the a axis, the same food obtained by pecking the right key. If the pigeon were indifferent between color and location of the keys, its indifference functions would be as in Fig. 1B, each line corresponding to a given amount of food distributed in various ways across the two keys.

At the other extreme we have complete nonsubstitutability illustrated in Fig. 1C. Commodities which are completely nonsubstitut-

---

[2] Indifference functions should not be confused with isohedonic contours (Young, 1961). Although both functions compare value of different commodities, isohedonic contours are determined by choosing between one commodity and the other while the indifference functions of demand theory involve choice between various packages containing both commodities together. Isohedonic contours always start at the origin and fan out while indifference contours are roughly hyperbolic in shape.

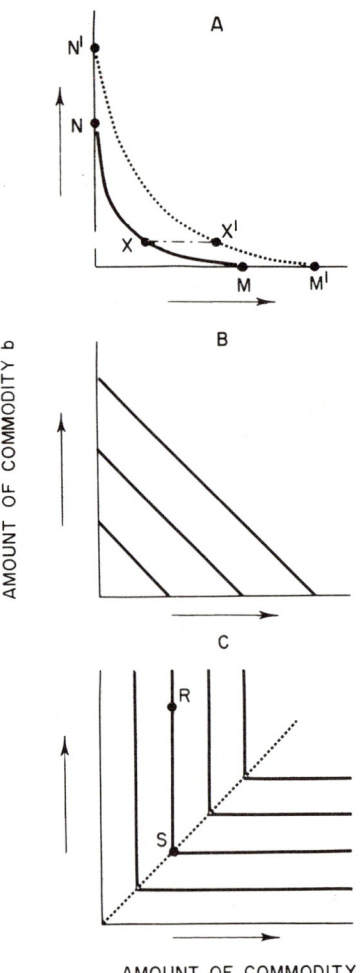

Fig. 1. Commodity space with two commodities, *a* and *b*. (A) Indifference functions with moderate substitutability. (B) Indifference functions with complete substitutability. (C) Indifference functions with complete nonsubstitutability.

able are also referred to as "perfect" complements. Figure 1C might describe a situation in which two commodities possessed different essential metabolites. Say a person were on a macrobiotic diet which must contain so much yin and so much yang. Suppose *b* is all yin and *a* is all yang; they have no common elements that are of any value, and there is no possibility of substituting one for the other. The commodities *a* and *b* must be consumed in a certain proportion, shown by the dotted line. If the individual has the package of a and b represented by point R, the amount of b between R and S is wasted since it cannot be consumed without more a. If any of the excess b were traded for a, the new package would be worth *more* than the old and hence be on a higher indifference line.

Most pairs of real commodities are somewhere between the extremes of complete substitutability and complete nonsubstitutability and are consequently described by indifference functions that are convex to the origin. The rate of substitution would be indicated by the degree of convexity (slope) of the indifference function. Even such items as food and clothing which seem nonsubstitutable may be substitutable to a certain extent. Eating more food when you are cold may keep you slightly warmer. To the extent that food keeps you warm it is substitutable for clothing. If not having a new hat makes you depressed perhaps you can forget your troubles with an ice-cream soda. Both food and clothing satisfy common emotional needs and are substitutable to that extent. Correspondingly, even items that seem completely substitutable, such as pecking the left and the right key of a two-key pigeon chamber, may be nonsubstitutable to a certain extent. Some muscles not used in one activity may be used in the other and it may be important to equalize exercise. Thus, eating from one side of the food hopper may be, to a slight extent, nonsubstitutable for eating the same food from the other side. It is evident that substitutability is not a fixed relationship between two commodities. Substitutability may vary depending on where in the commodity space it is observed.

When two commodities are highly substitutable the demand for one is said to be elastic with respect to the other. When the commodities are not substitutable the demand is said to be inelastic.[3]

The indifference functions of Fig. 1 are assumptions about what the individual organism brings to a choice experiment. Now we turn to the way economists suggest the functions interact with environmental contingencies.

Suppose that a and b now each have a unit price (P_a, P_b) and we give a person a fixed sum of money (M) that he may spend on the two commodities as he wishes. Figure 2 shows how he may spend his

---

[3] One characteristic of demand theory not emphasized here is that a given commodity may stand for a group of other commodities. For instance, one of the commodities might be "care packages" consisting in turn of a group of other commodities. In the extreme, one commodity might be "dollar bills." Elasticity of demand is not an absolute quality of a commodity but is relative to other commodities. Elasticity of a commodity with respect to money is just elasticity with respect to the other commodities that money can buy.

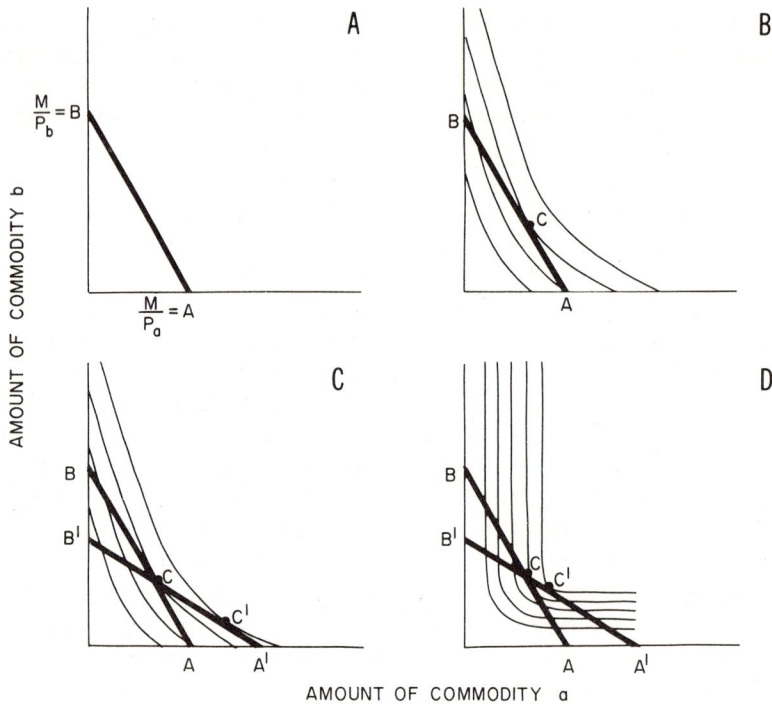

Fig. 2. (A) Budget line for two commodities, *a* and *b*. (B) Budget line superimposed on a set of indifference functions. Point C represents consumption of both commodities so as to attain the highest possible indifference function. (C) Shift in budge line (from A-B to A'-B') in which commodity *a* is now cheaper and commodity *b* is now more expensive. Point C' represents the new consumption with relatively substitutable commodities. (D) Shift in budget line and new consumption (Point C') with relatively nonsubstitutable commodities.

money (assuming he does not save any). The line in Fig. 2A (not to be confused with the indifference lines in Fig. 1B) is called a budget line. If all of the money is spent on *b* the amount of *b* bought is M/P_b and the location on the budget line is point B. If all the money is spent on *a*, the amount of *a* bought is M/P_a and the location is point A. If the money is distributed between *a* and *b* the location is elsewhere on the line. The budget line may be moved about by manipulating income and the relative price of *a* and *b*. Figure 2B shows a budget line superimposed on a set of indifference functions. According to demand theory, the individual will spend his money on *a* and *b* so as to attain the highest possible indifference function. Ordinarily this will be where the budget line is tangent to an indifference curve (point C).

Suppose we observe a distribution equal to C with the budget line A-B. We may now manipulate income and prices so as to produce the budget line A'-B' (Fig. 2C and 2D). Now a is cheaper and b is more expensive. Since A'-B' goes through point C, the same package of goods may be bought as before. The law of revealed preference (Samuelson, 1973) says that the new package cannot be bought between C and B' since Fig. 2B "reveals" a preference for C over any other package within the triangle formed by the origin and A-B, and all points on the line segment CB' are within this triangle. The new package, C', must be somewhere between C and A'. Figure 2C shows C' with relatively substitutable commodities. Figure 2D shows C' with relatively unsubstitutable commodities. The displacement of C' from C is greater, the greater the substitutability. This is another way of saying that when commodities are substitutable a sharp decrease in the price of one good will cause much more of that good to be bought. If goods are less substitutable, a decrease in the price will only cause slightly more to be bought. In fact, the displacement of C' from C may be used as a measure of substitutability. The experiments described in subsequent sections of this chapter attempt to apply this measure to rats' choices among various commodities.

II. The Purpose of the Experiments

Demand theory is not so much a psychological theory (in the sense that it specifies an internal mechanism or can be proven true or false) as it is a definition of psychological utility. If, in a given case, behavior does not conform to what demand theory predicts then our initial assumptions must have been wrong in that case (choice was intransitive or preference varied nonmonotonically with amount of reward). We know already that choices are not always transitive (Navarick & Fantino, 1974) and that preference does not always vary monotonically with amount (rats, for instance, prefer moderate to large concentrations of sugar). Nonconformance to demand theory is prevalent in human behavior (economists refer to behavior which is not in conformance with economic theory as "irrational" which, of course, puts all the blame on the subject and none on the economist) and may well be even more prevalent in the behavior of other animals whose more "primitive" behavioral mechanisms may not adjust smoothly to changes in price as demand theory requires. Nevertheless, it would be worthwhile to observe behavior of nonhumans in areas where the axioms of demand theory *are* satisfied. In these areas we have a biological system that could be used to test more complex economic theories, most of which are based on demand theory to which are added further assumptions about individual behavior (Samuelson, 1973). Further, any organism whose behavior conforms to the dictates of demand theory ought to be capable of interacting with another such organism so as to trade a commodity that it has in excess for commodity in which it is deficient (Newman, 1965). In a situation where behavior conformed to demand theory it would be possible, therefore, to study various systems of free distribution of goods, of taxation, and of trade. In the laboratory it will be possible to isolate and vary parameters that can only be guessed at in "real world" economic systems. The first step, however, is to discover whether demand theory applies at all to the behavior of laboratory animals and, if it does, what are the limits of its application.

III. Experiments on Substitutability: Procedure and Results[4]

We selected two pairs of commodities one of which we felt might be substitutable and the other, nonsubstitutable for a rat. The substitutable pair consisted of root beer and Tom Collins mix (without alcohol) that were allowed to go flat. The nonsubstitutable pair consisted of food pellets and water. The subjects were four male albino rats, two root beer/Tom Collins and two food/water. Each subject was kept 24 hr per day in a standard Gerbrands Co. operant chamber fitted with two levers. The chamber of the root beer/Tom Collins rats had two dipper feeders, one for each commodity, below the two levers. Food and water were continuously available in the chambers for the root beer/Tom Collins rats. The food/water rats were housed in chambers with a dipper feeder for water and a pellet dispenser for 45-mg food pellets situated below the levers. No other food or water was available for these rats.

A rat's income (M) was defined in terms of the total number of effective lever presses allowed per day. Each morning, after the rat's cage was cleaned, the reservoirs filled and the rat weighed, two sets of white lights, one over each lever, were lit. After the rat expended

---

[4] The experiments described here have been previously described in more detail in Kagel *et al.* (1975).

its lever-press income, distributed in any way over the two levers, the lights were extinguished and not lit again until the next day. Lever presses were ineffective when the lights above the levers were out. The price of each commodity (P_a or P_b) was the amount of that commodity obtained per lever press. Price could be varied in two ways: by changing the amount of the commodity delivered at each delivery and by changing the number of lever presses required per delivery. Essentially the rats were exposed to concurrent fixed-ratio (FR) schedules of reinforcement. The difference between these schedules and typical concurrent schedules of reinforcement is that sessions ended after a fixed number of lever presses rather than after a fixed number of reinforcements or time, and the rats were not removed from the chambers (except for cleaning the chambers and weighing the rats) after the session. Standard magazine training and shaping procedures were used to train the subjects to press the levers for the commodities. Each experimental condition (set of prices and income) was maintained for a minimum of 14 days. Conditions were changed after 10 consecutive days with stable performance. Average values for an experimental condition cover all but the first three days of that period.

The initial condition for the two root beer/Tom Collins rats was as follows: $M = 300$ lever presses; P (root beer) = 0.05 ml per press, FR 1; P (Tom Collins) = 0.05 ml per press, FR 1. The fluids remained available for 5 sec. Figure 3 shows the budget line for these conditions for the two rats as line A-B. Point C on each line represents that rat's consumption of the two commodities. Rat 1 preferred root beer

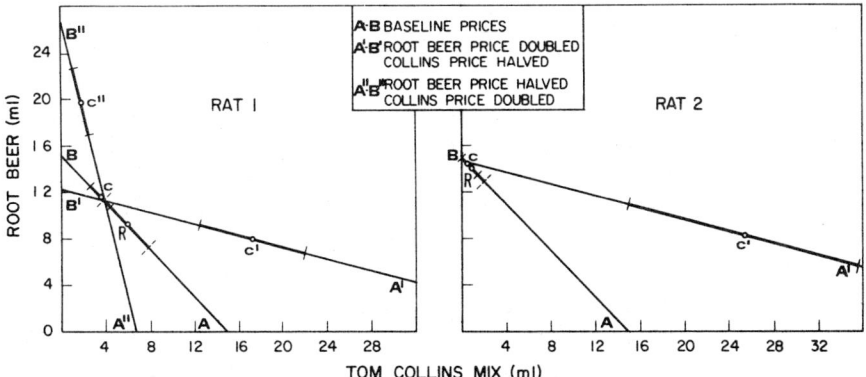

Fig. 3. Amount of root beer and Tom Collins consumed as budget lines were shifted by varying the price of each of the commodities and the total income. Brackets incidates the standard error of the mean.

to Tom Collins by a ratio of about 3:1. Rat 2 preferred root beer by a ratio of about 30:1. For the next condition we halved the price of Tom Collins, the less preferred commodity, and doubled the price of root beer for both rats. We adjusted the income of each rat so that the new budget line passed through point C thereby allowing the rat to obtain the same package of root beer and Tom Collins as before. The parameters of the new conditions were, for rat 1, M = 483 bar presses; P (root beer) = 0.025 ml per press; P (Tom Collins) = 0.10 ml per press. For Rat 2, M = 591 lever presses; P (root beer) = 0.025 ml per press; P (Tom Collins) = 0.10 ml per press. The amount of time the fluids remained available was changed proportionately with changes in price. The new budget lines are shown in Fig. 3 as A'-B'. Both rats greatly increased their purchases of Tom Collins as shown by the new distribution at point C'. Both rats now consumed more than twice as much Tom Collins as root beer.[5] The next condition was a return to the initial budget line A-B for both rats. Both rats returned at or near their initial performance as shown by point R on line A-B. Finally, for Rat 1, the price of root beer was halved and the price of Tom Collins doubled. The parameters were M = 267 lever presses; P (root beer) = 0.10 ml per press; P (Tom Collins) = 0.025 ml per press. This new budget line for Rat 1 is A''-B''. Again, the change of prices had a strong effect on amount purchased, the rat now buying 10 times as much root beer as Tom Collins (Point C'').

Two further control conditions were run. First, with Rat 1, holding prices and income constant at baseline values, we switched the levers producing root beer and Tom Collins mix. The rat switched its presses accordingly; we found no significant differences in purchase patterns. Second, using Rat 2, we put root beer behind both levers and varied the relative cost of root beer. Starting with the price of root beer lower on the left lever than on the right, the rat pressed the left lever almost exclusively. When we switched prices so that the lower price prevailed on the right lever the rat pressed exclusively on the right. The all-or-none behavior with concurrent fixed-ratio schedules for the same commodity is typical for these schedules (Herrnstein, 1958) and is consistent with demand theory as we will show later.

Evidently root beer and Tom Collins are highly substitutable as we suspected. We now turn to the results with food and water. After training a rat with the apparatus, we set the conditions at M = 2500

---

[5] The actual ratio of responses on the levers changed from .784 on the left lever to .653 on the left lever for Rat 1 and from .883 to .570 for Rat 2.

lever presses; P_{food} = FR 10, five pellets; P_{water} = FR 10, 0.10 ml. These conditions are shown as line A-B in Fig. 4. Point C on the line shows the rat's consumption. Then we increased the price of food 67% and simultaneously increased income so that the same amounts of food and water could be purchased as under baseline conditions. Now, M=3020 lever presses; P_{food} = FR 10, three pellets; P_{water} = FR 10, 0.10 ml. The new budget line is A'-B' in Fig. 4 and new consumption is shown as C'. The shift of consumption in response to the change in relative prices, while far less than in the root beer–Tom Collins studies still changed in favor of the cheaper water and away from the more expensive food.

We then increased the price of food again to determine if we could induce further substitution of water for food. The price of food was increased 400% over baseline while income was simultaneously increased so that the rat could continue to consume the baseline package (M = 5620 lever presses; P_{food} = FR 10, one pellet; P_{water} =

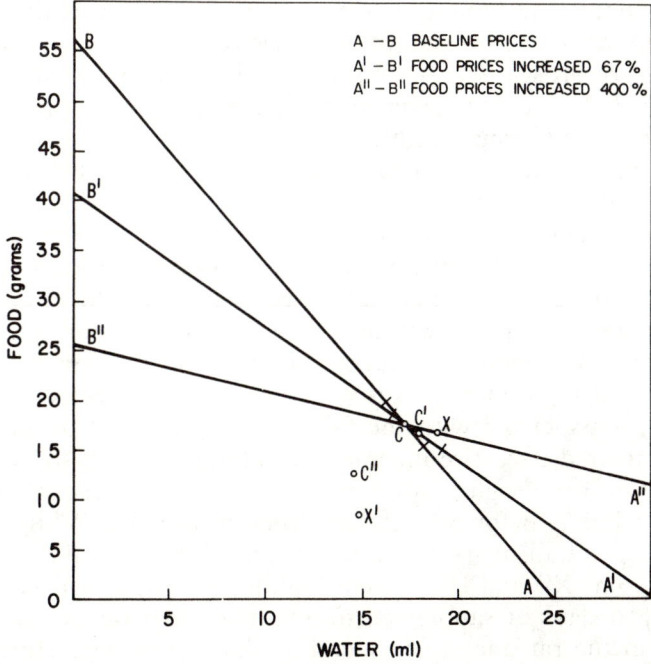

Fig. 4. Amount of food and water consumed as budget lines were shifted by varying the price of each of the commodities and the total income. Points X and X' represent results with a second rat (see text). Brackets indicate the standard error of the mean.

FR 10, 0.10 ml). This new budget line is A"-B" in Fig. 4. The ratio of food to water consumed decreased again but the rat now spent less than its total income in the 24 hr. This suppressed responding was immediate and continued for the entire experimental period, which was limited to 17 days since the rat steadily lost weight and spent an average of only 76.2% of its income each day. Mean consumption of food and water for this period is shown as point C" in Fig. 4.

The following manipulations examined why the rat lost weight when the price of food was increased. (Points not shown on figure). We first returned to baseline values (budget line A-B; M = 2,500 lever presses; P_{food} = FR 10, five pellets; P_{water} = FR 10, 0.10 ml). The rat, although initially spending all of its income in about 15 hours, continued to lose weight, drinking more water and eating less food than originally. We then halved the price of food again (P_{food} = FR 10, 10 pellets), adjusting income so that package C could still be purchased (M = 2110 lever presses) and the rat spent its income in about 5 hr. A return to baseline conditions now resulted in continued weight gain, a time spent consuming of about 8 hr (still double the time spent originally) and continued alteration in the composition of consumption, relative to baseline, away from food and towards water. A return to budget line A"-B" at this point reproduced the original behavior with the rat spending less than its total income and losing weight.

The failure of this subject to spend all of its income when the price of food was increased was unexpected. The suppressed responding cannot be attributed to the effort required to purchase the food and water since under budget line A"-B" average total presses remained below 5,000 per day, a number of presses which the same subject had consistently emitted within a period of 3–4 hr during a 5-week preexperimental period. To further study this behavior we placed a naive second rat under the price and income contingencies (budget line A"-B") associated with the failure of the first rat to finish. This second rat used its entire income under budget line A"-B" (point X) and did not lose weight. However, when this second rat was exposed to budget line A-B for 6 weeks and then returned to A"-B" again, it failed to spend all of its income, averaging 61% of total lever presses alloted (point X') and lost weight rapidly. Restoring budget line A-B following 6 days of suppressed responding under budget line A"-B" resulted in the rat once again spending all of its income. However, as with the first rat, the period of suppressed responding left marked residual effects on behavior as time spent purchasing increased and food purchases decreased compared with previous behavior under budget line A-B, and the subject continued to lose weight.

The results from the second rat provide further evidence that the first rat did not suppress its responding because of the contingencies of budget line A″-B″ itself. Rather the data from the second rat indicate that the severe disruption of the behavior of both rats resulted from the sharp increase in the relative price of food.

IV. Experiments on Substitutability: Discussion

A. EFFORT AS A COMMODITY

In the experiments described here we have been treating price as if it were a simple linear function of effort of response. This assumption can only be approximate at best and its violation may have been the cause of the "irrational" behavior of the rats when the price of food was increased. There are two ways in which this problem could have been avoided. One way would have been to discard lever presses as the measure of price and treat price wholly in temporal terms. That is, instead of giving a rat a fixed number of presses to distribute among commodities, we could have given it a fixed amount of time to distribute. The only response required (of insignificant effort) would consist of switching between the free delivery of one commodity and another. The rat could then spend its allotted time freely receiving one commodity or another depending on its indifference functions. The price of a commodity would be varied by changing its rate of delivery. Such a procedure resembles a variation of the Findley-type concurrent schedule (Brownstein & Pliskoff, 1968) in which a pigeon pecks a changeover key which serves to switch back and forth between two freely delivered rates of reinforcement. With such schedules pigeons' distribution of time to the two alternatives equalled distribution of pecks to normal concurrent schedules in which pecks produced food directly. We suspect, therefore, that a rat's distribution of time between two commodities would equal its distribution of lever presses. This modification of procedure might therefore preserve the various measures obtained in the present experiments and avoid the problem of response effort.

Alternatively we could have considered leisure itself as a commodity. This would have given us three commodities to consider and would have made analysis and explanation much more difficult. But the question of leisure itself as a commodity is important in economics. For instance, arguments against welfare or the negative income tax often hinge on their potential to decrease work. Imagine a diagram such as in Fig. 2B with some commodity (such as food) on the y axis and leisure on the x axis. The budget line would represent the contingency (for most people) that the more they work (less leisure) the more goods they can obtain. A negative income tax would lower the slope of the budget line (by raising point A or by curving the bottom part of the line outward depending on how the negative income tax was administered). This would move point C to the right thereby increasing leisure—people would work less. The rightward movement of point C is of crucial interest. Its degree would depend on the slope of the indifference lines and the budget lines around point C. It may be that at low income levels, because the goods on the y axis are necessities, the indifference curves would be sharply curved as in Fig. 2D rather than gradual as in Fig. 2C, and thus the movement of point C would be minimal. Such concepts could easily be tested by experiments with animals at various degrees of deprivation (various indifference functions) and various contingencies between work and reinforcement (budget lines).

B. THE PLACE OF PSYCHOLOGY IN ECONOMIC DEMAND THEORY

Macroeconomics refers to the economy of systems ranging from a family to a country. Microeconomics refers to the economy of the individuals comprising the macroeconomic system. It is apparent that microeconomics is macropsychology. The behavior of individual organisms is the province of psychology and it should not be surprising that psychologists and microeconomists should have something to say to each other about their common object of study.

The economists will object that their theories refer to the behavior of human beings and not to animals, especially ones so undignified as rats. But the axioms of demand theory are simple: transivity; more is better than less; the existence of indifference contours, etc. If these axioms cannot adequately account for the behavior of rats, they must be more inadequate when applied to the complex behavior of humans.

We have seen that demand theory accounts well for some of the behavior of our rat subjects. When choosing between the substitutable commodities, root beer and Tom Collins mix, rats behaved as demand theory would have them behave, buying more of the cheaper commodity and less of the dearer. With food and water, demand theory accounted for the rats' behavior as long as price changes of food were modest. When food became suddenly more expensive the rats did not spend their entire income and they lost weight. These deviations from "rational behavior" (i.e., behavior in accordance with demand theory) might have been expected by psychologists familiar with intransitivities (Navarick & Fantino, 1974), contrast effects and other restrictions on otherwise rational behavior (Staddon & Simmelhag, 1971; Rachlin, 1973; Green & Rachlin, 1975). No one expects that humans (or indeed any organism other than the rat) would show the particular biological peculiarities exhibited here. Nevertheless, the present experiments direct one's attention to the sort of situation where biological restrictions on economic behavior may be expected to act—sudden increases in price of commodities for which the demand is inelastic. Without pushing the analogy too far we might mention observations reported by clinical psychologists and sociologists (e.g., Brenner, 1973; Dublin, 1963; Henry & Short, 1954) of severe disruptions in human behavior, i.e., suicide, mental disorder, that often appear under similar economic circumstances. In fact, one behavioral theory of depression suggests that the onset of depression is accompanied by a reduction in response contingent positive reinforcement (Lewinsohn, 1974). Economists should consider such possibilities. (See, for example, Hamermesh and Soss, 1974, who have developed a theory of suicide based on economic variables.)

C. THE PLACE OF ECONOMIC DEMAND THEORY IN PSYCHOLOGY

If microeconomics and psychology are about the same subject (the behavior of individual organisms), we should be able to do more than simply design experiments such as those described here, suitable for analysis by economic demand theory. We should be able to translate psychology experiments into equivalent economic experiments. As an example of how this may be done, consider the findings with concurrent interval and ratio schedules of reinforcement. When two variable-ratio (VR) schedules are presented concurrently, subjects typically respond only on the shorter ratio or on the ratio that yields the larger reward. If both ratios are equal in all respects behavior is very variable. In experiments with pigeons with equal VR schedules, some subjects continue to respond only on one of the schedules and some distribute their responses in various proportions on the two alternatives (Herrnstein & Loveland, 1975). There seems to be no way of predicting what a given pigeon will do in such a situation. Let us consider the case from the point of view of demand theory. Since both concurrent schedules involve the same reward, we can regard the rewards as completely substitutable as in Fig. 1B. In this case each of the diagonal lines represents a given overall rate of reinforcement, higher lines corresponding to higher rates. As we pointed out, however, even identically programmed rewards may have actual idiosyncratic nonsubstitutable elements. Thus, there might be a very slight inward bow to the indifference functions. This slight bow would mean nothing when the concurrent ratio schedules differ. To see this, consider what the budget line would be with concurrent ratio schedules. Figure 5A shows such a budget line with one ratio schedule double the other (VR 2 versus VR 4). If the pigeon spent all its time pecking the key corresponding to the lower ratio it would get the food corresponding to point A. Assume now that the pigeon spent all its time pecking at the higher ratio key at the same rate as it pecked on the lower ratio key and that the session duration remained the same. Then it would get the amount of food corresponding to point B and the budget line resulting from various distributions of pecking on the two keys would be A-B. No point on this line is tangent to an indifference curve but point A intercepts the highest

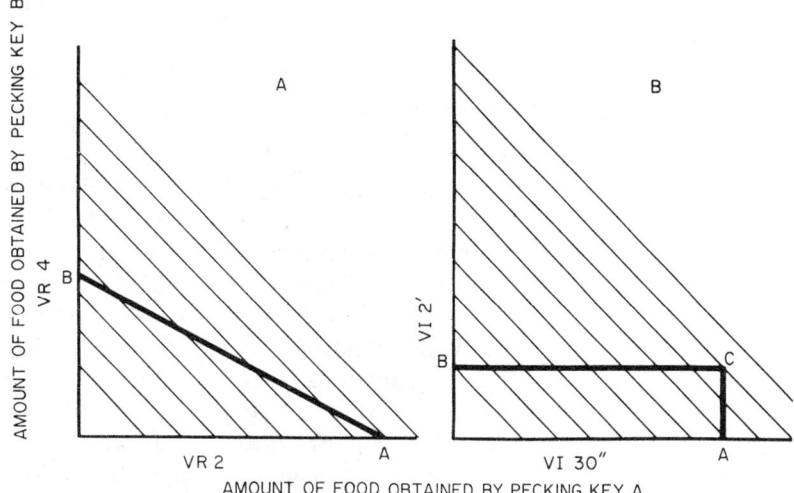

Fig. 5. (A) Budget line with concurrent variable-ratio schedules superimposed on indifference functions. (B) Budget line with concurrent variable-interval schedules superimposed on indifference schedules.

indifference curve. We should therefore expect that the pigeon would prefer point A to all other points and peck only on the lower ratio. If the pigeon pecked at a different rate at the two keys the budget line would be different but the rate on key B would have to be twice that on key A in order to rotate the budget line far enough to reverse key preference. While in certain situations pigeons peck faster with higher ratios (Boren, 1953), they do not generally peck fast enough to get as much food as they would with lower ratios.

When the two ratios are equal the budget line parallels the indifference lines. Here demand theory makes no prediction about choice. The variability of behavior found in Herrnstein and Loveland (1975) with equal VR schedules is explained by the instability of behavior predicted by the theory. Any tilt of the indifference lines such as might be provided by unequal spring tensions of the two keys or any bowing of the indifference lines such as might be provided by different key colors would determine the point on the budget line that maximized reinforcement.

Now let us consider concurrent interval schedules. For simplicity we will assume that the interval schedules are of the Findley-type where the subject switches between one schedule and another by responding on a changeover manipulandum (functionally equivalent to a toggle switch). Reinforcements in either schedule are delivered freely without the necessity of a further response.[6] As with the ratio schedules discussed above, the individual reinforcements provided by the two schedules are identical so there is complete substitutability. The indifference functions again look like those of Fig. 1B. But the budget line for concurrent variable-interval (VI) schedules is not straight. Figure 5B shows a budget line for concurrent Schedule A, variable-interval 30 sec (VI 30″) and Schedule B, variable-interval 2 min (VI 2′). Choosing only Schedule A provides 120 reinforcements per hour. Choosing only Schedule B provides 30 reinforcements per hour. But almost any distribution of time on the two schedules results in reinforcements at the rate of nearly 150 per hour, point C. However, most concurrent schedules are not studied in the simple form illustrated in Fig. 5B. In order to break up idiosyncratic

---

[6] In the more typical type of concurrent schedule reinforcements are dependent on pecks, and the rate of reinforcement will vary (albeit slightly) with the rate of pecking. The Findley-type schedules with free reinforcement that we will consider here would result in the same reinforcement as the more typical schedules if the response rates on the typical schedules were very high. Because results with the two schedules have been similar (Brownstein & Pliskoff, 1968) we assume that they are equivalent.

patterns of switching between manipulanda, a changeover delay is usually added. The changeover delay prevents reinforcement immediately after a switch from one schedule to the other. Figure 6 shows a series of budget lines determined by computer with various changeover delays. The schedules were VI 30" versus VI 2'. The computer, in the role of subject, switched back and forth between the schedules randomly. The relative time spent on the two schedules was varied. On the average the time to switch from A to B and back to A was 20 sec. With different relative times the computer spent different proportions of the 20 sec on A and B. Each point represents the reinforcement rate obtained with a different distribution of time on the two concurrent schedules. The budget lines were fitted to the points by eye. With higher changeover delays the budget lines come to deviate from that of Fig. 5B. As changeover delay increases the maximum obtainable rate of reinforcement decreases. Except with zero changeover delay, the maximum amount of reinforcement is

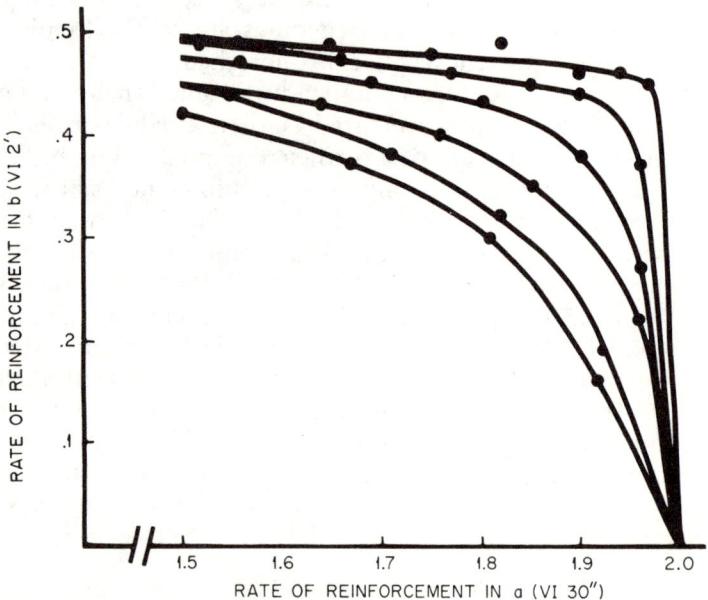

Fig. 6. Budget lines determined by computer for a concurrent VI 30-sec VI 2-min schedule of reinforcement with changeover delays of 0, 2, 4, 6, 8, and 10 sec. Each point represents rate of reinforcement obtained with a different distribution of time spent on the two concurrent schedules. The topmost curve represents the budget line with a changeover delay of 0 sec; the next curve with a changeover delay of 2 sec, then 4, 6, 8 sec; and the bottommost curve is for a changeover delay of 10 sec. All curves were fited to the points by eye.

obtained at a temporal distribution of 80:20 to the VI 30" schedule, exactly the distribution that matches the nominal rates of reinforcement. For example, Table I shows the actual rates of reinforcement obtained with various distributions of time on the two VI schedules for the 2-sec changeover delay condition. The maximum total reinforcement corresponds to a distribution of 80:20. Such matching, a pervasive finding with various organisms exposed to VI schedules (Herrnstein, 1970), is thus explained by demand theory as a maximization of overall rate of reinforcement. Table II presents maxima of Fig. 6, determined graphically by finding points of tangency between the budget lines and the indifference functions. The actual rates of reinforcement at these points were found by interpolation. Although the temporal distribution does not exactly match the distribution of reinforcements thus obtained, the two are about as close as usually obtained with experimental subjects. Of course, it does not require demand theory to assert that reinforcement is maximized. But demand theory focuses our attention on maximization and provides a convenient graphical way (Fig. 6) to determine whether maximization indeed occurs.

This simulation was then repeated with a different pair of concurrent VI schedules (VI 3' and VI 2'). Again, the points were determined at which overall rate of reinforcement was maximized.

TABLE I

REINFORCEMENTS OBTAINED WITH VARIOUS DISTRIBUTIONS OF TIME ON CONCURRENT VARIABLE-INTERVAL 30-SEC, VARIABLE-INTERVAL 2-MIN SCHEDULE[a]

Distribution of time on VI 30":VI 2' schedules	Rate of reinforcement on VI 30" schedule (reinfs./min)	Rate of reinforcement on VI 2' schedule (reinfs./min)	Total rate of reinforcement
100:0	2.00	.00	2.00
90:10	1.96	.37	2.33
80:20	1.90	.44	2.34
70:30	1.85	.45	2.30
60:40	1.77	.46	2.23
50:50	1.66	.47	2.13
40:60	1.52	.49	2.01
30:70	1.39	.49	1.88
20:80	1.18	.49	1.67
10:90	.83	.50	1.33
0:100	.00	.50	.50

[a]Changeover delay = 2 sec (computer simulation).

TABLE II

CONDITIONS AT POINT WHERE TOTAL RATE OF REINFORCEMENT IS MAXIMIZED[a]

Changeover delay (seconds)	Relative time spent in Schedule B	Relative rate of reinforcement obtained [B/(B+A)]
0	.10	.18
2	.15	.17
4	.22	.17
6	.22	.17
8	.19	.15
10	.19	.13

[a]Indifference curves tangent to budget lines of Fig. 6. Schedule A = VI 30″ and Schedule B = VI 2′.

The results were the same. Except for the zero changeover delay condition, overall rate of reinforcement was greatest when the hypothetical subject matched relative rate of responding to relative rate of reinforcement. Figure 7 shows the results for both conditions graphically. The open circles are medians for each condition of the various changeover delays (including zero changeover delay). These circles are the points of maximum overall reinforcement. The graph shows that they also fall on or near the matching line. The two solid points at the ends of the line are also points of maximization, the zero point, trivially, representing all responding on the nonextinction alternative with concurrent VI-extinction schedules and the .5 point representing equal VI schedules, because with equal VI schedules Fig. 6 would be symmetrical about a 45° line drawn from the origin. Imagine Fig. 6 with symmetrical curves. The tangents to the curves must be at the point where the 45° line crosses them. By symmetry with the present results the .6, .8, and 1.0 points must also lie on the matching line. Thus, we have shown, for seven points spread across the range of variation (0, .2, .4, .5, .6, .8, 1.0) that maximization of overall rate of reinforcement also results in matching of relative rate of responding to relative rate of reinforcement.[7]

---

[7] Shimp and associates (Menlove, Moffit & Shimp, 1973) have also explained matching as a form of maximizing but their account was quite different from ours. According to Shimp matching results from maximizing momentary reinforcement of responses where each interchangeover time is considered as a response. Our account is more molar. The exact pattern of changeovers is irrelevant so long as overall reinforcement is maximized.

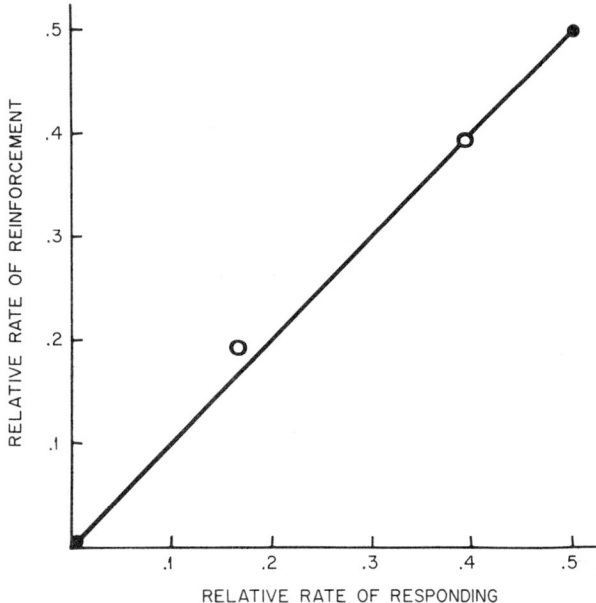

Fig. 7. Matching of relative rate of response to relative rate of reinforcement by computer programmed to maximize overall rates of reinforcement. As the hypothetical subject varied its relative rate of responding, the point was determined at which overall rate of reinforcement was maximum. The open circles are medians for the two conditions (VI 2-min versus VI 30-sec and VI 3-min versus VI 2-min) of the various changeover delays. The two solid points at the ends of the line are theoretical points of maximization.

One of the few psychological theories in which choice among different commodities plays an important part is that of Premack (1965). According to Premack choice between various commodities will predict whether access to one will reinforce access to another. For instance, suppose when choosing freely between several liquids a rat prefers a sugar solution to water. Then, if access to the sugar solution is contingent on drinking water the rat will drink more water (i.e., drinking water will be reinforced by drinking the sugar solution). Premack bases his theory on the notion that each commodity has a certain value as determined by the free-choice experiment, and that relative value of a commodity determines whether one will reinforce the other, the more valuable commodity reinforcing the less valuable. But, in its present form, Premack's theory does not take substitutability into account. For instance, it does not seem unreasonable that milk would be somewhat substitutable, for a rat, for both dry food and water; but we know that dry food and water are relatively unsubstitutable for each other. Suppose a particular rat consumed units of milk to dry food to water in a free-choice test in the ratio 70:20:10. Premack's prediction would be that drinking milk could strongly reinforce both eating dry food (50 units difference) and drinking water (60 units difference) but that eating dry food would only slightly reinforce drinking water (10 units difference). But because eating dry food and drinking water are not substitutable, demand theory would lead one to predict that dry food or water would reinforce each other strongly, whereas drinking milk, being substitutable to some extent for both eating dry food and drinking water, might reinforce either only slightly.

Such a result, if it did occur, might be explainable within Premack's theory by appropriate modifications. For instance, each pair of commodities might be theoretically separable into completely substitutable and completely nonsubstitutable elements. That is, degree of substitutability might be treated as a statistical artifact of the combination of the two extremes. Figure 1A would result from the combination of so many elements of Fig. 1B and so many of Fig. 1C. The substitutable elements could then be treated as equivalent and incapable of entering into a reinforcement relationship while Premack's theory, as it now stands, would account for relations between unsubstitutable elements only. As a crude attempt at such modification, let us assume that with a given (standard) budget line and a given set of indifference functions, a subject chooses the bundle at point C in Fig. 2B. A measure of substitutability might be the percentage of shift of C' from C in Figs. 2C and 2D as the budget line was rotated. Zero percent shift of C' from C toward A' would mean that none of the elements of the commodities were substitutable, 100% shift of point C', all the way to A', would mean that all of the elements of the commodities were substitutable; 50% shift, that half were substitutable and half, not, etc.

Now suppose, to take exaggerated values, the shift (of C' from C to A') with dry food and milk was 90%; with dry food and water, 1%; with milk and water, 90%. To calculate the power of one commodity to reinforce another we would have to consider nonsubstitutable units only. Thus when comparing milk and dry food in the free-choice test only 10% of the 70 units of milk actually consumed (7 units) and 10% of the 20 units of dry food actually consumed (2 units) should be compared in predicting milk—dry food reinforcement relationships. The difference is now 5 units instead of 50 units. Similarly, with milk and water, the difference would be 6 units instead of 60 units. But with dry food and water, 99% of the units are nonsubstitutable so the difference would be 9.9 instead of 10 units providing the strongest reinforcement relation.

As we indicated, this analysis is crude. A more sophisticated analysis might treat substitutability in terms of the ratio of common and unique aspects of Tversky's (1972) elimination-by-aspects theory.

We do not mean to say that "value" and substitutability exhaust all the factors that determine choice. We know that the assumptions of demand theory, especially transitivity, are often violated. But demand theory is formulated well enough so that violations come to light clearly. Psychologists might tend to attribute all food–water choice behavior to strong biological interactions between two needs. But there is a certain amount of substitutability in food–water choice. Demand theory allows us to separate the part that is biological from the part that is economic (or "rational").

Economic demand theory also has applications within the fields of ecology, ethology, and the biological sciences. Covich (1972) has used the concept of indifference curves to compare seed consumption between two species of mice. When pumpkin seed became scarce and sunflower seed abundant, both deer mice and beach mice increased consumption of the sunflower seed. However, when sunflower seed was scarce, the two species differed considerably in their consumption patterns. Deer mice showed substitution of pumpkin for sunflower seed, while beach mice, in fact, decreased consumption of now abundant pumpkin seed and increased consumption of the now scarce sunflower seed. Although such a result appears at variance with that predicted by demand theory, it does direct attention to variables that might previously have been neglected. Whether the result is due to inherent differences between the species or to different types of shifts in the budget lines themselves for the two species is a question that obviously requires further research. But an analysis based on demand theory focuses attention on the relationship between an organism and its environment and allows for testable hypotheses.

An indifference curve analysis has also been presented by Rapport (1971) in discussing a predator's selection of its optimal prey combination. Time is an important factor in such a model due to search time, capturing, and handling of the prey. The budget line is bounded by the quantity of prey species A and prey species B which the predictor can consume in a given time period. In the present series of experiments, time was not an important variable. However, both approaches make similar predictions and lead to similar conclusions.

Finally, we disclaim any attempt to enumerate all possible applications of economics in psychology. We have even ignored the logical sister of demand theory, exchange theory (Newman, 1965), and its many potential applications in social psychology (Rapoport, 1973). We have ignored the relationship between experiments in delay of reinforcement and commitment (Rachlin & Green, 1972) with economic theories about discount functions and how interest rates are determined. The potential areas of overlap between economics and psychology are too numerous to discuss fully here (see Castro & Weingarten, 1970, for an outline). Our purpose has been only to illustrate the ways in which a more complete interaction may be beneficial to both disciplines.

V. Summary

The relationship between psychology and economic demand theory was explored. Using economic concepts of budget lines, indifference curves, and substitutability, two series of experiments were conducted involving rats' choices between two *different* commodities. Consumption of the commodities changed as changes were introduced into the budget set—the rats consumed more of the lower priced commodity and less of the higher priced commodity. Large substitution effects were obtained when the choice was between nonessential commodities (root beer versus Tom Collins mix). When choice was between essential commodities (food versus water) some substitution was observed along with severe disruptions in behavior as relative prices were changed markedly. It was also shown how behavior on various schedules of reinforcement could be analyzed within the framework of economic demand theory. Through computer simulation, we found that maximization of overall rate of reinforcement results in matching of relative rate of responding to relative rate of reinforcement. Finally, we showed how demand theory could aid in separating substitutable from nonsubstitutable elements so as to better estimate reinforcement relationships according to Premack's theory of reinforcement.

REFERENCES

Boren, J. J. Response rate and resistance to extinction as functions of the fixed ratio. Unpublished doctoral dissertation, Columbia University, 1953.

Brenner, M. A. *Mental illness and the economy.* Cambridge: Harvard University Press, 1973.

Brownstein, A. J., & Pliskoff, S. S. Some effects of relative reinforcement rate and changeover delay in response-independent concurrent schedules of reinforcement. *Journal of the Experimental Analysis of Behavior,* 1968, **11**, 683–688.

Castro, B., & Weingarten, K. Toward experimental economics. *Journal of Political Economy,* 1970, **78**, 598–607.

Catania, A. C. Concurrent performances: Reinforcement interaction and response independence. *Journal of the Experimental Analysis of Behavior,* 1963, **6**, 253–263.

Covich, A. Ecological economics of seed consumption by *Peromyscus:* a graphical model of resource substitution. *Transactions of the Connecticut Academy of Arts and Sciences,* 1972, **44**, 71–93.

Dublin, L. I. *Suicide: a sociological and statistical study.* New York: Ronald Press, 1963.

Green, L., & Rachlin, H. Economic and biological influences on a pigeon's key peck. *Journal of the Experimental Analysis of Behavior,* 1975, **23**, 55–62.

Hamermesh, D. S., & Soss, N. M. An economic theory of suicide. *Journal of Political Economy,* 1974, **82**, 83–98.

Henry, A. F., & Short, J. F., Jr. *Suicide and homicide: Some economic, sociological and psychological aspects of aggression.* Glencoe, Illinois: The Free Press, 1954.

Herrnstein, R. J. Some factors influencing behavior in a two-response situation. *Transactions of the New York Academy of Sciences,* 1958, **21**, 35–45.

Herrnstein, R. J. On the law of effect. *Journal of the Experimental Analysis of Behavior,* 1970, **13**, 243–266.

Herrstein, R. J., & Loveland, D. Maximizing and matching on concurrent ratio schedules. *Journal of Experimental Analysis of Behavior,* 1975, **24**, 107–117.

Hollard, V., & Davison, M. C. Preference for qualitatively different reinforcers. *Journal of the Experimental Analysis of Behavior,* 1971, **16**, 375–380.

Kagel, J. H., Battalio, R. C., Rachlin, H., Green, L., Basmann, R. L., & Klemm, W. R. Experimental studies of consumer demand behavior using laboratory animals. *Economic Inquiry,* 1975, **13**, 22–38.

Lewinsohn, P. M. A behavioral approach to depression, In R. J. Friedman & M. M. Katz (Eds.), *The psychology of depression: comtemporary theory and research.* Washington, D.C.: Winston, 1974.

Luce, R. D. *Individual choice behavior: A theoretical analysis.* New York: Wiley, 1959.

Menlove, R. L., Moffitt, R. L., & Shimp, C. P. Choice between concurrent schedules. *Journal of the Experimental Analysis of Behavior,* 1973, **19**, 331–344.

Navarick, D. J., & Fantino, E. Stochastic transitivity and unidimentional behavior theories. *Psychological Review,* 1974, **81**, 426–441.

Newman, P. *The theory of exchange.* Englewood Cliffs, N.J.: Prentice-Hall, 1965.

Premack, D. Reinforcement theory. In D. Levine (Ed.), *Nebraska Symposium on Motivation,* Vol. 13. Lincoln: University of Nebraska Press, 1965.

Rachlin, H. Contrast and matching. *Psychological Review,* 1973, **80**, 217–234.

Rachlin, H., & Green, L. Commitment, choice and self-control. *Journal of the Experimental Analysis of Behavior,* 1972, **17**, 15–22.

Rapoport, A. *Experimental games and their uses in psychology.* Morristown, N.J.: General Learning Corp., 1973.

Rapport, D. J. An optimization model of food selection. *The American Naturalist,* 1971, **105**, 575–587.

Samuelson, P. A. *Economics: an introductory analysis,* 9th Ed. New York: McGraw-Hill, 1973.

Skinner, B. F. *Science and human behavior.* New York: MacMillan, 1953.

Staddon, J. E. R., & Simmelhag, V. L. The "superstition" experiment: a reexamination of its implications for the principles of adaptive behavior. *Psychological Review,* 1971, **78,** 3–43.

Tversky, A. Elimination by aspects: A theory of choice. *Psychological Review,* 1972, **79,** 281–299.

von Neumann, T., & Morgenstern, O. *Theory of games and economic behavior,* 2nd Ed. Princeton, N.J.: Princeton University Press, 1947.

Young, P. T. *Motivation and emotion.* New York: Wiley, 1961.

SELF-PUNITIVE BEHAVIOR

K. Edward Renner[1] and Jeanne B. Tinsley

UNIVERSITY OF ILLINOIS, CHAMPAIGN, ILLINOIS

I.	Introduction	156
	A. The Neurotic Paradox	156
	B. Early Learning Theory	156
	C. The Law of Effect	157
II.	Self-Punitive Behavior	157
	A. The Contribution of Judson Brown	157
	B. Description of the Empirical Effect	158
	C. Theoretical Accounts	158
	D. Issues and Problems	160
III.	Experimental Evaluation of the Discrimination-Expectancy Account	161
	A. Changes between Acquisition and Extinction	161
	B. Inferences of Preference and Choice	166
	C. Disrupting Self-Punitive Behavior	174
IV.	Effect of the Punishment	176
	A. Measurement Artifact Controversy	176
	B. Methodological Issues	178
	C. Prepunishment Data	178
V.	Empirical Constraints	183
	A. Abruptness of PE Extinction	184
	B. Response Style	185
	C. Intensity of Fear and Postshock Emotionality	186
	D. Goal Box Cues	188
VI.	Conclusions	188
	A. The Nature of Self-Punitive Behavior	188
	B. Active and Passive Views of the Subject	189
	C. Parallel Experiments with Humans and Rats	190
VII.	Implications for Punishment Theory and Research	190
	A. Value Learning	191
	B. Contingency Learning	191
	C. Response Selection as a Central State	192
	D. Similarity with Appetitive Processes	192
VIII.	Generalizations	194
	A. Disorders of Contingency—Confusion	194

[1] Present address: Department of Psychology, Dalhousie University, Halifax, Nova Scotia, Canada.

B. Disorders of Values—Motivation	194
C. The Case of Masochism	195
References	196

I. Introduction

It is a common clinical observation that people sometimes behave in self-defeating and self-punitive ways. When such behavior persists in the face of good advice and counsel, the person may be thought to be neurotic. A satisfactory psychological explanation for such behavior has remained elusive despite preoccupying nearly every major theory of psychopathology. Freud (1920) could not find any way out of the problem except through the postulation of a death instinct. Although his concept of a death instinct has never been generally accepted (Jones, 1957), a clearly more convincing alternative has not been forthcoming.

A. THE NEUROTIC PARADOX

Self-defeating and self-punitive behavior is paradoxical for psycological theory because it violates the article of faith that organisms should repeat those behaviors which result in positive outcomes and avoid or relinquish those which result in negative outcomes. Indeed, much of experimental psychology has been devoted to exploring the selective pressure of the consequences of one's actions on future behavior. If, in fact, it can be clearly shown that organisms sometimes behave in self-defeating and self-punitive ways, then this is as much a problem for experimental psychology as it is for abnormal psychology.

B. EARLY LEARNING THEORY

1. The Mowrer–Brown Finding

The serious efforts in the 1940's and 1950's to bridge the gap between experimental psychology and psychoanalytic theory led to the logical and experimental analysis of clinical phenomena. Mowrer (1947) reported an experimental analog of self-punitive behavior which had been observed by Judson Brown. Rats initially trained to avoid shock persisted in making the avoidance response even though it was now punished. Thus, the reality of self-punitive behavior was demonstrated and a theoretical challenge confronted experimental psychology.

2. Two-Factor Theory

A solution to the challenge was provided by two-factor theory (Mowrer, 1947). According to this theory, motivation for responding was provided by classically conditioned fear. The instrumental escape response was reinforced by the reduction or termination of the fear. When the instrumental response also produced the punishment, the effect was to maintain the fear, which in turn elicited the response that was reinforced through fear reduction. Two-factor theory provided an explanation of how self-punitive behavior could exist, although the proposal was neither subjected to experimental analysis nor was its generality to the clinical situation explored.

C. THE LAW OF EFFECT

The Mowrer–Brown contribution, although only a passing note in 1947, illustrates how the law of effect dominates psychological theory. By the law of effect we are referring only to the enhancement of behavior through reward, and the suppression of behavior through punishment without reference to the processes whereby the law operates. Such an analysis has been a topic of continued research throughout the history of experimental psychology. Thus, the problem is how to reconcile apparent natural or experimental contradictions with the assumptions of the empirical law of effect. Psychology has not been ready, with Freud, to go "Beyond the Pleasure Principle." If self-punitive behavior exists, psychological theory requires there to be an explanation which does not contradict the law of effect. The nature of this explanation with respect to self-punitive behavior will be the focus of this chapter.

II. Self-Punitive Behavior

A. THE CONTRIBUTION OF JUDSON BROWN

In the last decade, Judson Brown has effectively reintroduced the question of self-punitive behavior into experimental psychology. His first contribution was to provide a paradigm for the study of self-punitive behavior in the experimental laboratory, thereby eliminating the need to accept only a vague clinical description of the phenomenon (Brown, Martin, & Morrow, 1964). Second, he has pointed to the paradoxical or counterintuitive nature of the findings (e.g., Brown, Beier, & Lewis, 1971) and in so doing has generated an active research interest in obtaining a detailed experimental analysis and a thorough theoretical formulation of the phenomenon (Brown, 1969; Melvin, 1971). Third, he has raised the issue of the generality of the experimental work for human behavior as it is seen clinically (Brown, 1965), thus acknowledging the early origins of the problem.

B. DESCRIPTION OF THE EMPIRICAL EFFECT

Self-punitive behavior is the name given to a specific empirical finding which can be outlined as follows. During acquisition a rat is dropped onto the start area of a runway which has an electrified grid floor. The animal must learn to run the length of the runway to a safe goal area in order to escape the shock. Once this response has been learned, the experimenter turns off the shock in all but the middle part of the runway. If the subject continues to run it must cross the section containing shock to reach the goal box, thereby shocking itself, thus the name self-punitive. Most rats will do this for many trials, in contrast to control subjects which are given nonpunished extinction; these animals slow down and soon meet an arbitrary criterion.

The empirical finding is not limited to rats. Similar data have been obtained using human subjects (Dreyer & Renner, 1971). In the human counterpart, subjects press a telegraph key which advances a numerical readout screen until an arbitrary number is reached which is defined as the end. During acquisition trials key pressing results in escape from shock. Later, similar to the procedure used with rats, it is the key pressing itself which turns on the shock. Punished subjects persist in key pressing; nonpunished subjects do not. From a functional standpoint the human subjects, like the rats, shock themselves.

C. THEORETICAL ACCOUNTS

The question is how self-punitive behavior is to be conceptualized and reconciled with general punishment theory and research. Using past research on incentive motivation (Renner, 1967, 1972) as a basis for theorizing, we found we had a unique view of self-punitive behavior (e.g., Dreyer & Renner, 1971; Tinsley & Renner, 1975) which was quite different from the currently accepted vicious circle of fear explanation (e.g., Brown, 1969). To test our notions, we conducted a series of experiments, the results of which led us to question the need for theoretical distinctions between appetitive and aversive motivational systems, and whether classical and instrumental conditioning has a meaningful correspondence with the internal psychological processes of the organism. The details of our position must emerge from the data, but it may be useful at the outset to outline the general features of our discrimination-expectancy account and of the vicious circle of fear account which will provide a counterpoint for our analysis.

1. Discrimination-Expectancy

Our discrimination-expectancy account conceptualizes behavior in terms of two separate psychological processes. The first, a contingency process, reflects the acquisition of information about the relationship between situations, outcomes, and behaviors. The second, a value process, refers to the relative degree of desirability or aversiveness of outcomes.

We assume that the subject learns about response-outcome contingencies and, as part of this process, the subject has expectations about the outcomes associated with particular responses. Response selection occurs in accordance with these expectations and their anticipated value so as to obtain the most favorable outcome.

Self-punitive behavior is explained in terms of the specific contingency information acquired by the subject as a result of the self-punitive procedure. In acquisition, the subject learns the shock is painful (value information) and that the shock may be escaped by responding, but the consequence of nonresponding is continued punishment (contingency information). In extinction, the contingency relationships are altered and the two groups have different experiences and learn different things.

For subjects receiving the nonpunished extinction procedure, the old response-outcome contingencies are readily disconfirmed because the shock is no longer present. For subjects receiving punishment, shock and subsequent escape continue to be contigent upon running, while shock avoidance is contingent upon not running. The punished subjects continue to run during extinction because this change in the response-outcome contingencies between acquisition and extinction has not been discriminated. To discover the new response-outcome contingency that not responding is not punished, the subject must first fail to respond. Since the original expectancy that continuous shock is contingent upon not responding is still intact, the new outcome is effectively outside the range of response variation and hence no change in behavior will be observed.

Thus, self-punitive running as seen in the comparison of a punished extinction (PE) procedure to a nonpunished or regular extinction (RE) procedure is conceptualized as a discrimination-expectancy problem. The punishment used in extinction produces the empirical effect by preventing new contingency learning in the punished but not in the nonpunished extinction condition.

2. Vicious Circle of Fear

An alternative explanation is based upon the concept of a vicious circle of fear. In this account, it is asserted that during punished extinction the animal leaves the now safe start region because historically it has been associated with pain and fear. The pain the rat encounters in the runway sustains the fear. Entry into the goal box reduces the pain and the fear, reinforcing the running response. Alley fear then generalizes to the start area and the vicious circle is complete. This account (Brown, 1969) extends Mowrer's original version by explicitly including a generalization process, and it has been widely applied as an explanation of self-punitive behavior. The animal runs from the start area to escape fear and in so doing brings about the conditions that maintain fear of this area (e.g., Siegel, Melvin, & Wagner, 1971).

D. ISSUES AND PROBLEMS

The basic empirical self-punitive effect provides a forum to explore general conceptual issues of punishment theory and research. The main theme of this chapter will be to reassert a version of the law of effect which is not challenged by self-punitive behavior. A secondary theme will be to contrast the application of our discrimination-expectancy account with the currently more widely accepted account based on a vicious circle of fear.

We have conducted a series of self-punitive experiments for the purpose of determining the limits of our theoretical position (Section III). A second line of research is directed at methodological problems having a direct bearing on the theoretical issues under consideration (Section IV). In addition, there are a number of empirical features of self-punitive behavior, beyond running into shock, which have theoretical importance (Section V). These three parts constitute our analysis of self-punitive behavior and provide a basis for our conclusions (Section VI), the theoretical interpretations of our findings (Section VII), and a reanalysis of the neurotic paradox (Section VIII).

III. Experimental Evaluation of the Discrimination-Expectancy Account

A. CHANGES BETWEEN ACQUISITION AND EXTINCTION

Our discrimination-expectancy account simply asserts that it is the contingencies concerning the occurrence or nonoccurrence of shock that are the essential factors to be discriminated (Dreyer & Renner, 1971). Specifically, if the percentage or intensity of punishment is increased from acquisition to extinction, the subject may discriminate that it is now getting shock more frequently or more strongly but it may continue to respond because it is unaware that its own behavior produces the punishment. Until the subject is able to discriminate that it is no longer appropriate to respond to the fear situation with escape behavior, responding should continue. Tinsley & Renner (1975) tested this discrimination-expectancy interpretation in a design using human subjects in which the schedule of punishment was changed between acquisition and extinction.

1. Schedules of Punishment

a. Procedure. Human subjects were seated before a numerical readout screen. At the start of each trial the experimenter said "get ready" over an intercom, then the number 00 appeared on the screen, a buzzer sounded for 1 sec, and the subject was given a pulsating shock to the nondominant hand. Pressing a telegraph key advanced the numbers on the screen, and after 60 presses the shock was terminated.

During the 10 acquisition trials, half of the subjects were shocked on 100% and half on 50% of the trials. For extinction, one third of both groups were placed in a regular extinction condition in which the shock was turned off. The remaining groups encountered shock on either 100% or 50% of the eight extinction trials. After the eight extinction trials, all punished extinction subjects who were still key pressing (thereby shocking themselves) were informed as to the contingencies affecting the shock and given one additional trial. The subjects then filled out questionnaires to determine if they were able to discriminate the change in the percentage of shocked trials.

The expectation was that although subjects could discriminate the change in percentage of shock between acquisition and extinction this would not influence the occurrence of self-punitive responding. The critical discrimination for determining whether or not the subject responds is information regarding the response-outcome contingencies, not information about the percentage of shock trials.

b. The Self-Punitive Effect. Figure 1 presents speed data for the 100% shock acquisition subjects and Fig. 2 presents these same data for subjects shocked on 50% of the acquisition trials. As is clear from both figures, there are large group differences between the punished

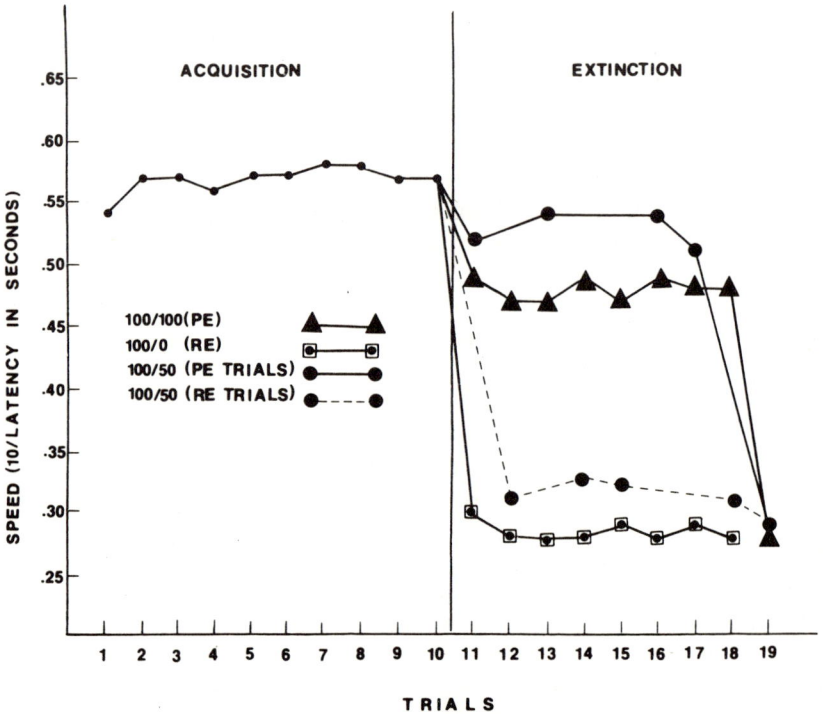

Fig. 1. Speed with which 60 telegraph key presses were completed for the ten acquisition and eight extinction trials for the regular extinction (RE) and punished extinction (PE) groups which received 100% shock during acquisition. The two PE groups were given a nineteenth trial after they were informed that it was their initial key press which turned on the shock. The 40-sec limit on each trial imposed a lower boundary of .25 on the speed score.

and regular extinction conditions. Punished extinction subjects shock themselves by continuing to respond regardless of what shock percentage condition they are in. Regular extinction subjects typically respond on each trial with a few key presses but soon stop since no shock is present. Punished subjects who are shocked on 50% of the extinction trials begin pressing, but like regular extinction subjects, stop when it is clear there will be no shock on that particular trial. On shock trials the 50% punishment subjects respond like the subjects who received 100% punishment.

  c. *Discrimination of Schedules.* On the postexperimental questionnaire, subjects were asked whether shock had been present on all, some, or none of the first 10 trials of the experiment. They were also asked the same question concerning the extinction trials. Subjects

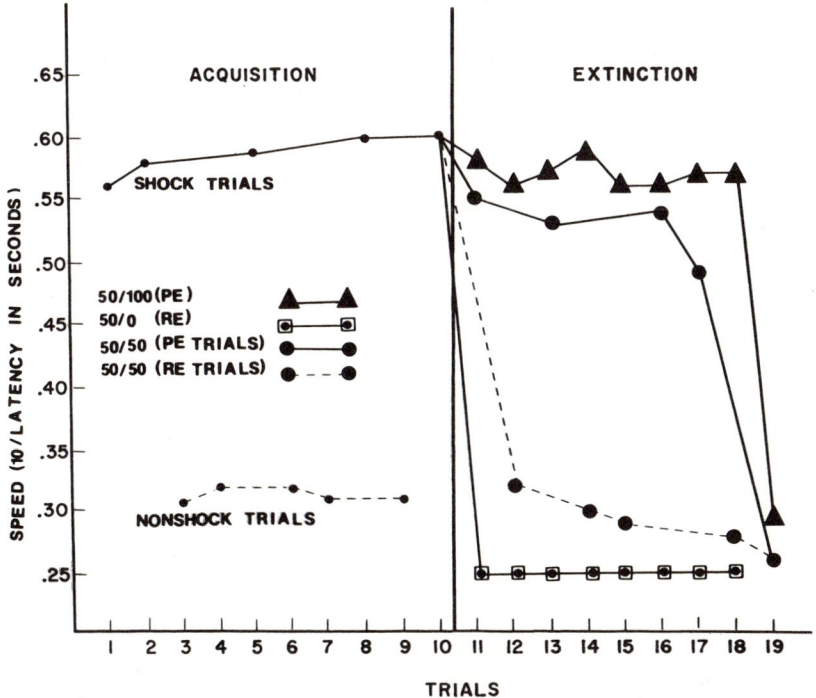

Fig. 2. Speed with which 60 telegraph key presses were completed for the ten acquisition and eight extinction trials for the regular extinction (RE) and punished extinction (PE) groups which received 50% shock during acquisition. The two PE groups were given a nineteenth trial after they were informed that it was their initial key press which turned on the shock. The 40-sec limit on each trial imposed a lower boundary of .25 on the speed score.

were able to correctly identify their experimental condition and discriminate what change, if any, had occurred between acquisition and extinction. Yet, this ability to discriminate the change between acquisition and extinction had no effect on the self-punitive phenomenon.

  d. *Discrimination of Contingencies.* Self-punitive key pressing in the punished extinction groups was allowed to continue through trial 18 at which time subjects still pressing were informed of the actual contingencies affecting the occurrence of the shock. On trial 19 when all punished extinction subjects were aware of the contingencies their data are indistinguishable from that obtained in regular extinction (see Figs. 1 and 2). Unless the subject is aware of (i.e., has discriminated) the response-outcome contingencies affecting the occurrence or nonoccurrence of the shock, key pressing and hence self-punitive behavior continues.

The standard self-punitive phenomenon usually obtained with rats was reproduced with human subjects. Therefore, the reliability of the phenomenon is not at issue, but rather the appropriate interpretation.

2. *The Concept of Discrimination*

Judson Brown (Brown *et al.,* 1964) had earlier proposed a different version of the discrimination hypothesis as a possible explanation, but rejected it (e.g., Brown, 1969) in favor of the vicious circle of fear account. He interpreted a discrimination process as requiring that the greater the similarity between the conditions of acquisition and extinction, the greater should be the resistance to extinction. If the conditions of extinction are not discriminated as being qualitatively different from those of acquisition, behavior appropriate to acquisition will be reinstated (Church, 1963). Thus, for Brown (1969) experiments in which there is a change between acquisition and extinction offer a direct test of this proposition. The discrimination hypothesis was found to be inadequate in part because of the results of one such study by Melvin (1964) on schedules of punishment.

Melvin used the basic self-punitive procedure except that during acquisition different groups of rats were shocked on 33%, 67%, or 100% of the trials. When some of the animals in the 33% and 67% groups were shifted to 100% schedules during punished extinction, they extinguished less rapidly than those groups kept on their original schedules. Melvin cites these findings as evidence against a discrimination hypothesis because rats which experience the greatest change in conditions between acquisition and extinction (33%/100% group) take longer to reach extinction than the rats which have no change whatever (33%/33% group).

We have just described with humans results similar to the animal study in question (Melvin, 1964), so the empirical facts are not disputed. At issue is the appropriate application of the concept of discrimination. Brown and Melvin have a definition of discrimination which is based on a generalization-decrement notion, and hence any stimulus change from acquisition to extinction should weaken the probability of the stimulus situation eliciting the associated response.

Our discrimination-expectancy account classifies behavior into different conceptual units than does the generalization notion. In our interpretation, discrimination can refer to either changes in the percentage or intensity of shock which influence its aversiveness, or to contingency processes, such as the relationship of outcomes to the alternative behaviors. Our use of the concept of discrimination does not imply that all changes between acquisition and extinction will result in faster extinction. In most learning situations it is possible to envision some change which, if discriminated, would retard rather than facilitate extinction. In the case of self-punitive behavior, if the subject learns that shock is present on an even greater percentage of trials than it was previously, one effect of the punishment might be to augment (i.e., reinstate) the highly specific escape response learned during acquisition.

Being able to recognize—as our subjects are—that the number of shock trials has increased or decreased does not bear on the issue of whether the subject will or will not respond in punished extinction. The discrimination of changes in the percentage of shock is irrelevant in that it gives subjects no information which might aid in redefining the original situation from one of active escape to one of passive avoidance. The critical discrimination in this case is quite specific and should not be facilitated by any manner of change between acquisition and extinction. The differences which the subject must detect are those which relate specifically to the contingencies which govern the occurrence of the shock.

In a similar fashion, self-punitive studies which shift or change shock intensity (Beecroft, Bouska, & Fisher, 1967; Melvin & Bender, 1968) or percentage (Beecroft, Fisher, & Bouska, 1967; Martin & Moon, 1968; Melvin, 1964) between acquisition and extinction do not offer an adequate test of the discrimination-expectancy hypothesis, since they provide no information specific to the response-outcome contingencies. Any facilitating effect such shifts might have would be indirect, by contributing to a change in the range of response variation.

Brown has criticized both the generalization version (Brown, 1969) and a contingency version (Crowell, Brown, & Lewis, 1972) of a discrimination explanation for being circular because discrimination can be demonstrated to have occurred only when the subject stops responding, and if the subject continues to respond discrimination, by definition, has not occurred. The same problem however, applies to the vicious circle explanation because fear is used to explain running, while running is itself taken as evidence of fear (Klare, 1974). For our discrimination-expectancy explanation the problem may be resolved by independently showing that as long as punished extinction subjects continue to respond they have not discriminated the change, yet once the discrimination is made, extinction occurs. In our study, as well as the one by Dreyer and Renner (1971), immediate extinction occurred with few exceptions when subjects were informed of the contingencies affecting the shock. This criticism can be discounted with respect to the response-outcome discrimination process.

B. INFERENCES OF PREFERENCE AND CHOICE

Perhaps the most important but confused issue in the area of self-punitive research is that the subject appears to be behaving in a paradoxical and stupid fashion. This perception is given tacit support through the use of the very term *self*-punitive, which implies that it is a deliberate, conscious, self-inflicted, self-controlled act.

The subject cannot be represented as choosing punishment over nonpunishment if the outcome the subject is supposedly rejecting is unknown. For example, if a rat were trained in a T-maze with one pellet on the right and nothing on the left, the rat would soon repeatedly choose the right side. If then, unknown to the rat, 10 pellets were put on the left and if the rat was observed to turn to the one pellet on the right, we would not be justified in saying that the rat chose one pellet over ten and therefore preferred one rather than ten pellets. Unknown and new contingencies which are outside the range of response variation, and thus not sampled, cannot be taken as elements of choice. In the case of self-punitive behavior, new expectancies must be acquired, and if the necessary information about the new contingencies cannot be acquired, then the subject has no logical reason to alter its behavior; and likewise, the experimenter has no logical basis on which to infer choice or preference with respect to the unknown outcome.

We have recently conducted two experiments which examine the role of choice by providing a nonpunished response alternative within the self-punitive situation. Both studies—the first with rats and the second with humans—support the assertion that when subjects are given a meaningful choice they neither choose nor prefer the punished alternative, although they will still show self-punitive responding. The results of both experiments also support the assertion that is the failure of the punished subjects to discriminate the new contingency associated with nonresponding that accounts for self-punitive persistence, and that extinction is dependent upon the acquisition of this contingency information. Consider first the animal experiment.

1. Animal Preference Experiment

a. Procedure. During acquisition, shock was present in two parallel alleys which opened off of a common start area. Subjects had some forced trials to each side and on other trials both runways were open and either could be chosen as a means of escape. During extinction one alley was designated as the punished extinction condition (PE) and the other as the regular extinction condition (RE). During acquisition and extinction free choice trials were followed by forced trials to the opposite sides thus maintaining equal exposure to both alleys.

Speed scores were used as the measure of performance. There was a 40-sec time limit for each trial and six consecutive 40-sec trials defined the extinction criterion. Six consecutive choices of the same side defined a preference criterion, and the first trial on which this criterion was achieved was taken as the beginning of preference. Extinction for PE and for RE was defined as the first 40-sec trial on which the subject never again responded to that alternative (i.e., thereafter always had a 40-sec criterion score for that alternative).

We wished to create a situation in which responding would continue long enough for a preference between the punished and nonpunished alternatives to be observed. We expected evidence of a self-punitive response but not a preference for punishment over nonpunishment.

b. Preference. Three subjects met the extinction criterion and therefore had no preference. The performance of these subjects was not relevant to the present problem since what is at issue is the relationship between preference and persistence during self-punitive responding, not the conditions of extinction. Sixteen subjects provided useful speed and preference data. Eleven of the 16 subjects met the preference criterion of six consecutive choices of one side. All 11 preferred the nonpunished alternative over the punished alternative. The emergence of this preference over trials is shown in Fig. 3, along with the choice data of the five subjects which did not achieve the preference criterion. No subjects preferred the punished (PE) over the nonpunished (RE) side.

c. *The Self-Punitive Effect.* The 11 subjects who developed a preference for the nonpunished alternative showed the standard self-punitive effect before the preference emerged ($p = .02$). As the preference emerged, the speed scores reversed ($p = .002$), reflecting a suppressive effect of punishment, and nine of the ten subjects completely stopped responding in the punished extinction alternative. This refusal to respond in the punished extinction alley only later extended to the regular extinction alley in the form of slower speeds, and eventually four of the ten subjects stopped responding there also. The relevant speed data before, during, and after the preference criterion are shown in Fig. 4. The five subjects without a preference persisted in both alleys, failing to meet any of the extinction or preference criteria.

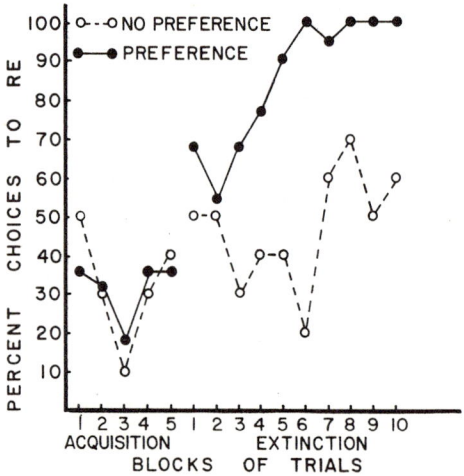

Fig. 3. Percentage of choices to the nonshock side over the five blocks of acquisition and 10 blocks of extinctions trials by the 11 subjects which did and the five subjects which did not meet the preference criterion of six consecutive choices of the same alternative.

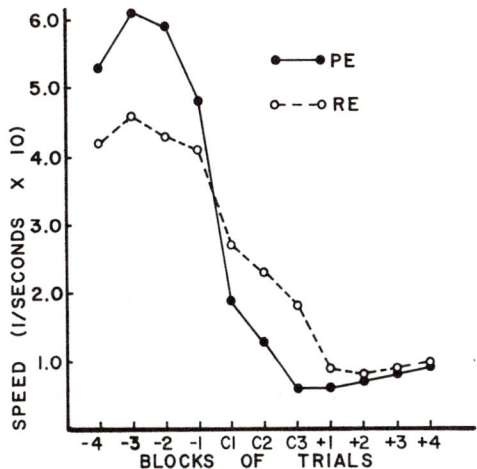

Fig. 4. Speed scores on the punished extinction (PE) and regular extinction (RE) alternatives. The standard self-punitive effect is demonstrated in the four trial blocks preceding criterion; the effect is reversed during the three blocks of trials on which the preference criterion is met, and these group differences continue at a reduced level for the four blocks following criterion.

2. Human Preference Experiment

a. Procedure. A similar experiment was carried out using human subjects. During acquisition, two telegraph keys provided the subjects with two equally salient escape routes. During acquisition it made no difference which key was used as both performed the identical function of providing escape from shock. During extinction, the contingencies were changed. One key now became a punished alternative where punishment was contingent upon responding, and the other key became an extinction (nonpunished) alternative. Choice and forced trials were given, and subjects could thus be observed under punished extinction, regular extinction, and on trials necessitating a choice between the two alternatives.

Acquisition was composed of three choice trials and two forced trials, one to each side. During extinction, the preferred key was made the punished alternative and the other key the nonpunished alternative. The 30 extinction trials were composed of five blocks of six trials, each block having both forced and choice trials. At the end of each block all subjects had equal exposure to both alternatives.

The time required for 50 key presses was recorded for each trial. The time limit on all trials was 20 sec and the extinction criterion was six consecutive 20-sec trials. The percentage of free choices to the nonpunished side provided the preference measure. Subjects filled out a questionnaire to determine whether they had learned that one key did not shock them

Self-punitive behavior was expected when only the punished extinction alternative was available, but a preference for the punished alternative was not anticipated.

b. Preference. Three subjects extinguished, leaving 21 subjects who failed to meet the extinction criterion within the 30-trial limit, thus giving the desired preference and speed data. On the basis of the questionnaire data, 10 of these 21 subjects were classified as being aware of the contingencies. Nine of the ten subjects (*a*) checked "yes" they had a preference; (*b*) indicated which key they preferred; and (*c*) when asked why they preferred a certain key wrote such responses as "no shock was associated with key A," "didn't receive shock," "that was the key I didn't get shocked from" or some equivalent version. These subjects verbalized, i.e., were aware of, the different conditions of the two keys. The tenth aware subject stated the actual punished extinction contingency: "If I didn't press a key I didn't get shocked."

On the final acquisition trial there were, as expected, no differences in the choices of the aware and unaware subjects, yet over the course of extinction all but one of the aware subjects developed a preference for the nonpunished key. The unaware subjects as a group neither reported the contingencies accurately nor developed a preference for the nonpunished key (see Fig. 5).

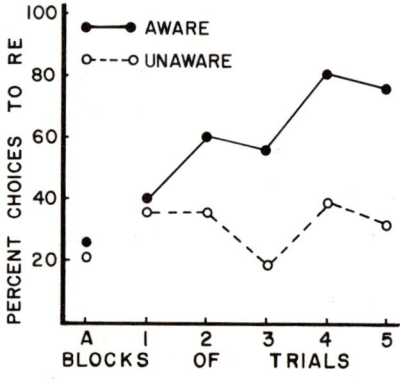

Fig. 5. Percentage of choices to the nonshock side over the five blocks of extinction trials by the 11 subjects who were aware and the 10 subjects who were not aware that one key was always shocked and the other key was never shocked.

At the start of extinction subjects had no reason beyond position bias or an erroneous hypothesis to prefer one key over the other. When the new contingencies were introduced the subject without knowing it was placed in a new problem-solving situation where new information about the relationship between the two keys and their new outcomes of either punishment or nonpunishment could be learned. Once this learning occurs, the subject's choice becomes psychologically meaningful and may be taken as unequivocal evidence that punishment is not preferred, even though (as discussed below) self-punitive responses are made when only the punished key is available. Thus, a self-punitive response in and of itself cannot be taken as evidence for choice or preference.

c. The Self-Punitive Effect. The standard self-punitive effect was obtained regardless of whether or not subjects were aware of the fact that one key was shocked (PE) and the other was not (RE) as is shown in Fig. 6. There is no significant effect due to awareness, but there is a significant difference between PE and RE conditions ($p < .001$). The self-punitive effect has been reproduced and the two-key procedure has not destroyed the phenomenon in question. The so-called self-punitive effect is present because there is an important conceptual and theoretical difference between making a response which results in shock and choosing to be shocked. Failure to learn

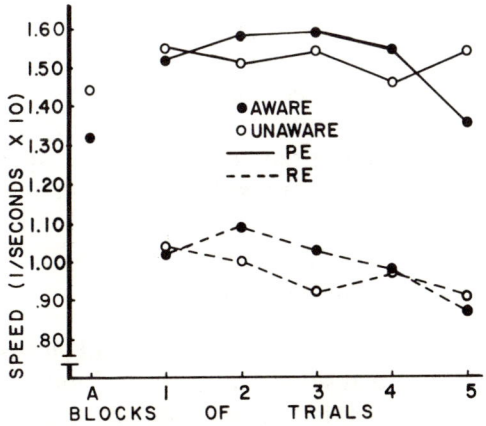

Fig. 6. Speed scores on the punished extinction (PE) and regular extinction (RE) trials over the five blocks of extinction trials by the 11 subjects who were aware and the 10 subjects who were unaware that one key was always shocked and the other key was never shocked.

the new contingency that not pressing results in nonpunishment does not imply a choice or a preference for punishment.

3. Differential Cues

An animal experiment similar in intent to our preference studies was carried out by Crowell *et al.* (1972). They obtained similar results, but but their interpretation differed from our own. In their study, the subjects had punished (PE) and nonpunished (RE) trials intermixed, each condition being associated with a distinctive tone. Animals ran faster in the presence of the shock tone than in the presence of the nonshock tone—identical to the faster response of our human subjects to the shock as opposed to the nonshock key. They reasoned that such differential responding was evidence that a discrimination had been formed. They concluded that this differential responding provided an appropriate behavioral criterion for the awareness required by the discrimination-expectancy account.

The essential point is that subjects can and do learn about their environment and make efforts to cope. For example, on punishment trials subjects continue to run fast to escape the anticipated punishment. In the regular extinction condition, however, new expectancies about the absence of punishment are acquired and are reflected in slower speeds and faster extinction. On the basis of our own data we would predict that if their subjects were given a choice they would have preferred the RE tone rather than the PE tone, while still responding in punished extinction. Crowell *et al.* (1972) did not carry out this essential procedural step for making a distinction between what the subject wants and what it does. Subjects are quite capable of learning a differential response to a signal that predicts shock without learning that nonresponding would avoid shock altogether.

4. A Behavioral Criterion of Self-Punishment

Previous researchers have assumed that the subject is choosing the punished alternative because it leaves a position of safety for a clearly known and discriminated punishment (e.g., Brown *et al.*, 1971). Because the previous research has taken the discrimination as a given, the subject was seen as masochistic (e.g., Brown, 1965), the shock as positive (Byrd, 1972), the process as paradoxical (Brown, 1969; Klare, 1974), and counterintuitive (Crowell *et al.*, 1972). Accordingly, theoretical emphasis was placed on fear and emotional factors as the critical elements which compel the subject to respond (e.g., Brown et al., 1971). This account contains two errors. The first is the assumption that discrimination about the shock (its intensity, location, signaled presence, frequency, etc.) is sufficient grounds for inferring that, for the subject, nonresponding is available as an alternative. The second is the failure to understand what constitutes an adequate behavioral criterion for the response of choosing to run.

Our data show that humans and rats neither prefer nor choose punishment although in a purely operational sense they do shock themselves. To the extent that the term "self-punitive" behavior has taken on theoretical meaning to imply a choice of or a preference for punishment, this conceptualization is in error. A more neutral term, such as the facilitative effects of response-contingent shock used by some investigators (e.g., Moorse, Mead, & Kelleher, 1967; Byrd, 1969, 1972; McKearny, 1972), would have been desirable.

A distinction must be drawn between contingencies known only to the experimenter and the information the subject has at its disposal for response selection. The subject does not choose the punishment in any psychologically meaningful sense of the term. On the contrary, subjects have a strong motivation to avoid the punishment and respond accordingly.

In our experiments there were two discriminations during extinction which could be learned: (a) the difference between the punished and the nonpunished alternatives; and (b) the fact that nonresponding is not punished. The respective theoretical issues are: (a) that inferences of choice rest on the first type of discrimination and require a preference methodology; and (b) that responding or failure to respond in punished extinction rests on the second type of discrimination.

The typical self-punitive study is done using a between-subjects design rather than a within-subjects design as were our preference experiments. In both designs, but especially in the typical between-subject design, subjects face a very different problem in the extinction condition from that encountered in the punishment condition. In nonpunished regular extinction, shock is discontinued altogether; therefore, the subject is directly confronted with the new contingency information that there is no shock to be escaped. Accordingly, these subjects abandon the active escape response.

In contrast, punished extinction subjects must abandon the active escape response which was specifically established during acquisition, and which even during punished extinction has its principal features maintained. In addition, they must acquire a passive avoidance response which was explicitly punished during acquisition. This new response cannot be learned if its outcome is never experienced.

C. DISRUPTING SELF-PUNITIVE BEHAVIOR

Since few punished extinction rats extinguish their self-punitive running, the mechanisms controlling the extinction process have been difficult to study, at least with rats. In the human self-punitive studies extinction can be manipulated by using verbal instructions. The human subject no longer responds once informed that it is his key pressing that is turning on the shock. We have attempted to explore a similar situation with rats by forcing a discrimination of the response-punishment contingencies by temporarily blocking the running response and forcing the rat to remain briefly in the now safe start box.

An extensive literature attesting to the effectiveness of response prevention to facilitate the extinction of avoidance responding already exists (for a review, see Baum 1970). O'Neil, Skeen, and Ryan (1970) have used response prevention procedures in the self-punitive apparatus. Rats which had undergone acquisition escape training were given a series of trials during which they were detained in the start area for 30 sec, a procedure which was effective in preventing self-punitive running on subsequent punished extinction trials.

Our purpose was to relate response prevention directly to the discrimination of the changed contingencies of punished extinction rather than to extinction of conditioned fear of the start area. Consequently we used a response prevention duration considerably shorter (i.e., 5 sec) than that used in previous response prevention studies.

a. Procedure. Thirty rats were given the standard self-punitive acquisition training in a straight alley runway. During extinction the subjects were divided into three groups: (a) PE with immediate blocking; (b) PE with the blocking procedure delayed for 20 trials; and (c) RE. In order to prevent the running response a panel was dropped between the lower portion of the start box and the runway for 5 sec and was then removed. The subject could then either remain in the start box or continue across the shock to the goal box. The following trial was a normal punished extinction trial and was not blocked. Blocked and nonblocked trials alternated until an extinction criterion of two consecutive 40-sec total time trials was met.

b. Results. The acquisition data are shown in the first panel of Fig. 7 and there are no differences among the three groups. The

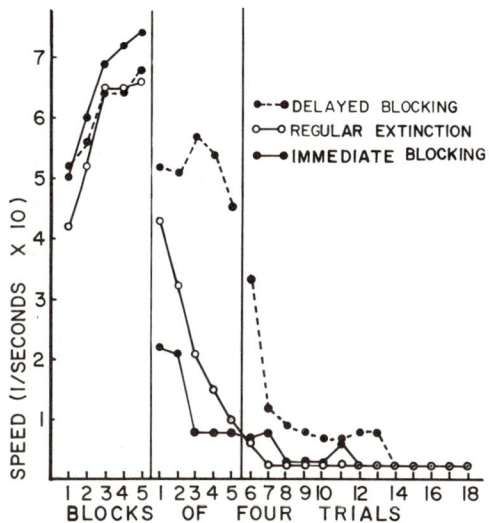

Fig. 7. Speed scores on nonblocked trials over five blocks of aquisition and 18 blocks of extinction for subjects in the regular extinction, immediate blocking and delayed blocking conditions.

second portion of the figure shows the speed scores for the first 20 extinction trials. At this point the delayed blocking group has received only punished extinction trials, and the standard self-punitive effect may be seen. The RE subjects (middle line) are gradually slowing down, and the subjects in the immediate blocking group (bottom line) are extinguishing most rapidly. In the third portion of the figure the delayed blocking subjects received blocking on alternate trials. Though these subjects had been responding self-punitively for the previous 20 trials, the blocking procedure is effective in stopping the already established self-punitive running.

Another notable feature of the data is the way in which response prevention affects extinction. The changeover from responding to nonresponding is quite abrupt. Of the 20 subjects in the blocking conditions, 18 met the extinction criterion within three blocks of trials once blocking began, whereas only three of the ten regular extinction subjects had extinguished within this same interval ($p < .05$).

Each subject was run for four additional trials after the extinction criterion had been met. Of the 20 PE subjects, 12 never responded on these postcriterion trials. Only one of the ten regular extinction subjects behaved this way (Chi-square Fisher exact $p = .017$, two-tailed). In other words, *the self-punitive effect is reversed on the trials following criterion.* This confirms our own and others' observations that when extinction does occur for a PE subject, the transition from responding to nonresponding is an abrupt process, unlike what happens in regular extinction.

   c. *Conclusions.* During acquisition the subject learns that running results in escape from shock. Once this expectancy is established it constrains the behavior of the subject until the expectancy is somehow disconfirmed and new ones are learned. For the RE subject this is a straightforward process; shock is no longer present in the runway, the subject learns this new contingency, and responding extinguishes. It is a slow and continuous process. This is not the case for the PE subject who continues to encounter shock in the runway and consequently the expectation that running will provide escape from shock is not disconfirmed. For most PE subjects, not running is simply outside the range of response variation and is not sampled. When appropriate new information about response-outcome contingencies becomes available to the subject this is no longer the case and extinction is abrupt.

   It can be argued that the effect of response prevention is to extinguish the conditioned fear of the start box. Though this possibility has not been directly discredited by our data, we feel it is less plausible than our own interpretation, especially in view of the very short response prevention times, the abruptness of the extinction, and the fact that RE subjects continue to leave the start area once they have met an extinction criterion.

IV. Effect of the Punishment

A. MEASUREMENT ARTIFACT CONTROVERSY

   Delude (1969) has raised an important methodological point the full importance of which has not yet been acknowledged or adequately dealt with Delude pointed out that the theoretical explanations invoked by the vicious circle of fear in accounting for the self-punitive effect are concerned primarily with the *pre*punishment area in that it is fear associated with this region which provides the motivation for the response. In self-punitive research the customary dependent measure is a speed score based on the reciprocal of the total elapsed time from the start of the trial until the subject reaches the goal box. Delude suggested that the use of this total time measure could itself provide evidence of a "vicious circle" effect which is in reality artifactual. The use of the total time criterion could allow the shock itself to produce the empirical difference between punished and nonpunished subjects. Specifically, both groups may leave the unpunished start area in a similar fasion. The punished subject will then find itself receiving shock, and as a consequence will run faster than if it was not being shocked. In contrast, the nonpunished subject will have a greater probability of making an abortive response, thus meeting an arbitrary extinction criterion.

If Delude is correct, the speed differential between the punished and nonpunished groups is the direct result of shock in the runway. It is not a result of the motivational effects of fear associated with the *pre*punishment area. The eliminate this possibility, Delude suggests that the prepunishment time is the appropriate measure, because this time cannot be influenced by the direct effects of the punishment. In his study he showed the typical self-punitive effect on speed scores based on total time, but not on those based on prepunishment time.

Delude also recorded the frequency of failures to leave the start box and failures to enter the goal box. Consistent with his analysis, punished subjects entered the goal box more frequently than non-punished subjects even though there were no differences in the frequency of their failures to leave the start box. In addition, for punished subjects the failure to enter the goal box was dependent upon failure to leave the start box. But, nonpunished rats left the start box as quickly on the trial on which criterion was achieved as they did on the previous trial.

In response to the Delude criticism, Siegel, Melvin, and Wagner (1971) agreed that the focus of the vicious circle hypothesis was on the prepunishment area and further than a more direct test of this hypothesis would utilize prepunishment measures. Siegel *et al.* countered the Delude criticism by arguing that Delude did not use the optimal procedures and had obtained a very weak self-punitive effect. In their own study the self-punitive effect was clearly evident when a prepunishment criterion was used, and therefore, they concluded the effect was not an artifact and that the data supported the vicious circle of fear explanation.

Some subsequent investigators (e.g., Crowell *et al.*, 1972; Delprato & Meltzer, 1974; Klare, 1974; Kruger, 1974) have acknowledged Delude's point that the prepunishment measure is more appropriate and have also reported these speeds. Similar to Siegel *et al.* they too found the self-punitive effect in both prepunishment and total time scores. The net result has been to accept both the rebuttal to Delude and the vicious circle of fear explanation. On closer examination both the rebuttal and the explanation can be questioned.

B. METHODOLOGICAL ISSUES

Consider first Delude's argument concerning prepunishment time. An inspection of the data used to refute Delude (Siegel *et al.*, 1971) shows that for the first 36 extinction trials there was no difference between PE and RE subjects in prepunishment speed, but a 33% reduction in the runway speed for the RE subjects. By the time 45 extinction trials had been completed these subjects were 60% extinguished on total time and a small difference was beginning to appear in the prepunishment speed. At this point Siegel *et al.* had replicated Delude. The ultimate difference in prepunishment speed between the punished and nonpunished procedure appeared only later, after the subjects had slowed down considerably in the runway.

We adopt the position that punished and nonpunished subjects initially leave the start box for the same reason. Namely, in acquisition both have learned the response-outcome expectancy that running escapes shock and that not running results in continued shock. But, with the start of extinction, the two groups are in a new learning situation and start acquiring different information. The nonpunished subjects begin to slow down first in the runway and learn the new contingency that nonrunning is not punished. It is not surprising that sometime *after* this information is acquired it generalizes to the prepunishment area. In contrast, punished subjects who leave the start area encounter shock and never experience in the runway the conditions necessary to learn the contingency that not running is not punished.

C. PREPUNISHMENT DATA

The prepunishment data on the pre- and postcriterion trials assumes theoretical importance because it is essential for the vicious circle of fear account that prepunishment differences exist which cannot be explained as due to the direct effects of the shock. If the speed differences between punished and nonpunished subjects are not associated with differences in generalized fear, as seen in prepunishment behavior, then the emotional basis of persistence is called into question and some other explanation must be found which is consistent with the data. Specifically, failures to observe either the self-punitive effect or, especially, reversals of the effect on prepunishment speeds prior to, during, or immediately after the total time criterion is achieved imply that a response-outcome discrimination process is the critical factor in self-punitive responding.

Our restatement of the critical issues about the direct effects of shock, the role of discrimination, and the inadequacy of a simple generalized fear concept can be evaluated directly by a reanalysis of our discrimination, preference, and blocking data. In addition, we conducted a standard self-punitive runway study using the standard punished (PE) and nonpunished (RE) groups to verify this interpretation in the basic paradigm.

1. Discrimination Study

In our discrimination study (Section III, A) using human subjects, frequency of response but not prepunishment speed data were available. Both groups which received partial punishment during extinction showed fast speed scores on punished trials and slow scores on nonpunished trials. Yet, all subjects who did not extinguish made several initial key presses on nonpunished trials, sometimes even finishing the sequence albeit at a slow rate. Thus, the subjects by leaving the start area behaved in a manner analogous to the rats; but it was whether or not they encountered shock that determined whether they showed the PE or the RE effect. The data support the notion that persistence is a result of being shocked, and that the initial expectancy and motivation are the same for both conditions. Responding in acquisition and in extinction is under the control of acquired information about contingencies. Fear of the shock is necessary in order to provide motivation, but is quite irrelevant as a critical process in the emergence of either persistence or extinction.

2. Rat Preference Study

In the preference study (Section III, B, 2) rats were exposed to both punished and nonpunished conditions. In the RE alley subjects continued to leave the start area, even after meeting the extinction criterion in the PE alley. Specifically, subjects met the PE criterion in an average of 28.55 trials, significantly less ($p < .01$) than the RE criterion of 46.36 trials. The subjects clearly had not acquired in regular extinction the same passive avoidance acquired in punished extinction.

The point can be examined in detail by considering the *pre*punishment speed scores for the same series of trials used to plot the total time scores of Fig. 4. As may be seen in Table I, initially there was a weak self-punitive effect in the *pre*punishment speeds, but as the preference criterion was being met these differences reversed and were maintained throughout the postcriterion trials. Subjects are not leaving the prepunishment area on PE trials, though these same subjects continue to do so when the RE alley is available.

3. Blocking Study

In our blocking study (Section III, C) there were three groups: RE, immediate blocking, and delayed blocking. The extinction criterion was based on a total time criterion of two consecutive 40-sec responses. The prepunishment speed scores were examined for those trials before, during, and after the total time criterion was achieved. On the trials before the criterion was reached the mean speed scores for all groups were similar as shown in Table II. However, on the criterion trials only the two punished groups were suppressed on *pre*punishment times, with the delayed blocking condition reaching the absolute floor, i.e., all subjects have the maximum time score all of which is accumulated in the prepunishment area. In addition, we

TABLE I

MEAN PREPUNISHMENT SPEEDS FOR TRIALS PRECEDING, DURING, AND FOLLOWING THE PREFERENCE CRITERION FOR THE ANIMAL PREFERENCE STUDY

	Mean prepunishment speed		
Experimental groups	Four blocks of precriterion trials	Three blocks of criterion trials	Four blocks of postcriterion trials
Regular extinction	7.17	4.40	2.90
Punished extinction	7.90	1.80	.84
t	$(6)^a = 2.11$	$(10) = 4.77$	$(9)^a = 4.49$
p	.08	.0007	.0015

[a] Because some subjects meet the criterion early and some late in extinction, data were not available for four subjects for the pre- and one on the postcriterion measures.

TABLE II

MEAN PREPUNISHMENT SPEEDS FOR TRIALS PRECEDING, DURING, AND FOLLOWING THE TOTAL TIME CRITERION FOR THE BLOCKING STUDY

Experimental groups	Mean prepunishment speed		
	Four precriterion trials[a]	Two criterion trials	Four postcriterion trials
Regular extinction	5.29	3.12	3.31
Punished extinction with immediate blocking	5.47	0.42	1.49
Punished extinction with delayed blocking	6.39	0.25	0.78
$F(2,27)$	1.39	5.23	2.99
p	.27	.02	.07

[a] Because two of the precriterion trials were blocked for the punished extinction conditions and did not provide a comparable measure, the means for these subjects were based on the two nonblocked trials.

ran four postextinction trials and the greater tendency of the RE subjects to respond on prepunishment times continued. This prepunishment data may be contrasted with the total time scores on the postcriterion trials which were suppressed for all three groups in which the means for RE, immediate blocking, and delayed blocking were .60, .61, .57 respectively; $F(2, 27) = 0.91; p = .985$.

The conclusion is obvious. Punished and nonpunished subjects are learning different things. If the RE subjects had been in a PE condition (even after extinction), they would have encountered shock and would have responded. Instead, both groups leave the start box at the same rate, up to the point at which a runway extinction criterion is met, at which time PE subjects stop responding altogether whereas RE subjects do not.

4. Runway Study

In our preceeding rat studies the speed data were obtained under the special circumstances of a preference and blocking procedure. Both of these procedures resulted in extinction in the punished condition, thereby providing us with an opportunity to directly examine our interpretation.

We felt it appropriate to consider the same kind of data from a standard self-punitive study conducted in a straight-alley runway. The difficulty, of course, is that under these conditions most punished (PE) subjects will not achieve a total time criterion and some nonpunished (RE) subjects will not extinguish. Thus, most punished and some nonpunished subjects will not provide useable data. This selection restricts the number of subjects but presents no bias because we are using the extinction process as a basis for inferences about the nature of the self-punitive phenomenon.

The total time acquisition and extinction data are shown in Fig. 8. In this study there was no difference between the mean acquisition speeds for RE and PE conditions ($p < .949$). There were, however, strong extinction differences replicating the standard self-punitive effect ($p < .001$). Six of the nine regular extinction subjects and three of the nine punished extinction subjects met the extinction criterion. For these nine subjects the prepunishment times were plotted for the trials preceding, during, and following the trials on which the total time criterion was achieved. The data are shown in Table III.

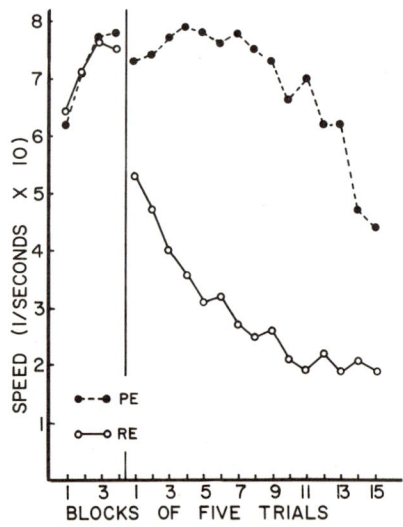

Fig. 8. Speed scores over four blocks of acquisition and 15 blocks of extinction for the regular extinction (RE) and punished extinction (PE) conditions.

TABLE III

MEAN PREPUNISHMENT SPEEDS FOR THE TRIALS PRECEDING, DURING, AND FOLLOWING THE TOTAL TIME CRITERION FOR THE RUNWAY STUDY

Experimental groups	Mean prepunishment speeds		
	Four precriterion trials	Two criterion trials	Four postcriterion trials
Regular extinction ($n = 6$)	.80	.71	.54
Punished extinction ($n = 3$)	.85	.15	.36
$t(7)$	.31	3.16	.58
p	.76	.0159	.58

There are no precriterion differences in the prepunishment speeds between the nonpunished and punished subjects, although the self-punitive effect is present in total time speeds (see Fig. 8). However, on the two criterion trials the punished subjects remain in the prepunishment area, whereas the nonpunished subjects continue to leave the start box even though they do not enter the goal box. Extinction is clearly being met in two different ways. If the nonpunished subjects had been in a punished condition they would have been shocked on leaving the prepunishment area and would not have met the total time criterion. The direction but not the magnitude of this reversed self-punitive effect was maintained on the postcriterion trials.

V. Empirical Constraints

A variety of studies on self-punitive behavior have been designed to assess the effects of specific variables such as shock intensity, trial distribution, goal box cues, etc. Though most of these investigations are parametric in nature, some consistent and reliable findings have emerged which need to be considered in their own right. Included in this latter category is the abruptness of PE extinction when it happens.

A. ABRUPTNESS OF PE EXTINCTION

In the self-punitive procedure some punished subjects will extinguish, and when this extinction occurs, it is generally an abrupt rather than a gradual process (e.g., Church, 1963; Delude, 1973; Kruger, 1974; Seward & Raskin, 1960). This finding was also reported in the present chapter for our preference and blocking experiments and by Dreyer and Renner (1971) and by Tinsley and Renner (1975).

In addition to our blocking study, the most extensively reported animal data on abruptness of extinction appears as a byproduct of the study by Kruger (1974) on the effects of shock intensity and start box fear on self-punitive running. In his study, PE subjects either stopped within the first three trials or ran for all 60 trials, with few exceptions.

If the occurrence of self-punitive responding is controlled by fear, extinction should result only when secondary start box fear is less than the primary runway fear (assuming a pure motivational interpretation), or when the punishment and inhibition of the instrumental response is more negative than the total reinforcement and the accumulated response strength of running is positive. This latter view is perhaps implicit in Brown's (1969) account because of his reliance on traditional two-factor theory, although the notion of accumulated response strength is not required nor critical to the vicious circle of fear account.

In either case, when extinction does occur for punished subjects it should be a gradual process reflecting an increase in fear associated with shock in the runway relative to the generalized fear component in the start box. Extinction should occur as these two components come into balance, causing a reduction in speed, which would further limit the generalization by fixing the spatial location of the shock. This conceptualization follows from the addition by Brown (1969) of a generalization process to the original two-process account (Mowrer, 1947). Neither the abrupt nature of extinction nor the speed data reviewed previously support this position.

If, however, responding is determined by the information provided by expectancy learning and not by fear, then the critical new learning is response-outcome contingencies, not emotions, and persistence will occur until this learning takes place. In other words, the shock must be painful and the animal must prefer to avoid it, but this condition of fear is not sufficient to explain the emergence of either persistence or suppression.

B. RESPONSE STYLE

The strength of the self-punitive effect depends upon a variety of procedural conditions, many of which have been specified for rats (Brown, 1969; Mackintosh, 1974). Based upon our research experience with humans, such variables as intensity, schedule, instructions, etc., seem to determine the strength of the self-punitive effect. Because relatively low levels of shock intensity must be used with humans, some subjects wait for shock onset before beginning to respond, even during acquisition. A stronger shock reduces this response style, but imposes selection on the subject population in that larger numbers will refuse to participate. With rats, a relatively strong punishment can be used without self-selection.

These procedural issues have theoretical implications to the extent that they influence the strength of the self-punitive effect. In our discrimination study 9 of the 11 PE subjects who extinguished were "waiters," and in the human preference study there were three waiters, all of whom extinguished. Because their typical response patterns—even during acquisition—were to respond to the shock only in a reactive (not anticipatory) way, they were immediately confronted with the new contingency and did not respond, even on the first extinction trial when there was no opportunity for fear to have extinguished. In contrast, anticipatory human subjects were pressing the key as soon as the warning began, even though this did not advance the numbers on the screen. As a consequence these subjects never had an opportunity to learn the new contingency.

Waiters are not seen with the same clarity in the animal studies, perhaps because of the timing of the events and the speed with which a rat reacts to landing on a shock. However, we do know the use of a guillotine door rather than an elevated start box considerably reduces self-punitive running by increasing the number of punished subjects who extinguish (Delprato & Meltzer, 1974; Delude, 1973; Siegel et al., 1971). There is one animal study in which waiting apparently did occur. Kruger (1974) used a fear conditioning procedure in the start box instead of the typical escape-runway training. In PE, waiting occurred in about 5% of the rats, and all of these subjects met the extinction criterion on the first extinction trial.

The most interesting aspect of this issue is that when waiting occurs it leads to abrupt extinction, usually on the first trial. Waiters learn that nonresponding is not punished. The waiters in a PE condition, however, remain *un*informed that *responding would be punished,* just as responders remain *un*informed that *nonresponding would not be punished.* The PE subject has a problem of "confusion" (Dreyer & Renner, 1971), not one of paradoxical or masochistic self-punishment.

C. INTENSITY OF FEAR AND POSTSHOCK EMOTIONALITY

The self-punitive phenomenon appears to be disrupted rather than facilitated by manipulations which should serve to increase the level of start box fear, such as foot shock to induce pretrial emotionality (Klare, 1974) or increased shock intensity during extinction (Kruger, 1974). Instead, these manipulations often appear to increase the number of subjects which abruptly stop running. These findings raise the question of whether the circle is at all vicious in an emotional or conditioned fear sense. It is our interpretation that the circle is vicious in a cognitive sense, i.e., the necessary discrimination about the new response-outcome contingency has not been made.

1. *Intensity of Fear*

One approach to the fear issue has been to show that a conditioned stimulus previously paired with shock can be used to elicit start box fear and the self-punitive effect is still obtained (Melvin & Stenmark, 1968). A further elaboration is to pretrain subjects to a CS using different frequencies of pairings (Galvani, 1969) or different intensities of punishment (Kruger, 1974), and to then use the CS as a secondary fear stimulus, measuring the differential effects on the strength of the self-punitive response.

There is no reason to doubt or to question either that fear is conditionable, or that a secondary aversive stimulus presented in the start box can be used to obtain self-punitive running, or that the level of initial fear can be manipulated through the use of a differential CS. The critical issue is whether the strength of the effect is related to the level of generalized fear.

In the most complete and carefully controlled study (Kruger, 1974), subjects were pretrained by giving them CS-shock conditioning in the start box to one of three intensities of punishment, and in addition a nonpunished control group was included. Each of these groups was divided into four subgroups in which the CS was present in the start box and one of the three levels of shock intensity was present in the runway for PE, the fourth group serving as a nonpunished control. The result was a 4 × 4 design in which three levels of shock intensity for conditioning and a nonshock control were crossed with the same four conditions for extinction.

A facilitative effect was found for the level of conditioned fear in the start box on self-punitive responding. This is not surprising because subjects with a stronger conditioned fear response should and do leave the start box at a higher rate than those with a weaker CS for fear, even those in the nonpunished control group. The critical data from the Kruger study are the intensity of shock used in the test for self-punitive behavior. This intensity effect is in the opposite direction to that predicted by the vicious circle of fear explanation; specifically, the weakest persistence was obtained with the strongest intensity which presumably should have produced the most fear.

2. Postshock Emotionality

The data on postshock emotionality are inconclusive and open to alternative interpretations. It was first reported that the introduction of a delay between acquisition and extinction disrupted self-punitive behavior (Martin, 1969; Melvin, Martin, & Parsons, 1965), suggesting that the effect is due largely to postshock emotionality. Next, Brown *et al.* (1971) obtained the self-punitive effect, although not as strongly, using a 24-hr intertrial interval. They concluded that the self-punitive effect was not just emotional but also had a conditioned fear aspect as required by the theory. In contrast, Klare (1974) directly induced emotionality by giving foot shock 1 min prior to a trial and found that it reduced the self-punitive effect. Klare suggested that his data ". . . illuminate the power of a 'pure' vicious-circle-of-conditioned-fear explanation of such paradoxical punishment effects [p. 382]." This illumination is relative only to a "non-pure" vicious circle of fear account, i.e., one which includes emotionality. In our view the emotionality problem is irrelevant. Emotionality may be expected to have an effect on self-punitive behavior to the extent that it increases or decreases response variability and, therefore, influences learning concerning the nonresponse-nonshock contingency.

D. GOAL BOX CUES

Delprato and Denny (1968) and Delprato and Meltzer (1974) have applied Denny's (1971) relaxation theory to the self-punitive findings. This theory holds that the reinforcement for running is relief which mediates the response and is necessary for self-punitive behavior. In their first study they varied the period of goal box confinement showing that the self-punitive effect was weaker with short goal box confinements because relief as a slow latency process did not have time to develop. Similarly, in Delprato's second experiment the self-punitive effect was weaker when the goal box was similar to the start box than when it was dissimilar. Under the dissimilar condition the feared (negative) start box and the relief (positive) goal box were not confounded by generalization effects and the relief could mediate the running response. Their version of the underlying process has the subject running toward a positive goal rather than away from a fear.

From the discrimination-expectancy view, accounts focusing on the emotional parts of the process simply miss the central features of punished escape situations. To the extent that goal conditions and emotional states affect the subsequent response variability they may be assumed to influence the strength of the self-punitive effect.

VI. Conclusions

A. THE NATURE OF SELF-PUNITIVE BEHAVIOR

The theoretical question is not whether the concept of discrimination of contingencies is necessary, but whether it is sufficient for conceptualizing the facts of persistence and extinction, and how the learning of information about contingencies should be interpreted and reconciled with the motivational role of fear.

If fear is viewed solely as a classically conditioned emotional response elicited by the cues of the start box, it should be eliminated only through a gradual extinction process. This view of fear plays an important role in the vicious circle of fear interpretation, but there are two problems: (a) When a punished subject discriminates the contingencies, extinction occurs abruptly, raising the question of whether it is reasonable to conclude that a classically conditioned fear of the start area is responsible for persistence; and (b) if the response-eliciting property of the fear is the result of a generalization process, stimulus-discrimination procedures should limit generalization, causing slower speeds which in turn should aid discrimination. This does not happen as a consequence of stimulus-discrimination (Brown *et al.*, 1971), even when there is direct behavioral evidence of the effectiveness of the stimulus-discrimination training.

Both problems can be avoided if fear is seen as a contingency relationship between a strong negative incentive and the subject's behavior. In this view, the significant motivational factor is fear of the shock, not fear of the start area, for the PE subject chooses to remain in the start area immediately upon learning that doing so will result in shock avoidance.

During acquisition the subject learns that responding results in escape from aversive electric shock. The shock and subsequent escape experienced in PE serve to keep this original learning intact, thus the response persistence. The subject has acquired a set of expectancies about how to escape an aversive stimulus, and continues to act in accord with these expectancies during PE. When new contingency learning redefines the original escape situation, the subject will extinguish.

Thus, we question whether fear plays any central theoretical role in understanding the self-punitive phenomenon. Clearly, fear is necessary. The shock must be aversive and the subject must prefer to escape or avoid it. Yet, for PE subjects fear motivation remains constant throughout acquisition, persistence, and extinction. In all three instances the subject's motivation is to minimize painful shock. Fear of the shock is necessary to produce the escape or avoidance responses but quite irrelevant as a critical process in determining the selection of the specific response during acquisition, persistence, or extinction. What distinguishes these three events are the kinds of expectancies the subjects have about the contingencies, not the motivational significance of fear of shock.

B. ACTIVE AND PASSIVE VIEWS OF THE SUBJECT

Our discrimination-expectancy account of self-punitive behavior is active in nature. The subject is conceptualized as operating on his environment in a problem solving way. When persistence occurs it simply reflects the fact that the environment is structured in such a way that the subject is deprived of information which, if available, would have caused him to alter his behavior. There is a sense of internal coherence and direction to the behavior, even if its outcome is more aversive than it need be.

In contrast, the vicious circle of fear account leaves the subject a passive victim, trapped in a cycle of external stimuli which elicit and reinforce a response chain that maintains itself in spite of known and anticipated punishment. This unflattering view of the subject's capacity for rational behavior seems to us to be inappropriate even for the rat. The "foolish" and "paradoxical" behavior appears such only because of the theory which has been imposed on the subject.

C. PARALLEL EXPERIMENTS WITH HUMANS AND RATS

Not all problems lend themselves equally well to parallel experiments with animals and humans. We were perhaps fortunate to find a human procedure which so directly paralleled the rat work. In our case the effort was well worthwhile.

The self-punitive problem immediately takes on different proportions once the experimenter is able to talk with a subject. The basic misleading nature of a *self*-punitive effect became very clear in our first conversations with human subjects (Dreyer & Renner, 1971). These subjects demanded of us—the experimenters—an explanation of how they could be expected to know that it was their own response which was producing the shock.

As we have seen, the appropriate analysis for the human subjects is also most suitable for the rats—they too suffered from an informational deficit. The consistency we found between rats and people, while encouraging for the notion of general behavior theory, does not speak well for the tendency of experimental psychologists to assert as generalizations those concepts which best fit our standard animal procedures (Lockard, 1968). A deliberate effort to conduct parallel experiments may help to impose useful constraints on the questions and procedures we use to address our animal subjects.

VII. Implications for Punishment Theory and Research

The results of our experiments and the analysis of self-punitive behavior add to the growing literature on a cognitive theory of punishment (e.g., Bolles, 1972; MacKintosh, 1974; Seligman & Johnston, 1973). We conclude that even the behavior of a rat is best conceptualized within a problem-solving framework. Responses are not compelled solely by external events, but arise primarily from within the animal based upon its evaluation and knowledge of the situation. Accordingly, our view of punishment involves these two components.

A. VALUE LEARNING

In a punishment situation a subject experiences aversive stimulation of which some negative evaluation is made. Though this evaluation takes place rather quickly it is not absolute or unchangeable. The relative degree of aversiveness depends upon a variety of other factors. For example, after a series of trials in which the intensity of a shock is gradually increased the final level is somewhat less aversive than if the full intensity is given immediately (Brown & Wagner, 1964; Miller, 1960). Other factors such as the uncertainty or delay of an inescapable shock can also make it more aversive than the same shock signalled or given immediately (e.g., Badia & Culbertson, 1972; Renner & Houlihan, 1969).

A variety of different mechanisms have been identified which mediate such effects. A stimulus which has been paired with an aversive event may be sought out if it allows the primary negative event to be reduced through preparatory responding (Perkins, 1968). In other situations, a warning signal provides the subject with knowledge that in the absence of the signal a shock free period is in effect (Rescorla, 1967; Seligman, 1968).

We are suggesting that these processes be viewed as having their effect on the relative value of the punishment or the situation. The important feature of evaluation is that the subject must acquire the information from its previous experiences and place these value judgments on anticipated future outcomes. It is an active process in which the subject attributes sign and magnitude to anticipated future consequences.

B. CONTINGENCY LEARNING

The second kind of learning suggested by our data is that the subject learns the relationship between various responses and situational conditions, and their outcomes. This second learning process requires a situation in which the subject encounters the relevant contingencies, although with humans this can be through observation rather than direct experience. A variety of factors, including the range of response variation, the motivation of the subject, and the schedule of events, will determine what information is acquired and how fast it is acquired.

C. RESPONSE SELECTION AS A CENTRAL STATE

The origins of behavior are thus located within the subject. The subject is oriented toward the future in terms of acquired values and the expected consequences of alternative behaviors. In this sense, actions are a series of choices based upon values and expectancies. The values are subjective, but lawful, with the specification of these relationships being an empirical question. The expectancies also reflect the history of the subject and are represented internally in the form of contingency information. External stimuli do not solely elicit responses directly but primarily provide the subject with an array of response-outcome alternatives. The particular response chosen depends upon internalized values and expectancies.

Thus, a response is not seen as growing in strength either through frequency or as a direct consequence of reinforcement. The effect of experience is to alter expectancies which provide information on the relationship between actions and outcomes, and to allow the subject to learn about the affective value of those specific outcomes.

D. SIMILARITY WITH APPETITIVE PROCESSES

One consequence of our view of the punishment process is that it is rendered compatible with the reinforcement process. The mechanisms which determine aversively motivated behavior can be conceptualized as the same ones which account for appetitively motivated behavior.

Appetitive research in our laboratory has explored situations in which the relative value of a food reward is dependent upon other variables, such as early deprivation experience (Renner, 1967) and level of depletion (Renner, Cravens, & Wooley, 1971). These values can be scaled and stated as the lawful effects of specific manipulations.

The operation of contingency and value learning as a central state can be illustrated by the fact that if a subject is given repeated experience in a two-choice situation with absolute certainty that one choice results in a given shock-plus-food outcome and the other choice results in neither, the subject will consistently choose one or the other depending on its level of depletion. If a level of depletion is selected so that the value of the food is more desirable than the aversiveness of the shock, the shock—food side will be selected. But, if the value of the food is lowered by decreasing the depletion level, the subject will immediately, on the first trial when less depleted, choose the nonshock—nonfood side. This result will be obtained, however, only if the subject has also previously eaten food at the lower depletion level so as to have an appropriate internal value system for that outcome (Renner, 1972). The process is similar to the self-punitive situation where the mere frequency of past behavior by itself does not determine response selection. The critical factor is the subject's information about contingencies and the value which is placed on the outcome.

An incentive-value and expectancy-contingency treatment of reward and punishment permit both to be seen in a similar context. In most real life situations both positive and negative consequences follow almost every action. The pleasure of going to the movies costs money, the effort of extra work provides overtime pay, and so on. There is an endless string of mixed consequences which contingently follow any action. The arbitrary distinction between appetitively and aversively motivated behavior is more one of experimental convenience than of ecological validity. An inescapable constraint for psychological theory is a theoretical view of punishment which operates within the organism through the same mechanisms and which is throughly integrated with the effects of reinforcement.

In sum, ours is a one-process theory with respect to reward and punishment. There are two components, one having to do with values and the other with response-outcome contingencies. Both are forms of associational learning and both take place in classical conditioning and instrumental learning situations. The former is typically more concerned with imparting value and the second with contingency information, though this need not be the case. Although psychology has two kinds of learning paradigms, we are suggesting that these are not parallel to the *value* and *contingency* processes which take place in the subject. The result is an internal incentive-value and response-outcome contingency system. Both kinds of information exist as a central state, allowing the subject to act upon the environment in an anticipatory, coherent, and integrated fashion, based upon knowledge of the relationship between acts and outcomes and needs and values.

VIII. Generalizations

Historically, the interest in self-punitive research came from the old problem of the neurotic paradox. Our current research, like this past research, has not addressed the question of whether the laboratory version of self-punitive behavior has any bearing on its clinical counterpart, other than by fiat.

In terms of such a fiat our empirical results have implications for how any apparent instances of self-defeating and self-punitive behavior are to be conceptualized. Our laboratory model, like those existing in general behavior theory, can be used for analytical purposes, although demonstrating the validity of the applied consequences is not, by current standards of pure science, an incumbent responsibility of the investigator.

The distinction between contingency and value learning made in this chapter has not been widely applied clinically. The tendency has been to conceptualize neurotic people as if they were perversely motivated to achieve the resulting outcome. As a consequence the conceptual task was to invent processes (e.g., unconscious motives, death wishes, masochism) which would make a negative outcome positive and which imply a choice of and preference for that outcome over other presumably better choices. The results of our research suggest that such cases are not "motivational" but rather are instances of "confusion."

A. DISORDERS OF CONTINGENCY—CONFUSION

Some instances of neurotic behavior may reflect instances of confusion. The rats in the self-punitive research were simply confused, lacking important information about contingencies. They were caught in a vicious circle of confusion, not in a vicious circle of fear. This is not to say that they were not frightened, but only that the key to breaking the circle was *knowledge.* Treatment to alter such response selection needs to be directed at contingency learning, not at the motivational state of the subject.

B. DISORDERS OF VALUES—MOTIVATION

There are undoubtedly a number of disorders where the key to understanding rests on the unique motivational states of the individual. Long and severe states of deprivation, be it food with rats (Renner, 1967) or maternal deprivation with children (Yarrow,

1961), can produce long and lasting effects on the values of the organism. In these cases, although the subject may be fully aware of the contingencies and is therefore not restricted by lack of information, response selection may yet be limited by the fact that total effort is directed at a few outcomes which, *normatively,* are given disproportionate value. The deviant nature of these values notwithstanding, their origins reflect the same principles and mechanisms that govern the acquisition of all values. In such cases, treatment is appropriately directed at the value process.

C. THE CASE OF MASOCHISM

Yet left unclarified is the case of masochism which deserves to be addressed directly. If a behavior is to be labeled masochistic we require that several objective criteria be met, the first of which is that the organism have alternative behaviors available. The prisoner incarcerated in the penitentiary, though living in unpleasant circumstances, is not a masochist by virtue of remaining in prison. We impose the additional restraint that the organism be aware of these alternative behaviors and their consequent outcomes. It is this second requirement which is not met in the usual self-punitive studies. These criteria insure that the masochistic choice of punishment is a meaningful one and not simple due to a lack of response alternatives or confusion or ignorance. It is only once these objective criteria have been met that we can then go on to determine whether a behavior is masochistic.

Consider the obvious fact that our human subjects show up for our experiments knowing they are to be shocked. In this instance the explanation seems clear. There are other considerations such as course requirements which influence our subject. The same logic must be extended to the religious devotee who engages in self-flagellation knowing full well that pain would be avoided by not responding. Response-outcome expectancies seem accurate in both cases, and it is presumably meeting the course requirement or relief from guilt which accounts for these behaviors. These are not violations of the law of effect but the selection of the least aversive outcome.

The logical implication of our position is that the concept of masochism is ultimately defined by social convention and is thus relative. The self-flagellator would not be deviant within the religious group, but probably would appear so to members of larger society. These judgments, however, are social and normative.

The term masochism, thus, retains its usefulness and can be invoked in situations which meet the following three conditions: (*a*) there are alternative behaviors available; (*b*) the individual is aware of these alternatives and their outcomes; and (*c*) our social normative values tell us the behavior is bizarre. In any case, the same processes which account for the acquired expectancies and values in all of us apply as well to the masochists, the self-flagellators, and the subjects who dutifully report for their experiments. The law of effect has once again been reasserted as an article of faith, though not in the simple sense of strengthening or weakening S-R associations.

ACKNOWLEDGMENTS

The authors would like to thank Robert Hendersen and Nancy Squires for their criticisms and suggestions in reference to an earlier draft of the chapter, and Lynn Fairlamb for helping to compile the references.

REFERENCES

Badia, P., & Culbertson, S. The relative aversiveness of signalled vs. unsignalled escapable and inescapable shock. *Journal of the Experimental Analysis of Behavior*, 1972, **17**, 463–471.

Baum, M. Extinction of avoidance responding through response prevention (flooding). *Psychological Bulletin*, 1970, **74**, 276–284.

Beecroft, R. S., Bouska, S. A., & Fisher, G. Punishment intensity and self-punitive behavior. *Psychonomic Science*, 1967, **8**, 351–352.

Beecroft, R. S., Fisher, G., & Bouska, S. A. Punishment continuity and self-punitive behavior. *Psychonomic Science*, 1967, **9**, 127–128.

Bolles, R. C. Reinforcement, expectancy and learning. *Psychological Review*, 1972, **79**, 394–409.

Brown, J. S. A behavioral analysis of masochism. *Journal of Experimental Research in Personality*, 1965, **1**, 65–70.

Brown, J. S. Factors affecting self-punitive locomotor behavior. In B. A. Campbell & R. M. Church (Eds.), *Punishment and aversive behavior*. New York: Appleton, 1969. Pp. 467–514.

Brown, J. S., Beier, E. M., & Lewis, R. W. Punishment-zone distinctiveness and self-punitive locomotor behavior in the rat. *Journal of Comparative and Physiological Psychology*, 1971, **77**, 513–520.

Brown, J. S., Martin, R. C., & Morrow, M. W. Self-punitive behavior in the rat: Facilitative effects of punishment on resistance to extinction. *Journal of Comparative and Physiological Psychology*, 1964, **57**, 127–133.

Brown, R. T., & Wagner, A. R. Resistance to punishment and extinction following training with shock or nonreinforcement. *Journal of Experimental Psychology*, 1964, **68**, 503–507.

Byrd, L. D. Responding in the cat maintained under response-independent electric shock and response-produced electric shock. *Journal of the Experimental Analysis of Behavior*, 1969, **12**, 1–10.

Byrd, L. D. Responding in the squirrel monkey under second-order schedules of shock delivery. *Journal of the Experimental Analysis of Behavior,* 1972, **18,** 155–167.

Church, R. M. The varied effects of punishment on behavior. *Psychological Review,* 1963, **70,** 369–402.

Crowell, C. R., Brown, J. S., & Lewis, R. W. Self-punitive behavior in the rat during successive-discrimination "extinction" trials. *Psychonomic Science.* 1972, **27,** 131–135.

Delprato, D. J., & Denny, M. R. Punishment and the length of nonshock confinement during the extinction of avoidance. *Canadian Journal of Psychology,* 1968, **22,** 456–464.

Delprato, D. J., & Meltzer, R. J. Type of start box and goal box distinctiveness in self-punitive running of rats. *Journal of Comparative and Physiological Psychology,* 1974, **87,** 548–554.

Delude, L. The vicious circle phenomenon: A result of measurement artifact. *Journal of Comparative and Physiological Psychology,* 1969, **69,** 246–252.

Delude, L. Factors affecting the strength of the vicious circle phenomenon. *Psychological Record,* 1973, **23,** 467–476.

Denny, M. R. Relaxation theory and experiments. In F. R. Brush (Ed.), *Aversive conditioning and learning.* New York: Academic Press, 1971. Pp. 235–295.

Dreyer, P. & Renner, K. E. Self-punitive behavior—masochism or confusion? *Psychological Review,* 1971, **78,** 333–337.

Freud, S. *Beyond the pleasure principle,* 1920. Translation in James Strachey (Ed.), *The standard edition of the complete works of Sigmund Freud.* Vol. 22. London: Hogarth and the Institute of Psycho-Analysis, 1953.

Galvani, P. F. Self-punitive behavior as a function of number of prior fear-conditioning trials. *Journal of Comparative and Physiological Psychology,* 1969, **68,** 359–363.

Jones, E. *The life and work of Sigmund Freud.* Vol. 3. New York: Basic Books, 1957.

Klare, W. F. Conditioned fear and postshock emotionality in vicious circle behavior of rats. *Journal of Comparative and Physiological Psychology,* 1974, **87,** 364–372.

Kruger, B. M. Self-punitive running in the rat following start box fear conditioning: Shock intensity effects. *Journal of Comparative and Physiological Psychology,* 1974, **87,** 555–562.

Lockard, R. B. The albino rat: A defensible choice or bad habit? *American Psychologist,* 1968, **23,** 734–741.

Mackintosh, N. J. *The psychology of animal learning.* New York: Academic Press, 1974.

Martin, R. C. Self-punitive behavior: One way to stop it. *Psychonomic Science,* 1969, **14,** 25–26.

Martin, R. C., & Moon, T. L. Self-punitive behavior and periodic punishment. *Psychonomic Science,* 1968, **10,** 245–246.

McKearney, J. W. Maintenance and suppression of responding under schedules of electric shock presentation. *Journal of Experimental Analysis of Behavior,* 1972, **17,** 425–432.

Melvin, K. B. Escape learning and "vicious-circle" behavior as a function of percentage of reinforcement. *Journal of Comparative and Physiological Psychology,* 1964, **58,** 248–251.

Melvin, K. B. Vicious circle behavior. In H. D. Kimmel (Ed.), *Experimental psychopathology: recent research and theory.* New York: Academic Press, 1971. Pp. 95–115.

Melvin, K. B., & Bender, L. Self-punitive avoidance behavior: Effects of changes in punishment intensity. *Psychological Record,* 1968, **18,** 29–34.

Melvin, K. B., Martin, R. C., & Parsons, G. Delayed extinction of escape responses: a parametric study. *Psychonomic Science,* 1965, **2,** 247–248.

Melvin, K. B., & Stenmark, F. H. Facilitative effects of punishment on the establishment of a fear motivated response. *Journal of Comparative and Physiological Psychology*, 1968, **65**, 517–519.

Miller, N. E. Learning resistance to pain and fear: Effects of overlearning, exposure, and rewarded exposure in context. *Journal of Experimental Psychology*, 1960, **60**, 137–145.

Morse, W. H., Mead, R. N., & Kelleher, R. T. Modulation of elicited behavior by a fixed-interval schedule of electric shock presentation. *Science*, 1967, **157**, 215–217.

Mowrer, O. H. On the dual nature of learning—A re-interpretation of "conditioning" and "problem-solving." *Harvard Educational Review*, 1947, **17**, 102–148.

O'Neil, H. F., Skeen, L. C., & Ryan, F. J. Prevention of vicious circle behavior. *Journal of Comparative and Physiological Psychology*, 1970, **70**, 281–285.

Perkins, C. C. An analysis of the concept of reinforcement. *Psychological Review*, 1968, **75**, 155–172.

Renner, K. E. Temporal integration: Modification of the incentive value of a food reward by early experience with deprivation. *Journal of Experimental Psychology*, 1967, **75**, 400–407.

Renner, K. E. Coherent self-direction and values. *Annals of the New York Academy of Sciences*, 1972, **193**, 175–184.

Renner, K. E., Cravens, R. W., & Wooley, O. W. Relative utility of food rewards as a function of cyclic deprivation or body weight loss in albino rats. *Journal of Experimental Psychology*, 1971, **90**, 102–112.

Renner, K. E., & Houlihan, J. Conditions affecting the relative aversiveness of immediate and delayed punishment. *Journal of Experimental Psychology*, 1969, **81**, 411–420.

Rescorla, R. A. Pavlovian conditioning and its proper control procedures. *Psychological Review*, 1967, **74**, 71–79.

Seligman, M. E. P. Chronic fear produced by unpredictable electric shock. *Journal of Comparative and Physiological Psychology*, 1968, **66**, 402–411.

Seligman, M. E. P., & Johnston, J. C. A cognitive theory of avoidance learning. In F. J. McGuigan, & D. R. Lumsden (Eds.), *Contemporary approaches to conditioning and learning*. Washington, D.C.: Winston, 1973. Pp. 69–110.

Seward, J. P., & Raskin, D. C. The role of fear in aversive behavior. *Journal of Comparative and Physiological Psychology*, 1960, **53**, 328–335.

Siegel, P. S., Melvin, K. B., & Wagner, J. D. Vicious circle behavior in the rat: measurement problems visited again. *Journal of Comparative and Physiological Psychology*, 1971, **76**, 311–315.

Tinsley, J. B., & Renner, K. E. Self-punitive behavior with changing percentages of reinforcement: The proper role of discrimination. *Learning and Motivation*, 1975, **6**, 448–458.

Yarrow, L. J. Maternal deprivation: Toward an empirical and conceptual reevaluation. *Psychological Bulletin*, 1961, **58**, 459–490.

REWARD VARIABLES IN INSTRUMENTAL CONDITIONING: A THEORY

Roger W. Black

UNIVERSITY OF SOUTH CAROLINA, COLUMBIA, SOUTH CAROLINA

I. Introduction 199
   A. Scope of the Theory 199
   B. Some Effects of Constant Reward Conditions 204
II. Basic Theoretical Formulation 207
   A. Basic Concepts and General Assumptions 208
   B. Specific Formulation 210
   C. Computational Procedures: Illustrative Results 216
III. Implications of the Theory 220
   A. Constant Reward Conditions 220
   B. Effects of Varied Reward Conditions: Shifts in MR 223
   C. Varied Reward Conditions 228
   D. Varied Reward Conditions: Concurrent Shifts in MR and PTR 232
   E. Temporal Factors 233
IV. General Discussion 236
   A. Evaluation of Theoretical Predictions 236
   B. Relationship to Other Formulations 238
   References 241

I. Introduction

A. SCOPE OF THE THEORY

The behavior of rats in the runway conditioning situation has been the subject of extensive experimental and theoretical interest for several decades. The training procedure most frequently employed with the runway is instrumental appetitive conditioning and the variables which have been manipulated most frequently may be described as "reward variables." For example, magnitude of reward (MR) is varied in terms of the physical quantity of food the rat obtains in the goal box. Delay of reward (DR) is defined by an interval which is allowed to elapse while the rat is in the goal box before reward is made available. If food is obtained in the goal box on every trial, then the number of rewards is equal to the number of trials and a consistent reward (CR) procedure is in effect. It is possible to vary the percentage of trials rewarded (PTR), however, so that a partial reward procedure is in effect. The relative frequency with which trials are rewarded may also be expressed as a proportion (P). Although these are the principal reward variables employed in appetitive runway conditioning experiments, numerous combinations of these variables may be employed.

Experiments concerned with reward variables in the runway generally involve administering a series of trials to two or more groups of rats with different reward conditions in effect for the different groups. Such experiments include one or more "phases," where a "phase" is a series of trials on which reward conditions are held constant within each group. For example, two-phase experiments may involve "acquisition" and "extinction" phases. Similarly, contrast-effect experiments often involve preshift and postshift phases, etc. Few runway experiments involve more than three or four phases but it is useful to conceive of a generalized experimental design which could describe most reward variable experiments, regardless of the particular variables involved or the number of groups, trials, or phases. Such a generalized design is presented in Table I. The design involves N trials conducted as m phases with reward conditions constant within each group during each phase. There are K groups with the differences among groups consisting of the particular reward conditions they receive during each phase. These reward conditions are indicated at T_{11} (treatment in Phase 1 for Group 1), etc., and

TABLE I

A GENERALIZED DESIGN FOR REWARD VARIABLE EXPERIMENTS

Trials	1	2	3	. . .	.	N
Phase	1		2		—	m
Group 1	T_{11}		T_{21}		·	T_{m1}
Group 2	T_{12}		T_{22}		·	T_{m2}
.	—		—			—
.						
	—		—			—
Group K	T_{1K}		T_{2K}		·	T_{mK}

they can include any of the reward variables previously discussed, in any combinations and in any order.

The theory described formally in Section II, B was designed to predict runway performance in experiments of the type described in Table I. The theory was developed in the context of several propositions which provide a less formal view of such experiments. The first of these general propositions is that runway behavior is essentially "adaptive" in the sense that the food-deprived rat tends to perform responses on which obtaining food is contingent and ceases to perform those responses if food reward subsequently is withheld. To a degree, this proposal merely affirms the law of effect, but the functions of rewards in the present formulation are quite different from those assumed by Thorndike. For Thorndike (e.g., 1932) the function of reward was to strengthen the "connections" between stimuli and responses. This "response strengthening" effect occurred at the time the reward was obtained and was relatively fixed or permanent. Measures of "response strength" thus provided a direct indication of the nature and amount of learning that had occurred in instrumental conditioning. The present analysis does not assume a simple relationship between "learning" and "response strength;" it does not assume that rewards have fixed or permanent effects; and it does not assume that the process responsible for runway performance is the "strengthening" of connections or associations between stimuli and the running response. These differences between the current position and "response strength" views will be noted several times in subsequent discussions.

A second general proposition is that runway behavior is "adaptive" in the sense that it tends to adjust or change appropriately when reward conditions are changed. The previous proposition concerning the effects of reward and nonreward may be considered a special case of this second proposal. In fact, it is proposed that the variance observed in runway performance may be accounted for largely in terms of the rat's response to reward conditions which are changing— from the rat's viewpoint. For example, an experiment might involve an initial training phase with large magnitude of reward (MR) followed by a phase in which MR is small. From the experimenter's viewpoint, MR is constant within each phase and only changes at the transition between phases, but the situation is assumed to be more complex for the rat. According to this view, the rat develops an expectancy of large reward during the first phase of the experiment. As a result, the reward in the second phase is smaller or "worse" than expected and obtaining this "unfavorable" reward is expected to adversely affect performance. At the same time, the rat is assumed to be "revising" its expectancy regarding MR to correspond to the current MR. Consequently, reward conditions in the second phase continue to change in the sense that they become less "unfavorable" and corresponding improvement in performance is expected. Both the reward conditions and performance should eventually become stable, however, when obtained reward and expected reward are approximately equal. The same analysis is proposed for performance in the initial training phase. When it is placed in the runway for the first time, the rat is assumed to have little expectation of finding food there. Whatever reward the rat obtains is assumed to be both "unexpected" and "larger than expected" and, therefore, a very "favorable" reward. As training progresses, however, the rat comes to expect the MR it obtains and reward conditions are viewed as changing in the manner described earlier. The theory assumes that when obtained reward and expected reward eventually become equal, "learning" ceases to occur.

The third general proposition concerns limitations or constraints on the degree to which runway behavior is expected to be "adaptive"—i.e., to change appropriately when reward conditions are changed. The basic proposal is that the *rate* at which runway performance changes when reward conditions are changed depends on the degree to which the rat discriminates the contingency between performing the instrumental response and obtaining food reward. If the rat recognizes that running to the goal box "produces" reward, then changes in reward should be reflected quickly in running speed. Conversely, when discrimination of the response-reward contingency is poor, changes in the contingency are not expected to produce rapid adjustments in performance. Similar assumptions appear to be implicit in the use of shaping procedures in operant conditioning. Such procedures presumably aid the animal in recognizing or discriminating the response which "produces" reward and thus increase the rate at which stable performance is achieved.

The current proposal is that the rate at which the rat adapts or responds to changed reward conditions is limited by its ability to discriminate the response-reward contingency. It is further proposed that the development of this discrimination is affected by reward variables such as MR, PTR, etc. A major portion of the formal theory is concerned with specifying the theoretical relationships between these reward variables and the development of this discrimination. In general, "favorable" reward conditions such as large reward and consistent reward are assumed to promote the development of the discrimination and rats trained under these conditions are expected to adjust their performance rapidly to prevailing reward conditions. Thus, "favorable" reward conditions should lead to both rapid acquisition and rapid extinction, both of which are "adaptive." This is another respect in which the current view differs from "response-strength" views: The current proposal is that rats which show rapid extinction have learned *more* than rats which are "resistant" to extinction; response-strength positions contend that such rats have learned *less*. Some of the basic effects of reward variables on runway performance are summarized briefly in Section I, B. This evidence is interpreted as being generally consistent with the present proposals and it provides the initial empirical basis for evaluating the implications of the formal theory.

The theory described in Section II is an attempt to formalize the preceding general propositions and assumptions. A basic premise in the development of the theory was that it should be possible to predict the effects of reward variables on the basis of the rat's experiences with those variables and a set of assumptions about the way in which the rat "processes" those experiences. The theory includes a set of equations which represent these assumptions about the way in which rats process their experiences with rewards. Additional equations relate these assumptions to runway performance. The goal was to make the theory sufficiently explicit and determinant that it could be reduced to a computer program which would predict runway performance on a trial-by-trial basis once the experimental conditions were specified. All of the theoretical data and implications presented in Section III were generated in this manner. In order to accomplish this, it was necessary to make detailed and specific assumptions about the processes theoretically involved in runway experiments. While I have made some attempt to provide informal descriptions of the major theoretical variables and assumptions, I have not attempted to defend or justify the specific assumptions which were made. These assumptions were made initially on an essentially intuitive basis, but specific assumptions were retained only if they appeared to generate predictions consistent with the experimental evidence. Some of the equations include terms to which it was necessary to assign arbitrary values. These values also were selected to provide the best agreement with experimental evidence. It is important to note, however, that all the theoretical implications which are presented were generated under the identical set of assumptions and assigned values. The only variable entries in the program which calculated theoretical data corresponded to the experimental variables manipulated in the hypothetical experiments for which runway performance was predicted.

B. SOME EFFECTS OF CONSTANT REWARD CONDITIONS

The results briefly summarized here are from runway experiments which investigated magnitude, delay or percent reward and in which reward conditions were constant during acquisition. The primary interest is in the effect of these variables on "rate of conditioning" and "rate of extinction," although much of the research cited was primarily concerned with absolute measures such as "asymptotic acquisition performance" and "extinction performance." For present purposes, a difference in "rate of conditioning" will be said to occur when the acquisition performance of two or more groups shows initial divergence followed by subsequent convergence. A difference in "rate of extinction" may be said to occur when groups enter extinction at similar performance levels but performance diverges early in extinction and tends to converge later. It should be noted that in the case of both acquisition and extinction, the final convergence may not occur unless a sufficient number of trials is conducted. Further, in the case of extinction, group differences in terminal acquisition performance may complicate the interpretation of results and require the use of "relative" measures of extinction performance (see Anderson, 1963), especially if the data are described in terms of "resistance to extinction" (RTE). In any case, the current view is that RTE and "rate of extinction" are inversely related measures and may differ from measures of extinction in terms of absolute performance. These matters are discussed further in Section III.

1. Magnitude of Reward

Hull's (1952) theory implied that the performance of groups trained under different MR should diverge with training to different asymptotes. Similar implications follow from Spence's (1956) formal assumptions, although Spence qualified his view by asserting that rats receiving small MR "should eventually reach the same asymptote as that attained with a group given a larger reward and allowed a longer consummatory period [p. 141]." Spence expected such convergence in performance to occur only after extended training. The expectation that the performance of groups trained with different MR should diverge early in acquisition has been confirmed repeatedly (e.g., Logan, 1960; Spence, 1956). Recent runway experiments, however, cast doubt on the view that different acquisition asymptotes are attained with different MR, when acquisition training is sufficiently extended. These experiments report that large MR does produce more rapid acquisition than small MR but equivalent asymptotes are eventually attained (Campbell, Batsche, & Batsche, 1972; Habley, Gipson, & Hause, 1972; Hammer, 1971; McCain, Dyleski, & McElvain, 1971; Ratliff & Ratliff, 1971). In addition to frequent failures to obtain asymptotic effects of MR, some investigations report an actual reversal in the effects of MR such that rats which receive the smaller MR come to run faster than rats receiving a larger MR (e.g., Black, 1969; Capaldi, 1973). Conversely, some experimenters do report that a large MR group continues to run faster than a small MR group, even after extended training (e.g., Ehrenfreund, 1971). Consequently, no conclusion regarding the effects of MR on asymptotic runway performance can be asserted with confidence. Nevertheless, it seems clearly established that rate of acquisition is a direct function of MR. Furthermore, a similar effect of MR on rate of extinction has been demonstrated, at least when training is with consistent reward. Thus, rats trained with large, consistent MR extinguish more rapidly than rats trained with small, consistent MR (see Sperling, 1965).

2. Percentage of Trials Rewarded

The classic, parametric research on the effects of PTR on acquisition and extinction performance was conducted by Weinstock (1954, 1958). Employing several percentage of reward, Weinstock found that early acquisition performance was directly related to PTR while asymptotic performance was inversely related to PTR. This latter effect of faster running for partial reward than consistent reward groups was replicated by Wagner (1961) and others and is referred to as the "partial reinforcement acquisition effect" (PRAE). While a number of experiments have obtained the effect, numerous experiments fail to find any evidence of PRAE and report that partial reward groups may approach but do not exceed the acquisition asymptote of the consistent reward group (see Robbins, 1971). The factors which account for the appearance or absence of the PRAE are not clear and the situation is complicated by the fact that most experiments which manipulate PTR are interested primarily in extinction effects and present little information on the acquisition effects of PTR. While the effects of PTR on the acquisition asymptote are unresolved, then, it does appear that the early acquisition performance of a consistent reward group diverges from that of a partial reward group—i.e., increasing PTR increases rate of conditioning. A similar effect of PTR on extinction performance is well established: RTE appears to be an inverse function of PTR (e.g., Weinstock, 1954). This result is generally referred to as the "partial reinforcement effect" (PRE). When stated in terms of rate, the PRE refers to the direct relationship between acquisition percent reward and rate of extinction and thus the principal effect of PTR apparently is to increase both acquisition rate and extinction rate.

3. Constant Delay of Reward

The constant DR procedure which is of current interest involves imposing a fixed delay interval between the response and reward on each trial. Although this procedure has been employed much less frequently than either reward magnitude or percent reward procedures, its effects on acquisition performance seem fairly well established. An early experiment by Perin (1943) which employed a discrete trial bar press response suggested that asymptotic acquisition performance was an inverse function of the delay interval. Subsequent runway experiments have confirmed this result (Renner, 1964). Thus, when the runway performance of a group trained under DR is compared with that of an immediate reward group, the curves diverge early in training and do not appear to show subsequent convergence. It is possible that DR might affect both asymptotic performance and rate of approach to the asymptote but at the present time there appears to be no evidence of an effect on acquisition rate. Furthermore, extinction rate also appears to be unaffected by constant DR. While there have been only a few experiments of this type, they consistently fail to find any strong effect on RTE attributable to acquisition DR (e.g., Habley et al., 1972; Logan, 1960; Logan, Beier, & Kincaid, 1956; Sgro, Dyal, & Anastasio, 1967). Thus, DR appears to affect asymptotic acquisition performance but not to affect strongly either rate of conditioning or rate of extinction. These effects are, of course, exactly the reverse of the effects reported for magnitude and percent reward.

4. Summary

It appears that in runway conditioning asymptotic performance in acquisition is inversely related to DR but DR does not appear to affect rate of extinction. The effects on the acquisition asymptote of both MR and PTR are controversial but both variables clearly affect rate of conditioning and rate of extinction. Specifically, rate of conditioning and of extinction both increase under favorable conditions of MR or PTR (e.g., larger MR or consistent reward). These results suggest that the effects of MR and PTR may be explained by a common process but a different process may be involved in DR. Further, since MR and PTR have the same effect on conditioning rate that they have on extinction rate, it is possible that conditioning rate and extinction rate both depend on a single process.

If these results are restated in terms of the concept of resistance-to-extinction (RTE), they may appear surprising or paradoxical since it appears that conditions which are favorable for the acquisition of the instrumental response are unfavorable for its persistence. The problem arises to the extent that RTE is considered a measure of the "response strength" which accumulated during acquisition. A response-strength interpretation of RTE appears to require a positive relationship between acquisition and extinction running speeds which generally is not obtained. For example, several influential theories of instrumental conditioning (Hull, 1943; Spence, 1936; Thorndike, 1932) traditionally considered the conditioning process to reflect the accumulation of the response-strengthening and the response-weakening effects of rewards and nonrewards. While more recent response-strength theories of conditioning can account for these experimental results (e.g., Amsel, 1958; Capaldi, 1967), the results appear problemmatical or exceptional only when extinction performance is viewed in terms of response strength. From the point of view of discrimination of reward conditions, it is the rat which shows little RTE which is showing "good responding," while the rat which persists in running is failing to discriminate the change in reward conditions. Similarly, in terms of the general "adaptiveness" of behavior, persistence in extinction responding is "poor" responding. Viewed in this manner, large and consistent reward promote adaptive behavior and good discrimination in both acquisition and extinction.

II. Basic Theoretical Formulation

This section describes a theory concerned with some of the effects of reward variables in appetitive, instrumental conditioning experiments. Section II, A introduces informally the major concepts and orienting assumptions, while Section II, B contains a more formal statement of the theory.

A. BASIC CONCEPTS AND GENERAL ASSUMPTIONS

1. *Expected Reward Magnitude (E(Sr))*

If rats were trained in a multiphase runway experiment (Table I) involving many reward conditions, their performance in any phase presumably would reflect the current reward conditions as well as those which prevailed in past phases. The present position is that rats "keep track" of their experiences with rewards by "averaging" those rewards. Further, the reward condition a rat learns to expect is assumed to be the result of such averaging. Thus, "average" MR determines "expected MR" which is identified in the theory as $E(Sr)$. These assumptions resemble those I made in dealing with incentive contrast effects (Black, 1968) but the present formulation modifies and extends those views. It is now proposed, for example, that in averaging rewards rats weight their experiences temporally so that recent rewards are assigned more weight than prior rewards in determining $E(Sr)$. Thus, the current MR will be weighted more heavily than the MR received in the previous phase, etc. Rewards are not viewed as producing relatively permanent changes in the organism such as an increment of habit strength (Hull, 1943) or the conditioning of $r_g - s_g$ (Spence, 1956); instead, the effects of past rewards are conceived as changing as the rat "revises" and "updates" $E(Sr)$ on the basis of intervening rewards (trials). This temporal-weighting assumption provides a theoretical means by which the rat may discount reward conditions that are temporally remote and irrelevant to currently prevailing conditions. Without such an assumption, average (mean) reward would become increasingly more resistant to change as experience with reward accumulates.

The present formulation emphasizes the properties of the reward as a stimulus (Sr) and the effectiveness of Sr is considered relative to $E(Sr)$—i.e., the difference, $Sr - E(Sr)$, is important rather than the absolute Sr. This difference appears in the theory in two forms. The absolute value of $Sr - E(Sr)$ defines the "distinctiveness" of reward which affects the degree to which the rat discriminates reward conditions. Additionally, when the difference is negative, so that reward is less than expected, a decremental effect on performance is expected.

2. Consistency of Reward (Cr)

In addition to learning about MR, rats are assumed to learn about the relative frequency of rewarded and nonrewarded runway trials— i.e., the consistency of reward. This expectation regarding the consistency of reward is identified as Cr and is a function of the proportion of trials which are rewarded. A temporally weighted averaging process is held to produce Cr in the same manner that $E(Sr)$ is produced. It should be noted, however, that the rat is assumed to form separate expectations on the basis of MR and PTR rather than "pooling" these aspects of reward.

3. Discrimination of Response-Reward Contingency (d)

This construct (d) has great importance in the formal theory but is difficult to describe intuitively. The basic notion is that reward conditions differ in the extent to which they permit the rat to learn what "produces" the food it obtains. Under favorable conditions such as large and consistent reward, the rat is assumed to quickly learn that the instrumental response "produces" food. Under less favorable conditions, such as partial reward, the rat is assumed to be less able to recognize or discriminate the response-reward contingency. Thus, d will be larger for consistent than partial reward. The function of d is to determine the rate at which performance reflects changes in reward conditions. For example, when extinction begins, rate of extinction will be greater for the rats trained under consistent reward since d is greater. Stated differently, the response is expected to change when reward changes only to the extent that the relationship between responses and reward is recognized. The present formulation differs from the "discrimination hypothesis" (Mowrer & Jones, 1945) in that the present view holds that RTE depends on what is learned in acquisition (d) while the "discrimination hypothesis" related RTE to the degree of difference between acquisition and extinction conditions. These hypotheses lead to different predictions (Section III).

4. Performance Variables

Running speed is assumed to vary directly with E. This theoretical variable is related to the concepts E, I, and $\bar{E}$ (Spence, 1936) which I employed in dealing with contrast effects. In that analysis (Black, 1968), reward variables contributed to E, nonreward and reduced reward produced I, and the variables combined additively to produce E. The present analysis assumes that both incremental and decremental (inhibitory) effects occur directly in E rather than indirectly through I or $\bar{E}$. Consequently, these latter theoretical variables are not retained and performance is related directly to the single variable E. The result is that the theory includes two performance equations.

$$\Delta E_i = d_i k_R (1 - E_i), \qquad (1)$$

$$\Delta E_j = d_j k_N (0 - E_j) = - d_j k_N E_j. \qquad (2)$$

Equation (1) indicates the increment in E on rewarded Trial i, while Eq. (2) indicates the decrement in E on nonrewarded Trial j. The rate at which E is expected to change is determined by d and by k_R or k_N which are constant for rewarded or nonrewarded trials, respectively. It is important to note, however, that d in Eqs. (1) and (2) is a variable rather than a constant. These assumptions are elaborated in the following section.

B. SPECIFIC FORMULATION

1. *Expected Reward Magnitude*

a. Scaling Assumption. The food used as reward in the goal box is considered a stimulus of variable intensity or magnitude (MR). The response or behavioral effect produced by reward is assumed to be some nonlinear function of MR which is approximated by

$$Sr = 1 - 10^{-a(MR)}, \qquad (3)$$

where a is an empirical constant dependent on type of food, units of MR, etc., and Sr is the "scale value" of MR. The relationship in Eq. (3) is similar to that employed by Spence (1956) to define K, but Sr is not assumed to have the incentive-motivational properties of K.

b. Temporal-Weighting Assumption. The "scaled MR" expected after n trials

$$E_{n+1} (Sr) = \sum_{1}^{n} Sr_i Wt_i \bigg/ \sum_{1}^{n} Wt_i \qquad (4)$$

where Wt_i is the temporal weight associated with a MR (Sr_i) obtained on a rewarded trial, Trial i. Three aspects of Eq. (4) require explanation. First, Wt_i always depends on a "temporal distance" involving two trials: The trial for which $E(Sr)$ is to be calculated and the trial for which Wt must be determined. The former will be referred to as the "current trial" and the latter as a "past" or "prior" trial. The second point involves the manner of defining the "temporal distance" on which Wt depends. The theory assumes that the "temporal distance" between the current trial and a past trial has two components: The actual time (T) which elapsed between the trials and the number of trials (t) which intervened between the current trial and the past trial in question. Since events occurring in runway conditioning are specified usually in terms of their location in the trial sequence rather than in time, and since the theory assigns greater significance to t than to T, the present discussion will define Wt in terms of t. Later (Section III) the role of T in the theory will be indicated. Finally, it should be noted that Eq. (4) reflects nonreward trials only to the degree that Wt is affected.

The general assumption regarding Wt is that it becomes smaller for trials as they are progressively more distant from the current trial in the trial sequence (or in time). The specific assumption is that

$$Wt_i = t_i^{-b}, \qquad (5)$$

where b is a constant that determines the rate at which Wt_i decreases as the number of trials (t_i) intervening between the current trial and Trial i increases. If all trials in an experiment are numbered in consecutive order as in Table I, then t_i is the difference between the ordinal position of Trial i and the current trial. Thus, if Trial 20 is considered "current," then t for Trial 5 is $20 - 5 = 15$, etc. As either b or t increases, of course, Wt decreases.

c. *Initial Value of $E(Sr)$.* The theory assumes that when the rat is first placed in the runway (Trial 1), it has some expectation of finding food there—i.e., $E_1(Sr) > 0$. This initial $E(Sr)$ is assumed to contain the quantities in Eq. (4) but is the result of the preexperimental history of the animal. This history is assumed to result in an initial expectation of some small reward which involves the sum of the Wt's accumulated during a history of considerable length (L). Although the theory specifies ways in which $E_1(Sr)$ can be manipulated experimentally (Section III), there appears to be no way in which the components $E_1(Sr)$ and L can be calculated. Therefore, a constant but arbitrary value will be assigned to each of these theoretical quantities in subsequent calculations of $E(Sr)$. It will be noted that the value of $E_1(Sr)$ has a negligible effect on $E_n(Sr)$ beyond the early training trials, since this quantity is treated as "Trial 0" in assigning Wt—i.e., in calculating $E_n(Sr)$, t for the quantities in $E_1(Sr)$ is equal to n.

d. *Calculation of $E(Sr)$.* The preceding assumptions are incorporated in and summarized by a general equation for $E(Sr)$ on Trial $n + 1$ as follows:

$$E_{n+1}(Sr) = \frac{\sum_{1}^{n} Sr_i t_i^{-b} + LE_1(Sr) t_{n+1}^{-b}}{\sum_{1}^{n} t_i^{-b} + L t_{n+1}^{-b}}, \qquad (6)$$

where Sr_i is the reward on the rewarded trial, Trial i; t_i is the number of trials intervening between Trial i and the current trial; $E_1(Sr)$ is the reward expected on Trial 1; L is the sum of Wt for $E_1(Sr)$; and $n + 1$ is the ordinal position of the trial considered current. It must be noted that for each trial on which $E(Sr)$ is to be calculated, the Wt assigned each past trial must change. Thus, when $E_{20}(Sr)$ is calculated, t for Trial 5 is $20 - 5 = 15$; but, when $E_{21}(Sr)$ is calculated, t for Trial 5 is $21 - 5 = 16$, etc.

2. Consistency of Reward

a. Relationship to $E(Sr)$. The basic assumption is that rats average MR on rewarded trials to arrive at $E(Sr)$ while Cr is based on all trials and reflects the relative frequency with which there was reward or no reward. Thus, while these theoretical variables are not strictly independent, they are considered to result from separate averaging processes.

b. Temporal Weighting Assumption. The assumption made for Cr is identical to that for $E(Sr)$ in Eqs. (4) and (5). For Cr the value of Sr in Eq. (4) is either 0 (nonrewarded trials) or 1.0 (rewarded trials). Thus, the equation for Cr becomes

$$Cr = \sum_{1}^{m} t_{R_i}^{-b} \bigg/ \left(\sum_{1}^{m} t_{R_i}^{-b} + \sum_{1}^{n-m} t_{N_j}^{-b} \right) \qquad (7)$$

where t_{R_i} is the value of t for rewarded Trial i and t_{N_j} is t for nonrewarded Trial j. The denominator in Eq. (7) obviously is the sum of Wt for all trials.

c. Initial Value of Cr. In the case of $E(Sr)$, the rat was assumed to have an initial expectation of reward for which the sum of Wt was L. In the case of Cr it is assumed that based on the same "length" (L) of experience, the rat initially expects reward for some low probability which reflects the relative frequency of reward in that experience, i.e., Cr_1. The value of Cr_1 must be assigned arbitrarily, and the considerations discussed with respect $E_1(Sr)$ are appropriate here as well.

d. *Calculation of Cr.* These assumptions are incorporated into a general equation for Cr on Trial $n + 1$ as

$$Cr_{n+1} = \left(\sum_1^m t_i^{-b} + LCr_1 t_{n+1}^{-b} \right) \bigg/ \left(\sum_1^{n-m} \sum_1^m t_{ij}^{-b} + Lt_{n+1}^{-b} \right) \qquad (8)$$

where $n + 1$ is the current trial and m of the n prior trials were rewarded. As in the case of $E(Sr)$, calculation of Cr requires reassigning Wt for past trials each time a new trial is considered current.

4. Development of d

a. *Specific Assumption.* The concept, d, is defined in terms of the change in d on rewarded Trial n as

$$\Delta d_n = |Sr_n - E_n(Sr)| (Cr_n - d_n). \qquad (9)$$

b. *Role of Distinctiveness of Reward.* To the (absolute) degree that a stimulus differs from, or contrasts with, the background or context in which it occurs, the stimulus may be considered "distinctive." The "context" in which Sr is assumed to occur is provided, in part, by $E(Sr)$. Thus, when Sr is obtained, it will be distinctive relative to $E(Sr)$ and the more distinctive Sr is, the more readily the rat will learn to recognize the relationship between Sr and the instrumental response. Consequently, the absolute difference between Sr and $E(Sr)$ will be a determinant of the rate at which d develops in Eq. (9). It is Sr, however, which is assumed to be "distinctive" and when Sr is absent the value of $|Sr - E(Sr)|$ is assumed to be 0. Therefore, on nonrewarded trials no change in d occurs in Eq. (9), although the value of Cr will change on such trials. This view of nonrewarded trials is consistent with the assumption that the rat separately averages MR and PTR. It is also consistent with the general assumption that d reflects the extent to which the animal learns to recognize the conditions under which reward occurs, since such learning presumably occurs only when those conditions (and reward) occur.

c. *Regularity of Reward.* The current view is that the rat's ability to discriminate or recognize the response-reward contingency will be limited generally by the degree to which a regular or predictable relationship actually exists. Any source of variability or irregularity in the reward conditions which follow the instrumental response will be expected to detract from the discrimination of the response-reward contingency (d). Since d is a principal determinant of extinction rate, variable reward conditions should tend to retard extinction—i.e., to increase resistance to extinction. For example, if acquisition reward magnitude is unpredictably variable, then poorer extinction performance (i.e., greater resistance to extinction) is expected. Similiarly, a random sequence of delayed and immediate rewards (partial delay of reward) should also increase resistance to extinction. For present purposes, the concept of "regularity of reward" has been reduced to "consistency of reward" which can be specified unambiguously in terms of PTR, etc. Thus, Cr provides the limit toward which d changes on rewarded trials. If d exceeds Cr, it will tend to become smaller and if Cr exceeds d, d will tend to increase. The rate at which these changes occur in d, however, will depend on the distinctiveness of reward $|Sr - E(Sr)|$. Conversely, regardless of the distinctiveness of reward, d will not change if $Cr = d$.

d. *Calculation of d.* The value of d is calculated successively for each rewarded trial of an experiment. Although some initial nonzero value was assumed to $E(Sr)$ and Cr, d is considered 0 on Trial 1—i.e., the rat is not assumed to have acquired a discrimination of the response-reward contingencies in the runway prior to Trial 1. While d changes only on rewarded trials, both $E(Sr)$ and Cr may change on nonrewarded trials. Thus, the value of all three variables for any trial depends on all of the preceding trials.

5. *Performance: Incremental Effects*

The incremental effect on E of a rewarded trial is indicated in Eq. (1). Performance (running speed) is assumed to be a direct function of E but no attempt has been made in the present formulation to relate E more precisely to empirical measures of performance. Once d has been determined, the calculation of ΔE on rewarded Trial i requires only the specification of k_R. A single value for this constant has been employed in all current calculations.

6. *Performance: Decremental Effects*

a. *Reduced Reward.* The theoretical effect of nonreward indicated in Eq. (2) reflects the view that rats respond "adaptively" to nonreward by ceasing to perform the instrumental response. This "inhibitory" effect of nonreward may be considered a special case of the decremental effects predicted whenever reward is reduced to a level below that which the rat expects. For example, continuous nonreward (extinction) following consistent reward might be described as a "complete" reduction of PTR, while a shift from consistent to partial reward involves a "fractional" reduction in PTR. The theory provides equivalent treatment of all cases of reduced reward: Whenever reward is reduced below the level expected by the rat, a decremental effect proportional to the quantity in Eq. (2) is assumed to occur. The magnitude of this effect is assumed to depend on the difference between expected reward and the prevailing reward condition. Thus, when PTR is reduced, the decremental effect will depend on $Cr - P$; when MR is reduced, the effect will depend on $E(Sr) - Sr$. Specifically, if on Trial i reward magnitude Sr is less than expected, a decrement in E is expected such that

$$\Delta E_i = - d_i k_N E_i(E(Sr) - Sr). \tag{10}$$

Since a reduced-reward trial is, nevertheless, a rewarded trial, an increment in E should also occur as indicated by Eq. (1). Further, since these incremental and decremental effects are considered additive, the combined effect on E on Trial i will be

$$\Delta E_i = d_i [k_R (1 - E_i) - E_i k_N (E(Sr) - Sr)] \tag{11}$$

The rat is assumed to respond in an analogous fashion to a reduction in percent reward. On rewarded trials, E will increase in accordance with Eq. (1); on nonrewarded trials a decrement in E occurs as a function of the difference between the Cr and the current proportion of trials rewarded, P, in accordance with

$$\Delta E_i = - d_i k_N E_i(Cr - P). \tag{12}$$

The formulation represented by Eq. (12) can be considered general—i.e., it is applied to all nonrewarded trials in experiments of the type described in Table I. Thus, Eq. (2) is a special case of Eq. (12) which applies when $P = 0$ and $Cr = 1.0$—e.g., at the beginning of an extinction phase following extended acquisition under consistent reward.

b. Delay of Reward. The experimental results reviewed in Section I, B clearly indicated that constant DR has decremental effects on acquisition, but unfortunately, these results provide limited guidance among the alternative assumptions that could be made to incorporate DR into the present theory. While all of the current assumptions obviously are tentative in nature, this is especially true for the proposal regarding DR. In any event, it will be assumed that the effect of DR is to alter the "distinctiveness" of reward—i.e., the quantity $|Sr - E(Sr)|$. Specifically, it is proposed that DR has effects which subtract from the "distinctiveness" of reward. This delay-produced effect that can be viewed as reducing the effective value of MR by being subtracted from Sr or, alternatively, it could be held that during the delay interval expected MR increases in that the effects of DR are added to $E(Sr)$. In either case, the algebraic result is the same and, for present purposes, it is assumed that the "distinctiveness" of delayed reward is defined by $[Sr - \log(1 + D) - E(Sr)]$, where D is the delay interval in minutes. Since the delay intervals employed in the relevant experiments rarely exceed 30 seconds, the present proposal in limited to cases where $D < 1.00$. Thus, under constant delayed reinforcement,

$$\Delta d_i = |Sr - \log(1 + D) - E(Sr)|(Cr - d_i). \qquad (13)$$

Under Eq. (13) the effect of DR early in acquisition will be to reduce "distinctiveness" of reward and, thus, retard the development of d. Later in acquisition, however, $E(Sr)$ will become greater than $[Sr - \log(1 + D)]$ and "distinctiveness" will increase and facilitate d. Furthermore, when $E(Sr)$ exceeds $[Sr - \log(1 + D)]$, the theory treats the situation as a case of "reduced reward" and applies Eq. (11) with $[Sr - \log(1 + D)]$ as the value of Sr in that equation.

C. COMPUTATIONAL PROCEDURES: ILLUSTRATIVE RESULTS

1. General Considerations

The formal theory presented in Section II, B essentially involves only four theoretical variables: $E(Sr)$, Cr, d, and E. Quite independently of their informal or intuitive aspects (Section II, A), these theoretical concepts are each defined by an equation which allows the calculation of their numerical values for any trial, of any phase, of any experiment of the type represented in Table I. The calculation of these values is conceptually simple but it is complicated by the temporal weighting aspect of the theory which requires frequently reassigning the temporal weights associated with prior trials. All of the theoretical data were calculated using an iterative computer program which provided exact solutions to the relevant equations. All of the theoretical results are for three-phase "experiments" consisting of 150 "trials" (Table I), with the last 50 trials as an extinction phase in all cases.

2. Development of $E(Sr)$ and Cr

The development of $E(Sr)$ is presented in Fig. 1 for two values of Sr ("large MR" = .75 and "small MR" = .25) and two values of b, the temporal weighting factor. The solid lines indicate $E(Sr)$ for "groups" which receive the same MR on all 100 trials. The broken curves indicate $E(Sr)$ following a shift (reversal) in MR. In all cases, the value of $E_1(Sr)$, the reward expected initially, was assumed to be .05, while the value for the weight or length of experience associated with $E_1(Sr)$ was assumed to be 15 (i.e., $L = 15$). The theoretical data were calculated by Eq. (6).

The effects of the temporal-weighting assumption are quite apparent in Fig. 1, since when $b = 0$ (upper half of figure) such temporal weighting does not occur and $E(Sr)$ is simply mean Sr, including $E_1(Sr)$. Under this condition, a shift from large to small MR at Trial 50 results in a gradual change in $E(Sr)$ and by Trial 100, $E(Sr)$ for the hypothetical shifted-MR groups is equal and intermediate to the values of Sr involved. The lower portion of Fig. 1

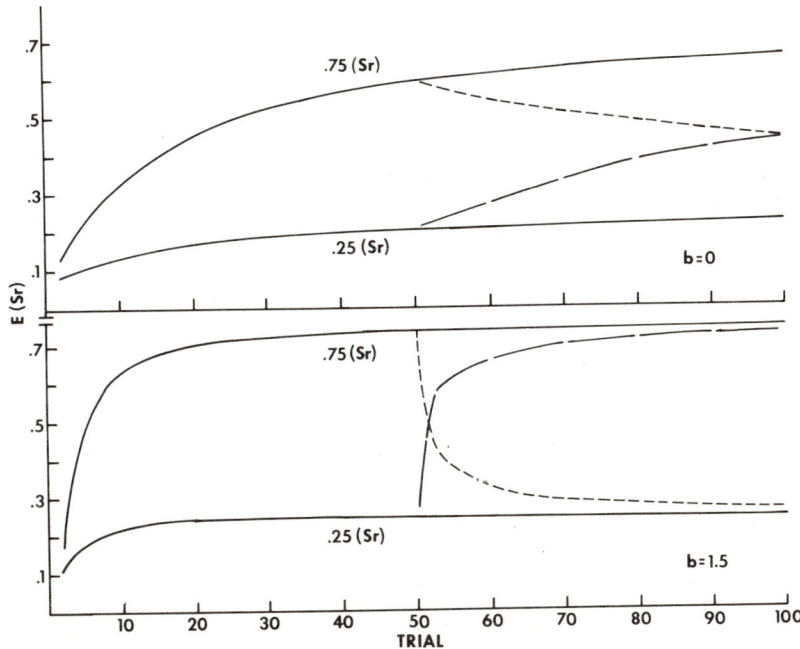

Fig. 1. Development of $E(Sr)$ for two reward magnitudes (Sr) and two temporal-weighting assumptions (b). Solid lines indicate $E(Sr)$ for "groups" which receive the same MR on all 100 trials. Broken curves indicate $E(Sr)$ following a shift (reversal) in MR.

represents the effects of assigning a relatively large value to the temporal-weighting factor ($b = 1.50$). Under this assumption, a shift in MR produces a very rapid change in $E(Sr)$ followed by relatively complete adjustment to the new value of Sr. Although they are not presented, an analogous set of theoretical results obtains in the case of Cr. If hypothetical groups are trained under 100% and 50% reward, and PTR is then reversed, slow and incomplete adjustment occurs in Cr if $b = 0$, but rapid and essentially complete changes occur if $b = 1.50$. Thus, with respect to both MR and PTR, the assumption that temporal weighting does occur produces theoretical expectations which resemble the empirical effects of shifts in these variables (see Section III). In all subsequent calculations, the values noted above have been assumed—i.e., $b = 1.5$, $L = 15$, $E_1(Sr) = .05$ and, in calculating Cr (Eq. 8), it is assumed that $Cr_1 = .1$.

3. Development of d and E

The development of "discrimination" (d) and "performance" (E) are illustrated in Figs. 2 and 3, respectively, for the case of a hypothetical experiment in which two levels of MR ($Sr = .25$ or $.75$) are combined factorially with two levels of PTR ($P = 1.0$ or $.5$). Inspec-

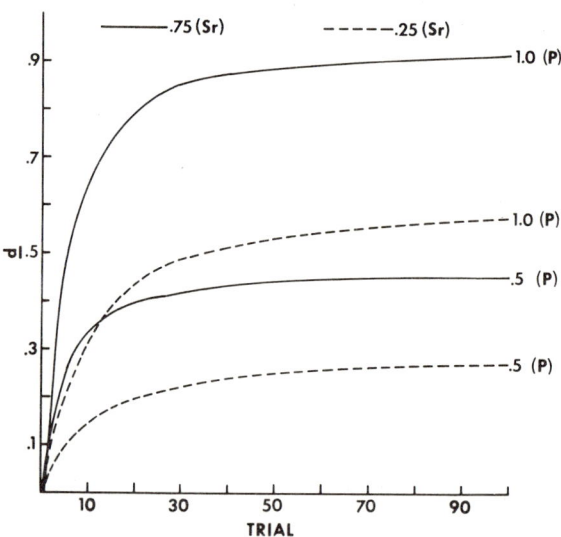

Fig. 2. Development of d for two reward magnitudes (Sr) and two proportions of rewarded trials (P).

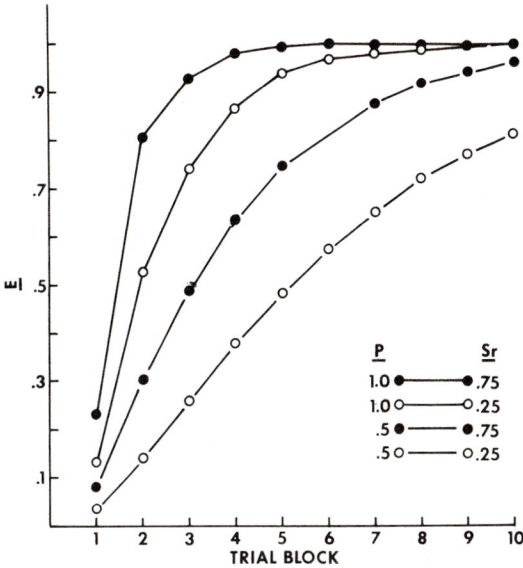

Fig. 3. Development of E for two reward magnitudes (Sr) and two proportions of rewarded trials (P).

tion of Fig. 2 indicates that both MR and PTR have strong effects on the development of d. Both of these variables also affect the development of E, but Fig. 3 indicates that the effect primarily is on the rate at which E develops rather than on its asymptote. Had the development of E been extended beyond "Trial Block 10," all of the groups would have reached the same asymptote ($E = 1.00$) as Eq. (1) requires. The values of d in Fig. 2 were calculated by Eq. (9) and the values of E were calculated by Eq. (1) for the hypothetical CR groups. For this latter purpose, the value of k_R was set at .15 which is the value of k_R employed in all subsequent calculations. The values of E for the hypothetical 50% reward groups were calculated by Eq. (1) for rewarded trials and by Eq. (12) for nonrewarded trials. For Eq. (12) the value of k_N was .4 and this value of k_N is employed in all applications of Eq. (12) including partial reward, extinction and changes in PTR, as well as for all applications of Eq. (11) to reduced reward, delay of reward, etc. In short, k_R (= .15) is employed whenever "incremental effects" on E are involved and k_N (= .4) is employed for all "decremental effects" on E. These values were arbitrarily selected to allow most changes in E to be complete within the 50 trials that constitute most "phases" in the hypothetical experiments discussed here. Thus, it should be clear that no significance is attached to the particular number of "trials" over which effects on E are indicated as occurring theoretically. To emphasize this, most predictions involving E are related to "trial blocks" (e.g., Fig. 3) which can be considered ordinally related to the actual trial sequence in genuine experiments. All calculations continue to be performed, however, in terms of phases of 50 trials each.

III. Implications of the Theory

A. CONSTANT REWARD CONDITIONS

1. *Acquisition Effects of* MR *and* PTR

The basic implications of the theory for acquisition under constant MR and PTR were presented in Fig. 3. (The experimental results relevant to these predictions are discussed in Section I, B.) It is expected that rate of conditioning will be greater for large reward than for small reward and greater for consistent than partial reward. These expectations agree, of course, with the results consistently obtained in runway experiments. The theory also implies that the difference between large and small reward groups should begin to decline with extended training and should ultimately disappear, if training is sufficiently extended. This prediction is consistent with the results of several recent runway experiments but conflicting results have also been obtained. A similar situation exists regarding the asymptotic effects of PTR. The present prediction is that groups trained under partial reward will converge upon, but not exceed, the asymptote attained under consistent reward. The asymptotic effects of PTR, however, are controversial to a degree that precludes definitive evaluation of the current predictions. Nevertheless, where the effects of MR and PTR are clear, these effects agree with the current predictions.

2. *Extinction Effects of* MR *and* PTR

Extinction data are sometimes presented in relative terms which are intended to correct for initial differences in performance and to reflect the rate at which extinction occurs (see Anderson, 1963). The present formulation readily generates predictions for rate of extinction. It is apparent in Eq. (12) that during a series of extinction trials, where $P = 0$, the rate of extinction (i.e., $\Delta E_i/E_i$) will be directly proportional to $d_i Cr_i$. A convenient measure of RTE, in relative terms, is $(1 - d_i Cr_i)$ and this quantity will define RTE for present purposes. It must be noted, however, that extinction data are presented more commonly in terms of absolute performance (running speed) rather than in relative terms. Predictions regarding absolute extinction performance also can be made from the present theory by use of Eq. (12). Since it is measures of absolute extinction performance which are commonly presented, the current discussion will emphasize predictions made for such measures, although predicted RTE in relative terms will also be indicated.

The levels of extinction performance predicted for the four groups of the hypothetical MR–PTR factorial experiment are presented in Fig. 4. Inspection of this figure indicates the following theoretical expectations: (a) For consistent reward groups (solid lines) extinction performance should be an inverse function of acquisition MR; (b) a partial reinforcement effect (PRE) should occur for both large MR (filled circles) and small MR (open circles) groups; and (c) the PRE should be larger for the large MR groups. The first two predictions are consistent with the relevant experimental results summarized in Section I, B. The third prediction also has been confirmed by several investigators (see Robbins, 1971). The theory predicts

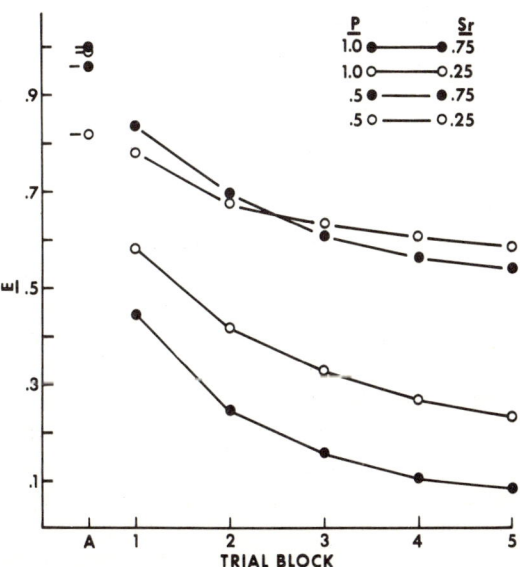

Fig. 4. Predicted extinction performance (E) following training under one of two reward magnitudes (Sr) and one of two proportions of rewarded trials (P).

rapid extinction for groups trained with consistent reward and large MR because these groups attain good discrimination of the response-reward contingency during acquisition (Fig. 2). When the contingency is altered in extinction, the changed reward conditions are recognized more readily by such groups and reflected in rapid performance decrements [Eq. (12)]. On the other hand, extinction performance for partial reward groups is not expected to differ substantially as a function of MR (Fig. 4), in spite of the somewhat greater d developed by the partial reward group which receives the larger reward (Fig. 2). This implication is dependent, however, on the level of acquisition training involved and will be considered in relation to that variable.

3. Extinction Effects of Amount of Training

Since the theory defined RTE as a direct function of $(1 - d_i Cr_i)$, it is apparent that the increasing either d or Cr will decrease RTE—i.e., the better the discrimination of the response-reward contingency and the more consistently reward is expected, the more rapidly will performance decline when reward is discontinued. Further, to the degree that d and Cr increase with increasing training, the theory predicts that RTE will decline as a function of amount of training. To illustrate these theoretical expectations, predictions were generated for a hypothetical experiment which factorially combines two levels of MR, two levels of percent reward, and five levels of training. The predicted RTE for the 20 groups of such an experiment are presented in Table II. Inspection of this table indicates that RTE should decline with increasing training for all four reward combinations, but the decline in RTE is expected to be substantially larger for consistent reward groups than for partial reward groups.

Predicted performance in extinction (i.e., mean E) for the hypothetical 20-group experiment is presented in Table III which indicates that (a) for consistent reward groups, extinction performance should first increase and then decrease as training level increases; (b) for consistent reward groups, the extinction decrement produced by extended training should occur earlier for a large MR group; (c) for partial reward groups, extinction performance increases monotonically as training level increases (although with further increases in training some decline would occur); (d) for partial reward groups large MR results in increased extinction performance but this effect decreases and disappears as training is increased. Each of these expectations is consistent with the relevant experimental literature.

TABLE II

PREDICTED RESISTANCE-TO-EXTINCTION
$(1 - dCr)^a$

	Number of training trials				
Group	10	30	50	70	100
.75(Sr)/1.0(P)	.875	.787	.757	.741	.727
.75(Sr)/.5(P)	.969	.947	.939	.935	.932
.25(Sr)/1.0(P)	.984	.877	.853	.840	.827
.25(Sr)/.5(P)	.987	.972	.966	.962	.959

[a]The value of Cr declines during extinction at a rate which is partly determined by the amount of acquisition training on which Cr is based. For purposes of this table in which training level is a variable, RTE was calculated on the basis of mean extinction Cr for each training level. Elsewhere, when training level is not variable, RTE is estimated on the basis of the value of Cr on Extinction Trial 1.

Thus, extinction performance does appear to increase monotonically for partial reward groups (see Robbins, 1971). While a decrement in extinction performance occurs following extended consistent reward training (see Sperling, 1965), increasing training initially increases extinction performance for consistent reward groups (e.g., Clifford, 1964) and the subsequent decrement is obtained more readily with large MR (e.g., Traupmann, 1972). Finally, when partial reward training is limited or moderate, large MR produces a higher level of extinction performance than small MR (e.g., Hulse, 1958; Wagner, 1961) but this effect of MR may be eliminated following more extended training (see Capaldi & Freese, 1974). Thus, the detailed implications of the present formulation receive considerable empirical support.

B. EFFECTS OF VARIED REWARD CONDITION: SHIFTS IN MR

1. *Immediate Reward*

For expository purposes, a hypothetical two-phase experiment will be considered which involves training four groups of rats with either large MR ($Sr = .75$) or small MR ($Sr = .25$). Group .75 and Group .25 are control groups which receive large or small MR, respectively, in

TABLE III
PREDICTED EXTINCTION PERFORMANCE (E)

Group	Number of training trials				
	10	30	50	70	100
.75(Sr)/1.0(P)	.284	.318	.275	.249	.227
.75(Sr)/.5(P)	.144	.443	.566	.633	.667
.25(Sr)/1.0(P)	.203	.429	.442	.420	.392
.25(Sr)/.5(P)	.062	.269	.437	.556	.664

both phases. Group .75–.25 receives large MR in Phase I and small MR in Phase II, and Group .25–.75 receives small MR in Phase I and is shifted to large MR in Phase II. This experimental design allows the investigation of incentive contrast effects which may occur in Phase II performance. Specifically, if Group .75–.25 performs at a lower level in Phase II than Group .25, a negative contrast effect (NCE) is said to occur. Similarly, if Group .25–.75 exceeds the Phase II performance of Group .75, a positive contrast effect (PCE) has occurred.

a. Effects of Reduced MR. According to the present view, MR contributes to runway performance in two ways: To the degree that reward Sr differs from expected reward $E(Sr)$, it promotes the recognition of the response-reward contingency as indicated by Eq. (9); to the degree that Sr is less than $E(Sr)$, it produces a decrement in E as indicated by Eqs. (10) and (11). Both of these effects are "relative" in the sense that they depend on the relationship between Sr and $E(Sr)$ rather than the absolute value of reward. Nevertheless, a special significance is attributed to reduced reward which is not attributed to increased reward—i.e., Eq. (11) applies to cases where reward is less than expected but not to cases where reward is greater than expected. The status afforded reduction in reward in the present formulation is analogous to the assumption I made in a previous analysis of contrast effects (Black, 1968). The general view which I am suggesting is that rats respond to a reduction in reward as though it were a cue to the discontinuation of reward, and the decremental changes in their performance can be viewed as comparable to the changes associated with nonreward (i.e., extinction). Indeed, this is precisely the formal treatment of reduced reward expressed in Eq. (10)—the decrement produced by reduced reward is a fraction of the decrement produced by nonreward in Eq. (2). The other assumptions of the theory apply equally to reduced reward such that, for example, the decremental effects of reward reduction will depend on the level of d attained at the time reward is reduced and these effects will diminish as $E(Sr)$ adjusts to the reduced MR, etc.

The effects of reduction in MR for the hypothetical contrast effects experiment under discussion are presented in Fig. 5 for reductions occuring at two levels of Phase I training—i.e., MR is reduced on Trial 21 for one hypothetical group and on Trial 51 for a second group. The predicted effects of reduction in MR include that an NCE will occur following by recovery in performance and that the NCE will be larger following extended Phase I training than following limited training. Reference to Eq. (11) indicates the further prediction that the magnitude of the NCE will be a direct function of the degree of reduction in MR. Each of these expectations receives substantial support in the experimental literature (e.g., see Black, 1968; Cox, 1975; Durham, 1968). It may be shown also that, while the theory predicts a large NCE following 50 CR trials, a NCE is not

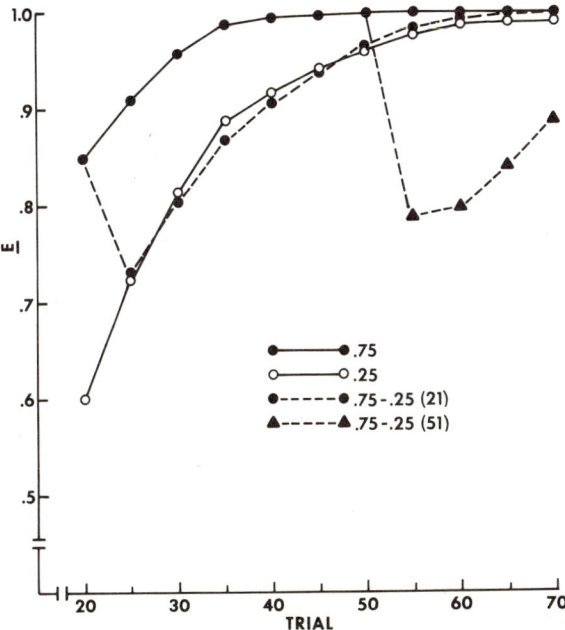

Fig. 5. Predicted performance (E) in a hypothetical NCE experiment (immediate reward). The numbers not enclosed in parentheses are the reward magnitudes received by different groups. The numbers in parentheses indicate the trial on which shifted-reward groups began to receive the second reward magnitude.

predicted when a group is shifted to .25 (Sr) from .75 (Sr) following 50 PR trials (P = .5). A NCE is expected, however, if the shift in MR is greater (e.g., from Sr = .9 to Sr = .1). These implications are in agreement with the relevant results (see Peters & McHose, 1974).

b. *Effects of Increased* MR. Under immediate reward conditions in an experiment of the type hypothetically considered, shifts from small to large reward rarely result in PCE (see Cox, 1975). It was for this reason that I did not assume that increased reward resulted in "special" incremental effects on E symmetrical to the inhibitory effects assumed to result from reduced reward (Black, 1968). It is for the same reason that Eq. (11) is not applied on trials where Sr exceeds $E(Sr)$. The result is that the current formulation does not predict PCE in "standard" experiments involving immediate reward, although it does predict that increased MR will result in a rapid increase in performance to a level appropriate to the new MR.

2. Delayed Reward

While PCE seldom have been obtained with immediate reward shifts, PCE have been reported when reward is delayed (e.g., Mellgren, 1971, 1972). The rationale in such experiments has been that PCE typically fail to appear because of a "ceiling effect" such that the performance of control rats trained with large, immediate reward cannot be exceeded by rats shifted to large reward from small reward (Bower, 1961). The introduction of a constant delay is employed to depress performance below this "ceiling" and allow the PCE to be observed. In any event, a PCE does appear to occur under delayed reward circumstances.

a. *General Effects of Constant* DR. As indicated earlier, the present analysis treats constant DR as a case of reduced reward. Specifically, it was assumed that under DR "effective MR" is reduced by the quantity log (1+D), where D is the delay interval in minutes. For either immediate or delayed reward, $E(Sr)$ will rapidly approach Sr during acquisition training as specified in Eq. (4). Thus, early in acquisition, $E(Sr)$ will come to exceed $Sr - \log(1 + D)$ for DR groups, and the decremental effects in Eq. (11) will depress acquisition performance such that asymptotic performance for DR groups will be an inverse function of DR. This prediction agrees with the acquisition results summarized in Section I, B. Further, since the effects of DR and MR combine additively, no interaction of these variables is predicted and, apparently, no interaction is obtained experimentally (e.g., Shanab, Sanders, & Premack, 1969; Shanab & Biller, 1972).

With respect to extinction effects, the implications of the current analysis of DR again agree with the relevant experimental evidence (Section I, B): Training under constant DR is not expected to increase RTE relative to a comparable group trained under immediate reward. This prediction results from the theoretical effect of DR on the "distinctiveness" of reward and the consequent development of d as indicated in Eq. (13). Rewards are "distinctive" to the degree that they differ from $E(Sr)$. For immediate reward this difference is maximal early in training while $E(Sr)$ is small and it decreases as $E(Sr)$ approaches Sr. For DR, however, the quantity, $\log(1 + D)$, will reduce this difference early in training, thereby making reward less distinctive; but later, as $E(Sr)$ approaches Sr, this quantity will result in a continuing difference between $E(Sr)$ and $Sr - \log(1 + D)$. In a sense, the theory assumes that delay intervals require the rat to continue to "attend" to the reward conditions. In any case, Eq. (13) predicts that a high level of d will develop eventually under DR and, as a result, a good rate of extinction (i.e., low RTE) is predicted. For example, assuming that $\log(1 + D) = .20$ ($D = 35.1$ sec), predicted RTE following 100 CR trials with large MR ($Sr = .75$) is .42 for a DR group, compared with .47 for a comparable immediate-reward group. Because asymptotic acquisition performance for the DR group ($E = .66$) is depressed relative to the immediate-reward group ($E = 1.00$), however, extinction performance for the DR group is expected to be lower than that for the immediate-reward group (mean extinction E of .10 and .23, respectively). These predictions are in excellent agreement with the relevant experimental results cited in Section I, B (see Tarpy & Sawabini, 1974).

b. *Shifts in Magnitude of Delayed Reward.* A hypothetical contrast effect experiment of the type discussed in relation to Fig. 5 will be considered with a constant DR (35.1 sec) assumed for all groups. The predicted effects of shifts in MR for such an experiment are presented in Fig. 6. The usual large MR ($Sr = .75$) and small MR ($Sr = .25$) control groups are employed—Group LL and Group SS. It is apparent in Fig. 6 that a shift from large to small MR (Group LS) is expected to produce a NCE and a shift from small to large MR (Group SL) is expected to produce a positive contrast effect (PCE). The basis for these predictions has been discussed earlier. For example, following the shift to large reward, Group SL will exceed the performance of Group LL because for Group SL reward will be large relative to expected reward following the shift, thus "offsetting" the decremental effect of delay in the expression, $[Sr - \log(1 + D) - E(Sr)]$. As $E(Sr)$ increases toward the value of the new MR, however, the performance of Group SL will decline toward that of Group LL.

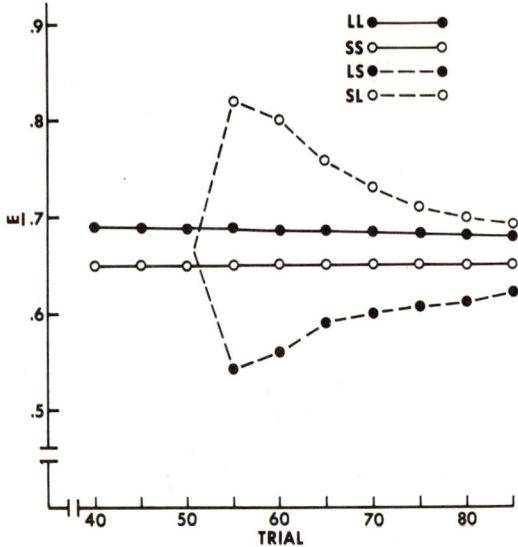

Fig. 6. Predicted performance in a hypothetical CE experiment (constant delayed reward). The letters indicate the reward magnitude received in the two phases (L = large reward; S = small reward).

Thus, in a sense, the PCE results from the fact that temporarily for Group SL the reward the rats obtain will not be less than expected. In this connection, an additional implication of this analysis of DR is of interest: While shifts in magnitude of delayed reward are expected to produce PCE, a shift (decrease) in delay per se is not expected to result in PCE. Instead, shifting from long to short delay (with MR constant) simply reduces $\log(1 + D)$ to a level of a short-delay control group and the performance of the shifted group will not exceed that of the control group. Experimental support for this prediction has been provided by a number of experiments (see Cox, 1975). It appears, therefore, that the present analysis provides a rather comprehensive account of the relationship between DR and incentive contrast effects, as well as of the more general effects of constant DR.

C. VARIED REWARD CONDITIONS

1. *Shifts Between Partial Reward and Consistent Reward*

Several experiments have been concerned with the magnitude of the PRE when partial reward training is followed by consistent reward training (a P-C sequence) or when partial reward training is preceded by consistent reward training (a C-P sequence). Theios (1962) reported that the PRE was not eliminated by P-C training, although RTE was reduced when consistent reward training was extended. A PRE following both P-C and C-P training sequences was reported by Sutherland, Mackintosh, and Wolfe (1965) who also reported lower extinction performance for the C-P group than for the P-C group. When relative extinction measures were employed by Elstad (1966) and by Theios and McGinnis (1967), however, greater RTE was found following C-P training than following P-C training. Elstad also reported that, for both training sequences, RTE was directly related to the amount of partial reward training and inversely related to the amount of consistent reward training.

The initial purpose of the preceding experiments (Theios, 1962) was to test the "discrimination hypothesis" interpretation of the PRE (see Section II, A). Since this view relates RTE to the amount of change in reward conditions which occurs at the transition from acquisition to extinction, it seems to imply that RTE will be equal for groups which receive the same percent reward at the end of acquisition. Consequently, no difference in RTE would be expected between a P-C group and a C-only control group. This implication of the "discrimination hypothesis" differs from the predictions generated by the current formulation and serves to illustrate some of the differences between these positions. According to the present analysis, the preceding investigations are three-phase experiments in which Phase III (extinction) performance will depend upon the reward conditions which prevailed in both prior phases. Specifically, RTE is proportional to $1 - dCr$ and, as a consequence of temporal weighting, the value of Cr will depend mostly on PTR in Phase II. When MR is constant, the value of d, however, will depend primarily on percent reward in Phase I. This is because $E(Sr)$ will approach the value of Sr during Phase I and Sr will cease to be "distinctive," so that subsequent changes in percent reward will have minimal effects on d, as indicated in Eq. (9). Although percent reward in both phases of acquisition will be expected to affect RTE, Cr effects will diminish during extinction while d will remain constant. Thus, the effects of Phase I percent reward will be expected to be larger than the effects of percent reward in Phase II. These predictions assume that Phase I training is sufficiently extended to allow expected reward to approximate obtained reward and that Phase II training is sufficiently extended to allow the expected consistency of reward (Cr) to adjust to the percent reward in Phase II. If Phase I training is limited, for example, then Sr will remain "distinctive" for some portion of Phase II and d will be affected by percent reward in Phase II.

These theoretical expectations are summarized in Fig. 7 which indicates predicte RTE $(1 - dCr)$ for the 12 groups of a hypothetical experiment which compares P-C and C-P groups and C-only and P-only control groups for two levels of MR (Sr = .25 or .75). All groups theoretically receive 100 acquisition trials, with the number of trials under each percent reward indicated in parentheses. Inspection of Fig. 7 indicates the following theoretical expectations: (a) RTE should be greatest for PR-only training and least for C-only; (b) a PRE is expected following partial reward training, whether that training is preceded or followed by consistent reward training; (c) the C-P sequence should produce greater RTE than P-C; (d) RTE should

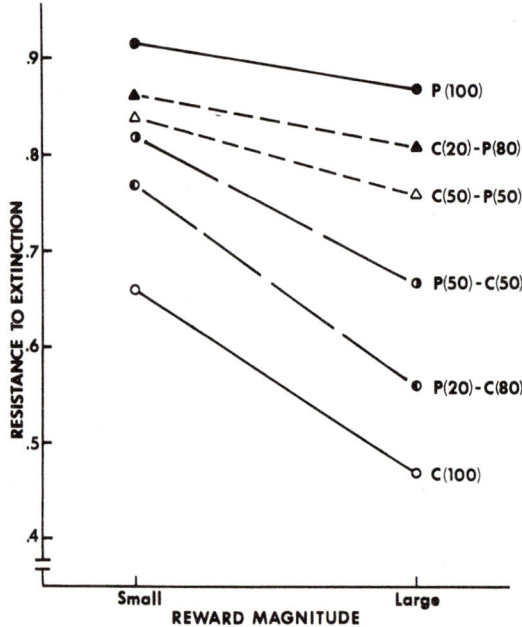

Fig. 7. Predicted RTE $(1 - dCr)$ for 12 groups trained under one of two reward magnitudes and one of several sequences of partial (P) or consistent (C) reward. The numbers in parentheses indicate the number of trials of the procedure indicated which the group received.

be directly related to the amount of PR training and inversely related to the amount of CR training. These expectations agree with the relevant results previously discussed. A further implication of the theory which is apparent in Fig. 7 is that these predicted effects should be enhanced when MR is large. Unfortunately, data bearing directly on this prediction do not appear to be available.

2. Effects of Initial Nonreward

Several experiments have involved administering an initial series of nonrewarded runway trials prior to runway training under CR (e.g., Robbins, Chait, & Weinstock, 1968; Spear, Hill, & O'Sullivan, 1965). These experimenters report that a group which received the initial nonreward showed greater RTE than a control group which received only the regular training phase. This result is predicted by the present analysis and is of some interest because the procedure of giving an initial series of nonrewarded trials should have the effect of experimentally manipulating Cr_1 — i.e., the "initial value" of Cr on the first (regular) training trial. It was assumed earlier that the rat begins runway training with some expectation of obtaining reward in that situation and that this initial value of Cr must be included in the calculation of subsequent values of Cr by Eq. (8). Since Cr_1 is presumably the result of undefined, preexperimental experience, its value cannot be calculated and an arbitrary value was assigned. Whatever the value of Cr_1, however, the effect of an initial series of nonrewarded trials should be to reduce Cr_1 while increasing its "weight." In other words, at the end of such a series, the animal should have less expectancy of reward and this expectation should be more resistant to change by subsequent experience with reward.

The theoretical effect of reducing Cr_1 and retarding the subsequent development of Cr can be determined from Eq. (9). Since Cr will be small early in training for an initially nonrewarded group, a reduced amount of d will develop. With continued rewarded training, the temporal-weighting process eventually will "discount" the initial nonrewards; but, concurrently, $E(Sr)$ will develop and Sr will become less "distinctive." The theoretical result is that the development of d will be limited by the small value of Cr in early training and later in training by the small difference between Sr and $E(Sr)$. The increased RTE for the initially nonrewarded group is the theoretical result of this reduction in the degree to which these animals discriminate the response-reward contingency.

D. VARIED REWARD CONDITIONS: CONCURRENT SHIFTS IN MR AND PTR

In discussing the theoretical effects of shifts in PTR, it was noted that such shifts will have minimal effects on d if they occur when reward has ceased to be "distinctive"—e.g., after extended training with constant MR. An obvious way in which the effects of shifts in PTR might be enhanced theoretically is to concurrently shift MR, thereby ensuring that obtained and expected reward will differ and that d will change as Cr adjusts to the new PTR, as indicated in Eq. (9). The general effect of such concurrent shifts in MR and PTR will be that d will tend toward the value characteristic of the postshift reward conditions and RTE will reflect these later conditions more than the preshift conditions.

A recent experiment by Capaldi (1974) provided a test of these implications of the theory. To clarify these implications, the predicted results of a hypothetical experiment are presented in Table IV. The hypothetical experiment consists of training five groups of rats in a three-phase experiment with interest centering on RTE (Phase III). Phases I and II each consists of 50 runway trials conducted under 50% reward (P) or 100% reward (C) with MR either large ($Sr = .75$) or small ($Sr = .25$). The specific treatments hypothetically received by each group are indicated in Table IV along with the RTE expected following training under the indicated conditions. Two of the groups receive concurrent shifts in MR and PTR (Groups C/S-P/L and P/L-C/S); percent reward is shifted with MR constant for two of the groups (Groups C/L-P/L and P/L-C/L; and Group P/L-P/L receives constant reward conditions in the two phases of training. The predicted effects of these treatments on RTE presented in Table IV may be described as follows: (*a*) A shift from consistent to partial reward should produce a greater increase in RTE when it is combined with an increase in MR; indeed, there is little difference between Group C/S-P/L and the P/L control group; (*b*) a shift from partial to consistent reward should produce a greater reduction in RTE when it is combined with a reduction in MR; thus, Group P/L-C/S is expected to show much less RTE than the other groups;

TABLE IV

PREDICTED RESISTANCE TO EXTINCTION ($1 - dCr$)

Group	P/L-P/L	C/S-P/L	C/L-P/L	P/L-C/S	P/L-C/L
RTE	.867	.831	.750	.549	.670

(c) shifts in PTR under constant MR should produce intermediate levels of RTE.

The experiment reported by Capaldi (1974) resembled the hypothetical one described above. In a manner similar to Table IV, three of the groups were designated as Groups C1-P6, P6-C1, and P6, where the number refers to the number of food pellets used as reward. The least RTE was reported for Group P6-C1 while Group C1-P6 displayed as much or more RTE than Group P6. With respect to the first two groups, these results agree with the predictions in Table IV. Further, the similarity in RTE for the latter two groups is also predicted, although Group C1-P6 is not expected to exceed Group P6 in RTE. It is not clear, however, whether the observed difference between these groups was reliable nor whether it was attributable to the fact that Group P6 received training only during the second acquisition phase. The remaining two groups, Groups C12-P6 and P6-C12, showed RTE intermediate to that of the preceding groups. This may have resulted from an insufficient variation in MR—i.e., experimental evidence (Section I, B) suggests that there may be very little difference between 6 and 12 pellets for rats. In this case, these groups may have been effectively under constant, large reward and would then be comparable to Groups L/C-L/P and L/P-L/C in Table IV. Intermediate levels of RTE for such groups are predicted in Table IV. In any event, general agreement obviously exists between Capaldi's (1974) results and the implications of the theory for concurrent shifts in MR and PTR. These implications serve to illustrate the interactive relationship assumed to exist between these variables.

E. TEMPORAL FACTORS

In the preceding discussion, temporal weights (Wt) are specified in terms of the number of trials intervening between the current trial and a prior trial (t) rather than the amount of time elapsing between those trials (T), as indicated in Section II, B and Eq. (5). A complete specification of the "temporal distance" between trials, however, should include both t and T as components. A simple, preliminary assumption is that the "total, effective temporal distance" (t') between Trial $_i$ and the current trial is

$$t'_i = t_i + \log(1 + T_i) \qquad (14)$$

where T_i is the time between the trials in appropriate units—e.g., in minutes. The logarithmic relationship assumed between t' and T reflects the view that t makes a relatively large contribution to "temporal distance" and it is consistent with the treatment of delay in Eq. (13). The inclusion of $\log(1 + T)$ in Eq. (14) makes t' progressively larger than t as T increases, but this effect will be relatively greater on more recent trials. The exponential relationship which is assumed between Wt and t (and t') also makes the effect of including T relatively greater on recent trials, since Wt decreases as a negatively accererated function of t'. For example, if the current trial is 20 and a unit intertrial interval (ITI) is assumed, t' for Trial 19 is 1.30 and t' for Trial 10 is 11.04. Based on t', and assuming that $b = 1.50$, Wt for Trial 19 is .674 and for Trial 10 Wt is .027. If these temporal weights are calculated on the basis of t alone, then Wt for Trial 19 is 1.0 and Wt for Trial 10 is .032. Therefore, the inclusion of T results in a reduction of 33% in Wt for the most recent trial but a reduction of only 16% in Wt for a trial nine trials earlier. Further, as the ITI or T increases, this differential effect becomes more pronounced while differences in ordinal position (t) become relatively less significant. Another effect of T will occur if t' is substituted for t in calculating $E(Sr)$ or Cr by Eqs. (6) and (8), respectively. As time is allowed to elapse following a training series, t' increases for all prior trials and sums based on temporally weighted quantities will decrease. This reduction in the "weight" of prior experiences with reward will make new experiences more effective in changing both $E(Sr)$ and Cr.

Although the formal assumption regarding T is indicated in Eq. (14), no attempt will be made to present quantitative predictions based on this assumption, but some general effects theoretically expected of T will be indicated. Some of the theoretical effects of T can be illustrated in terms of a procedure widely used in runway experiments. This procedure involves conducting trials in daily "blocks" such that a fairly constant ITI is maintained within a block of trials but a long "rest" interval occurs between daily blocks. A hypothectical experiment might involve runway training on three consecutive days, with a small MR on Day 1 and a large MR on Days 2 and 3. On Day 1 $E(Sr)$ is expected to develop toward the level of the small reward and may approach that level at the end of Day 1, since temporal weighting will "discount" the low, initial level of $E(Sr)$. At the beginning of Day 2, T (elapsed time) will be large for Day 1 trials which will reduce Wt for those trials and allow $E(Sr)$ on Day 2 to adjust rapidly to the large reward. Another effect of the long rest interval, however, will be a reduction in $E(Sr)$ at the beginning of Day 2 training relative to its value at the end of Day 1. This will occur because the increase in T will reduce the difference between Wt for Day 1 trials and Wt for the initial, low level of expected reward. A similar effect is expected to occur between Days 2 and 3. At the end of Day 2, $E(Sr)$ will approach the level appropriate to large reward, because of the greater weight of Day 2 rewards than the smaller rewards obtained on Day 1. During the rest interval between Days 2 and 3, however, the difference in Wt between Days 1 and 2 will decrease and $E(Sr)$ will "regress toward the (unweighted) mean"—i.e., it will assume a value more intermediate to the MR obtained on Days 1 and 2. This illustrates a general implication of the current treatment of T: When a long rest interval follows a training session, reward expectancies should "regress" somewhat toward their values prior to the training session. For example, in a NCE experiment in which a long "rest" interval occurs between the large and small reward phases, $E(Sr)$ should "regress" toward $E_1(Sr)$ and a smaller NCE should occur. Similarly, NCE should be more pronounced when ITI is short. Experimental support exists for both of these expectations (e.g., Capaldi, 1972; Gonzales, Fernhoff, & David, 1973).

Any attempt to derive precise predictions regarding the effects of T would require specifying the role of temporal factors in the development of E. While the role of temporal weighting has been made explicit for $E(Sr)$, Cr and, therefore, d, this process had been assumed to affect E only indirectly through d. A more complete statement of the present formulation, however, would include the assumption that E is also affected by the temporal-weighting process. This assumption was omitted so as not to further complicate the current discussion and is mentioned now only briefly and in a general way. In the present analysis, the value of E on any trial is simply the algebraic sum of the incremental effects indicated in Eq. (1) and the decremental effects indicated in Eqs. (10), (12), and (13). When temporal factors are included in this analysis it is assumed that each increment or decrement in E is weighted temporally in a manner similar to that assumed for $E(Sr)$ and Cr. In the case of E, of course, each temporally weighted quantity contributes to a sum rather than a mean. The effects of including temporal effects in E are negligible unless reward conditions are changed or the ITI is not constant. If reward conditions are changed, the assumption that E is temporally weighted "intensifies" expected effects to the degree that those effects depend on current or recent trials, since such trials will be weighted heavily. For example, larger contrast effects and faster extinction are predicted, since these decremental effects are pro duced by current reward conditions. The most interesting implications, however, involve situations in which the intertrial interval (ITI) is not constant—e.g., when training is conducted in daily trial blocks separated by long "rest" intervals. Such "rest" intervals are expected to have effects on performance which resemble those described for $E(Sr)$—i.e., the relative contribution to E of ordinally recent trials should decline as T increases. For example, if a block of acquisition trials is conducted on Day 1 and a block of extinction trials follows on Day 2, the value of E at the end of the Day 2 extinction trials will be lower when the temporal effects of t are included than if temporal factors are ignored. This will occur as a result of the differences on Day 2 between the weights assigned to Day 1 trials as opposed to Day 2 trials. If an additional trial block is conducted on Day 3, T will reduce the difference between Day 1 and Day 2 temporal weights—i.e., these weights become more similar. Since the effects which are reduced more are decremental or negative, E will show some "recovery" or "regression" to its earlier (acquisition) value. Further, less "spontaneous recovery" in E should occur between successive days as extinction is continued. A similar analysis might be applied to the "warm-up effect" sometimes observed between successive days of acquisition training. In any event, these examples serve to illustrate the general effect on E which occurs as T increases: The importance of the recency of reward conditions and of the order in which they were presented should decline. Thus, effects resulting from earlier stages of training may "reappear."

IV. General Discussion

A. EVALUATION OF THEORETICAL PREDICTIONS

The theory was designed to predict the effects of MR, PTR, and DR in experiments of the type described in Table I. The principal expository device consisted of generating theoretical data for hypothetical experiments analogous to those which provided the relevant empirical evidence. These theoretical data illustrated the major effects expected when these variables are manipulated individually or in various combinations. Thus, the effects of training under constant levels of MR, PTR, or DR were predicted for both acquisition and extinction performance. Further, the effects expected where these variables are shifted in acquisition were indicated. These effects included the contrast effect associated with shifts in both immediate and delayed MR and shifts in DR. The effects of PR-CR and CR-PR training sequences and the effects of initial nonreward were also predicted. A number of implications were derived for cases involving variations in more than one of the reward variables, including the expected interactions of these variables with training level in determining acquisition performance and RTE. Similarly, the expected effects on RTE of joint variations in MR and PTR were discussed, both for cases in which these variables are constant in acquisition and cases in which they are shifted concurrently. Additional discussion included some general expectations regarding temporal factors. It is apparent, then, the theory generates explicit, testable predictions for numerous sets of experimental conditions. Nevertheless, certain procedures have been excluded in the current analysis which have been studied extensively in runway conditioning experiments. These procedures include the systematic manipulation of food-deprivation level and the use of regular or "patterned" sequences of rewarded and nonrewarded trials as opposed to random partial reward procedures. While it may not prove difficult to extend the analysis to include those procedures, I did not feel that it was necessary to attempt to do so in this initial statement of the theory.

The theoretical implications presented in Section III generally agreed with the experimental results with which they were compared and the numerous specific points of agreement will not be reviewed here. A more precise conclusion regarding the general degree of agreement is a matter of judgment, since in many cases the empirical effects and relationships are uncertain. Where substantial conflict exists in the experimental results, the most reliably obtained results were emphasized in evaluating the theory. For example, it appears certain that runway conditioning is more rapid when reward is large, but it is not clear that an MR effect persists during extended training. Similarly, the conditions under which a partial reinforcement acquisition effect occurs are not certain, although other effects of percent reward are well established. The theory predicts that neither MR nor PTR should have effects on asymptotic, acquisition performance. Since the empirical evidence is equivocal, however, these predictions provide little basis for evaluating the theory. Conversely, the fact that the reliable effects of these variables on rate of conditioning and extinction are predicted correctly does provide substantial support for the theory.

The theory predicts that NCE following reward reduction should be obtained generally, while PCE are expected for shifts in delayed, but not immediate, reward. These predictions are consistent with most of the relevant experimental results, although PCE are reported occasionally for shifts in immediate reward. If PCE prove to be more general than the present assumptions imply, it may be necessary to allow Eq. (11) to apply symmetrically to increments and decrements in MR. Revisions also may be required in the role tentatively assumed for DR, but assumptions which were made do appear to predict correctly the effects of constant delay on acquisition and extinction performance as well as predicting both PCE and NCE for shifts in delayed reward.

B. RELATIONSHIP TO OTHER FORMULATIONS

The theory described in this chapter and, especially, the general viewpoint from which it was developed are related to several other theoretical formulations. Considerable similarity exists, for example, between the current viewpoint and a set of proposals made previously by Bolles (1972). Bolles describes animal learning experiments as involving adaptation to new sets of contingencies between stimuli as well as between responses and their environmental consequences. He proposes that animals "process" and "store" information about events in the environment which allows them to respond appropriately to new contingencies. Learning is said to involve a "direct appreciation" of these new contingencies. The general propositions which I describe informally appear to resemble Bolles' position in several respects. More specific comparisons of these positions are considered in the following discussion. A primary difference between these positions appears to be the goals involved. Bolles is concerned with describing learning principles which he believes have considerable generality but which he admits do not generate detailed predictions about performance; I have attempted an analysis which leads to detailed predictions but for a circumscribed experimental context.

A fundamental assumption in the present analysis is that rats learn about reward conditions in the goal box and come to "expect" these conditions when they are placed in the runway. The view that animals acquire such "S-S expectancies" was introduced into learning theory by Tolman (1932). A functionally similar concept, the "anticipatory goal response," was employed extensively in "S-R" learning theory by Hull (1952) and Spence (1956). Recently, a number of theorists are again arguing that S-S expectancies are an important part of what is learned in learning experiments (e.g., Bindra, 1972, 1974; Bolles, 1972; Estes, 1969; Rescorla & Solomon, 1967). According to Bindra (1974), for example, animals acquire "central contingency organizations" which are central representations of contingent relationships between environmental stimuli. Bindra argues that these S-S contingencies are all that the animal learns, that they are learned simply through observation, and that certain of these S-S contingencies are responsible for producing responses—i.e., observable behavior. Bolles (1972) also assumes that animals learn expectancies corresponding to S-S contingencies, such as the contingencies between environmental stimuli and other "biologically significant" stimuli. In addition to these S-S expectancies, Bolles assumes that animals can learn predictive relationships between their responses and the consequences of those responses—i.e., R-S expectancies. These R-S expectancies are combined with S-S expectancies to produce overt behavior.

The current theory assumes that rats learn two expectancies regarding reward conditions—$E(Sr)$ and Cr. The former concept presumably would be considered an S-S expectancy, since it involves the expectancy of a stimulus (food reward), it occurs in the presence of runway stimuli, and it develops only on trials on which this S-S sequence occurs (i.e., rewarded trials). The latter concept, Cr, might be considered an R-S expectancy, since it develops with each response as a result of the consequence of that response, and it reflects the "expected consistency" with which the response will be followed by reward. Thus, the present formulation appears to resemble Bolles' (1972) proposals to the degree that it involves both S-S expectancies and R-S expectancies.

Several differences exist between the analyses of instrumental learning proposed by Bindra and Bolles and the assumptions made by the theory described in this chapter. For example, Bindra (1974) attributes the function of "response production" to certain S-S contingencies. Bolles (1972) assumes that S-S expectancies and R-S contingencies combine in such a manner that response probability varies directly with the strength of each of these expectancies. In the current analysis, however, expectancies regarding reward interact in more complex ways. A primary function theoretically attributed to these expectancies is that of determining the rat's ability to recognize the conditions which produce reward and to discriminate changes in those conditions—i.e., the development of d depends on $E(Sr)$ and Cr. The contribution of these expectancies to d, however, is not simple or direct. For example, during initial acquisition training, the increasing value of Cr (a "R-S expectancy") will permit corresponding increases in d; but, at the same time, the growth of $E(Sr)$, an "S-S expectancy," will retard the development of d. Additional effects of these expectancies in the present theory occur when reward conditions are reduced below the expected level. Under these conditions, the "stronger" the expectancies are, the *worse* the resulting performance will be. The greater complexity assumed for the effects of expectancies in the present analysis simply may reflect the greater elaboration of this analysis for the more limited cases to which it applies. The formulations of Bolles and Bindra, however, do not appear to involve any theoretical concept analogous to d. This theoretical variable is not considered an expectancy but is rather the acquired ability to discriminate changes in reward conditions and respond appropriately. Training under favorable reward conditions promotes the development of d and allows the rat to quickly adjust its performance when reward conditions are changed. Conversely, training under unfavorable reward conditions reduces the adaptiveness and flexibility of behavior. The substantial "resistance to extinction" which often follows training with small and inconsistent reward presumably illustrates the failure of these unfavorable reinforcement conditions to promote the discrimination of the response-reward contingency. Indeed, great persistence in extinction responding seems conceptually related to the "learned helplessness" which follows exposure to uncontrollable aversive events (Overmier & Seligman, 1967). Thus, Maier and Seligman (1976) suggest that such unfavorable, aversive reinforcement conditions interfere "with the organism's tendency to perceive contingent relationships between its behavior and outcomes [p. 3]."

In the present analysis an attempt has been made to specify a theoretical mechanism by which rats process their experiences with different reward conditions to arrive at an expected reward which is representative of "recent" or "current" reward conditions. The assumption that the expected reward results from an "averaging process" is similar to views I have previously described (Black, 1968) and the view is obviously related to Helson's (e.g., 1964) concept of "adaptation level." While Helson originally developed this concept in dealing with psychophysical and perceptual data, he has applied it to a variety of other behavioral phenomena. An adaptation-level analysis specifically of phenomena associated with reinforcement magnitude has been proposed by Bevan and Adamson (1963). While the specific assumptions differ, the concept $E(Sr)$ clearly is related to the Bevan and Adamson proposals regarding the averaging of reinforcers and their proposal that the effective magnitude of a reinforcer depends on its relationship to this average. Similiarly, the present view that unexpected (distinctive) reinforcers are more effective than expected reinforcers resembles assumptions made by Rescorla and Wagner (1972) in the context of classical conditioning.

The "temporal-weighting process" assumed in the current analysis is more difficult to relate to other formulations. These temporal-ordinal effects were assumed in order to provide a theoretical means by which the rat could rapidly adjust expected reward to correspond to current reward conditions. The informal proposal was that rats continuously "review" their experiences with reward and revise their expectancies by "discounting" experiences that have become "irrelevant." Such a process presumably would require memory and part of the "discounting" assumed to occur presumably could result from forgetting. To the extent that such forgetting might result from interference, it would be consistent with the relative importance assumed for t (ordinal position) and T (time). Thus, intervals of time would be expected to produce more forgetting when "conflicting" experiences with reward occur during those intervals.

ACKNOWLEDGMENT

I am indebted to Mary Kay Busemeyer who wrote the computer programs which generated the theoretical data presented in this chapter.

REFERENCES

Amsel, A. The role of frustrative nonreward in noncontinuous reward situations. *Psychological Bulletin,* 1958, **55,** 102–112.

Anderson, N. H. Comparison of different populations: Resistance to extinction and transfer. *Psychological Review,* 1963, **70,** 162–179.

Bevan, W., & Adamson, R. E. Internal referents and the concept of reinforcement. In N. F. Washburn (Ed.), *Decisions, values and groups.* Vol. 2. New York: Pergamon, 1963. Pp. 92–139.

Bindra, D. A unified account of classical conditioning and operant training. In A. H. Black & W. F. Prokasy (Eds.), *Classical conditioning.* New York: Appleton, 1972. Pp. 453–481.

Bindra, D. A motivational view of learning, performance, and behavior modification. *Psychological Review,* 1974, **81,** 199–213.

Black, R. W. Shifts in magnitude of reward and contrast effects in instrumental and selective learning: A reinterpretation. *Psychological Review,* 1968, **75,** 114–126.

Black, R. W. Incentive motivation and the parameters of reward in instrumental conditioning. In W. J. Arnold & D. Levine (Eds.), *Nebraska symposium on motivation: 1969.* Lincoln: University of Nebraska Press, 1969. Pp. 85–137.

Bolles, R. C. Reinforcement, expectancy, and learning. *Psychological Review,* 1972, **79,** 394–409.

Bower, G. H. A contrast effect in differential conditioning. *Journal of Experimental Psychology,* 1961, **62,** 196–199.

Campbell, P. E., Batsche, C. J., & Batsche, G. M. Spaced-trials reward magnitude effects in the rat: Single versus multiple food pellets. *Journal of Comparative and Physiological Psychology,* 1972, **81,** 360–364.

Capaldi, E. D. Effects of shifts in body weight on rats' straight alley performance as a function of reward magnitude. *Learning and Motivation,* 1973, **4,** 229–235.

Capaldi, E. J. A sequential hypothesis of instrumental learning. In K. W. Spence & J. T. Spence (Eds.), *The psychology of learning and motivation*. Vol. 1. New York: Academic Press, 1967.

Capaldi, E. J. The successive negative contrast effect: Intertrial interval, type of shift and four sources of generalization decrement. *Journal of Experimental Psychology*, 1972, **96**, 433–438.

Capaldi, E. J. Partial reward either following or preceding consistent reward: A case of reinforcement level. *Journal of Experimental Psychology*, 1974, **102**, 954–962.

Capaldi, E. J., & Freese, M. Partial reward training level and reward magnitude: Effects on acquisition and extinction. *Learning and Motivation*, 1974, **5**, 299–310.

Clifford, T. Extinction following continuous reward and latent extinction. *Journal of Experimental Psychology*, 1964, **68**, 456–465.

Cox, W. M. A review of recent incentive contrast studies involving discrete trial procedures. *Psychological Record*, 1975, **25**, 373–393.

Dunham, P. J. Contrasted conditions of reinforcement: A selected critique. *Psychological Bulletin*, 1968, **69**, 295–315.

Ehrenfreund, D. Effect of drive on successive magnitude shift in rats. *Journal of Comparative and Physiological Psychology*, 1971, **76**, 418–423.

Elstad, P. Resistance to extinction of a running response as a function of shifts in percent reward and number of acquisition trials (Doctoral dissertation, University of Iowa, 1966). *Dissertation Abstracts International*, 1966, **27**, 3563B.

Estes, W. K. Reinforcement in human learning. In J. T. Tapp (Ed.), *Reinforcement and behavior*. New York: Academic Press, 1969.

Gonzalez, R. C., Fernhoff, D., & David, F. G. Contrast, resistance to extinction, and forgetting in rats. *Journal of Comparative and Physiological Psychology*, 1973, **84**, 562–571.

Habley, P., Gipson, M., & Hause, J. Acquisition and extinction in the runway as a joint function of constant reward magnitude and constant reward delay. *Psychonomic Science*, 1972, **29**, 133–136.

Hammer, L. R. Reinforcement magnitude effects with overtraining. *Psychonomic Science*, 1971, **22**, 295–296.

Helson, H. *Adaptation-level theory*. New York: Harper & Row, 1964.

Hull, C. L. *Principles of behavior*. New York: Appleton, 1943.

Hull, C. L. *A behavior system*. New Haven: Yale University Press, 1952.

Hulse, S. H., Jr. Amount and percentage of reinforcement and duration of goal confinement in conditioning and extinction. *Journal of Experimental Psychology*, 1958, **56**, 48–57.

Logan, F. *Incentive*. New Haven: Yale University Press, 1960.

Logan, F. A., Beier, E. M., & Kincaid, W. D. Extinction following partial and varied reinforcement. *Journal of Experimental Psychology*, 1956, **52**, 65–70.

McCain, G., Dyleski, K., & McElvain, G. Reward magnitude and instrumental responses: Consistent reward. *Psychonomic Monograph Supplements*, 1971, **3**, (16, Whole No. 48).

Maier, S. F., & Seligman, M. E. P. Learned helplessness: Theory and evidence. *Journal of Experimental Psychology: General*, 1976, **105**, 3–46.

Mellgren, R. L. Positive contrast in the rat as a function of the number of preshift trials in the runway. *Journal of Comparative and Physiological Psychology*, 1971, **77**, 329–336.

Mellgren, R. L. Positive and negative contrast effects using delayed reinforcement. *Learning and motivation*, 1972, **3**, 185–193.

Mowrer, O. H., & Jones, H. M. Habit strength as a function of the pattern of reinforcement. *Journal of Experimental Psychology*, 1945, **35**, 293–311.

Overminer, J. B., & Seligman, M. E. P. Effects of inescapable shock upon subsequent escape and avoidance learning. *Journal of Comparative and Physiological Psychology,* 1967, **63,** 28–33.

Perin, C. T. A quantitative investigation of the delay of reinforcement gradient. *Journal of Experimental Psychology,* 1943, **32,** 37–51.

Peters, D. P., & McHose, J. H. Effects of varied preshift reward magnitude on successive negative contrast effects in rats. *Journal of Comparative and Physiological Psychology,* 1974, **86,** 85–95.

Ratliff, R. G., & Ratliff, A. R. Runway acquisition and extinction as a joint function of magnitude of reward and percentage of rewarded acquisition trials. *Learning and Motivation,* 1971, **2,** 215–227.

Renner, K. E. Delay of reinforcement: A historical review. *Psychological Bulletin,* 1964, **61,** 341–361.

Rescorla, R. A., & Solomon, R. L. Two process learning theory: Relationships between Pavlovian conditioning and instrumental learning. *Psychological Review,* 1967, **74,** 151–182.

Rescorla, R. A., & Wagner, A. R. A theory of Pavlovian conditioning: Variations in the effectiveness of reinforcement and nonreinforcement. In A. Black & W. F. Prokasy (Eds.), *Classical conditioning II, Current theory and research.* New York: Appleton, 1972. Pp. 64–99.

Robbins, D. Partial reinforcement: A selective review of the alleyway literature since 1960. *Psychological Bulletin,* 1971, **76,** 415–431.

Robbins, D., Chait, H., & Weinstock, S. Effects of nonreinforcement on running behavior during acquisition, extinction, and reacquisition. *Journal of Comparative and Physiological Psychology,* 1968, **66,** 699–706.

Sgro, J. A., Dyal, J. A., & Anastasio, E. J. Effects of constant delay of reinforcement on acquisition asymptote and resistance to extinction. *Journal of Experimental Psychology,* 1967, **73,** 634–636.

Shanab, M. E., & Biller, J. D. Positive contrast in the runway obtained following a shift in both delay and magnitude of reward. *Learning and Motivation,* 1972, **3,** 179–184.

Shanab, M. E., Sanders, R., & Premack, D. Positive contrast obtained with delay of reward. *Science,* 1969, **164,** 724–725.

Spear, N. E., Hill, W. F., & O'Sullivan, D. J. Acquisition and extinction after initial trials without reward. *Journal of Experimental Psychology,* 1965, **69,** 25–29.

Spence, K. W. The nature of discrimination learning in animals. *Psychological Review,* 1936, **43,** 427–449.

Spence, K. W. *Behavior theory and conditioning.* New Haven: Yale University Press, 1956.

Sperling, S. E. Reversal learning and resistance to extinction: A review of the rat literature. *Psychological Bulletin,* 1965, **63,** 281–297.

Sutherland, N. S., Mackintosh, N. J., & Wolfe, J. B. Extinction as a function of the order of partial and consistent reinforcement. *Journal of Experimental Psychology,* 1965, **69,** 56–59.

Tarpy, R. M., & Sawabini, F. L. Reinforcement delay: A selective review of the last decade. *Psychological Bulletin,* 1974, **81,** 984–997.

Theios, J. The partial reinforcement effect sustained through a block of continuous reinforcement. *Journal of Experimental Psychology,* 1962, **64,** 1–6.

Theios, J., & McGinnis, R. W. Partial reinforcement before and after continuous reinforcement. *Journal of Experimental Psychology,* 1967, **73,** 479–481.

Thorndike, E. L. *The fundamentals of learning.* New York: Teachers College, Columbia University, 1932.

Tolman, E. C. *Purposive behavior in animals and men.* New York: Appleton, 1932.

Traupmann, K. L. Drive, reward, and training parameters, and the overlearning-extinction effect (OEE). *Learning and Motivation,* 1972, **3**, 359–368.

Wagner, A. R. Effects of amount and percentage of reinforcement and number of acquisition trials on conditioning and extinction. *Journal of Experimental Psychology,* 1961, **62**, 234–242.

Weinstock, S. Resistance to extinction of a running response following partial reinforcement under widely spaced trials. *Journal of Comparative and Physiological Psychology,* 1954, **47**, 318–322.

Weinstock, S. Acquisition and extinction of a partially reinforced running response at a 24-hr. intertrial interval. *Journal of Experimental Psychology,* 1958, **56**, 151–159.

SUBJECT INDEX

A

Abstraction, 119–121
  decontextualization and, 118–119
Acquisition, of self-punitive behavior, 161–166
Appetitive processes, similarity with punishment, 192–194
Associative coding model, 21–24
  parameter estimates and choice probability, 24–29
  scale properties of, 29–30
Attention, spacing effect and, 74–80

C

Choice
  in economic demand theory, 129–136
  substitutability and, 136–152
  in self-punitive behavior, 166–174
Comprehension, linguistic, 107–111
Consolidation, spacing effect and, 73
Contextual encoding variability, 71–72
Contingency learning, self-punitive behavior and, 191–192, 194

D

Decontextualization, 114–118
  abstraction and, 118–119
Deficient processing, spacing effect and, 72–80
Demand theory, choice in, 129–136
  substitutability and, 136–152
Differential reward learning, 30–31, 38–42
  within disjoint training pairs, 37–38
  under full information condition, 31–35
  under partial information condition, 35–37
Discrimination-expectancy, in self-punitive behavior, 159–160, 166
  acquisition and extinction of, 161–166
  disruption of, 174–176
  preference and choice in, 166–174

E

Economic demand theory, choice in, 129–136
  substitutability and, 136–152
Effect, law of, self-punitive behavior and, 157
Effort, as economic commodity, 141–142
Emotionality, self-punitive behavior and, 187
Encoding variability
  contextual, 71–72
  semantic, 69–71
Extinction, of self-punitive behavior, 161–166, 184–185

F

Fear, self-punitive behavior and, 160, 186–187
Frequency information
  independence of, 52–54
  retrieval of, 59–62
  status of, 62–64

H

Habituation, spacing effect and, 73–74

I

Information, *see also* Frequency information
  as basis of predictive behavior, 6–20
Instrumental conditioning, reward variables in basic theoretical formulation, 207–220

constant reward conditions, 204–207, 220–223
scope of theory, 199–204
theoretical perspectives, 236–241
varied reward conditions, 223–236

L

Linguistic comprehension, stage setting and, 107–111

M

Masochism, self-punitive behavior and, 195–196
Meanings, uniqueness of, 107–111
Measurement, of punishment effect, 176–178
Memory, *see also* Retrieval
novelty and, 94–102
Memory trace(s)
identifiability of, 54–59
multiple, 50
propositional encoding versus, 59–64
strength versus, 52–59
Motivation, self-punitive behavior and, 194–195

N

Neurotic paradox, of self-punitive behavior, 156
Novelty, 94
memory metaphor and, 94–102

O

Observation-transfer paradigm, for predictive behavior, 3–6

P

Predictive behavior
information basis of, 6–20
observation-transfer paradigm, 3–6
Preference, in self-punitive behavior, 166–174

Probability learning, 20–21
associative coding model, 21–24
parameter estimates and choice probability, 24–29
scale properties of, 29–30
with homogeneous blocks of observation trials, 7–10
with joint variation of stimulus frequency and outcome probability, 15–17
with overlapping observation pairs, 17–20
with observation trials with a common losing alternative, 12–15
with randomized training trials and delayed tests, 10–12
Propositional encoding, 50–52
memory traces versus, 59–64
Punishment, *see also* Self-punitive behavior
effect of, 176–183

R

Rehearsal, spacing effect and, 72
Repetition, 47–48
representation of frequency, 48–49, 64–65
multiple traces versus propositional encoding, 59–64
strength versus multiple traces, 52–59
theories, 49
retrieval and, 84–87
study-phase, 80–84
spacing effect in
definition and generality, 65–69
theories and evidence, 69–80
Response selection, as central state, 192
Response style, self-punitive behavior and, 185–186
Retrieval
of frequency information, 59–62
repetition and, 80–87
Reward, in instrumental conditioning, *see* Instrumental conditioning
Reward sets, *see* Differential reward learning

S

Self-punitive behavior
active and passive views of, 189–190

Subject Index

changes between acquisition and extinction, 161–166
contingency learning and, 191–192, 194
disruption of, 174–176
early learning theory and, 156–157
effect of punishment in, 176–183
empirical effect, 158
extinction of, 184–185
goal box cues and, 188
intensity of fear and postshock emotionality and, 186–187
issues in, 160–161
law of effect and, 157
masochism and, 195–196
nature of, 188–189
neurotic paradox of, 156
preference and choice in, 166–174
rats and humans compared on, 190
response selection and, 192
response style and, 185–186
similarity with appetitive processes, 192–194
theoretical aspects, 158–160
value learning and, 191, 194–195

Semantic encoding variability, 69–71
Spacing effect
definition and generality, 65–69
theories and evidence, 69–80
Stage setting effect
learning and, 112–113
abstraction and, 118–121
decontextualization and, 114–119
shaping and clarifying knowledge and, 113–114
of past experience, 102–107, 111–112
linguistic comprehension and uniqueness of understood meanings and, 107–111
Strength, of memory trace, 49–50
multiple traces versus, 52–59
Study-phase retrieval, 80–84
Substitutability, in economic demand theory, 136–152

V

Value learning, self-punitive behavior and, 191, 194–195